HUMAN TARGET

PETER MILLIGAN
Writer

EDVIN BIUKOVIĆ
Artist

LEE LOUGHRIDGE
Colorist/Separator

ROBERT SOLANOVIĆ
Letterer

TIM BRADSTREET
Cover Artist

HUMAN TARGET created by
LEN WEIN and CARMINE INFANT[...]

HUMAN TARGET Published by DC Comics. Cover and compilation copyright © 2000 DC Comics. All Rights Reserved. Originally published in single magazine form as HUMAN TARGET 1-4. Copyright © 1999 DC Comics. All Rights Reserved. All characters, their distinctive likenesses and related indicia featured in this publication are trademarks of DC Comics. The stories, characters, and incidents featured in this publication are entirely fictional. DC Comics, 1700 Broadway, New York, NY 10019. A division of Warner Bros. - A Time Warner Entertainment Company

Printed in Canada. First Printing. ISBN: 1-56389-693-1

Cover illustration by Tim Bradstreet.

Publication design by Louis V Prandi.

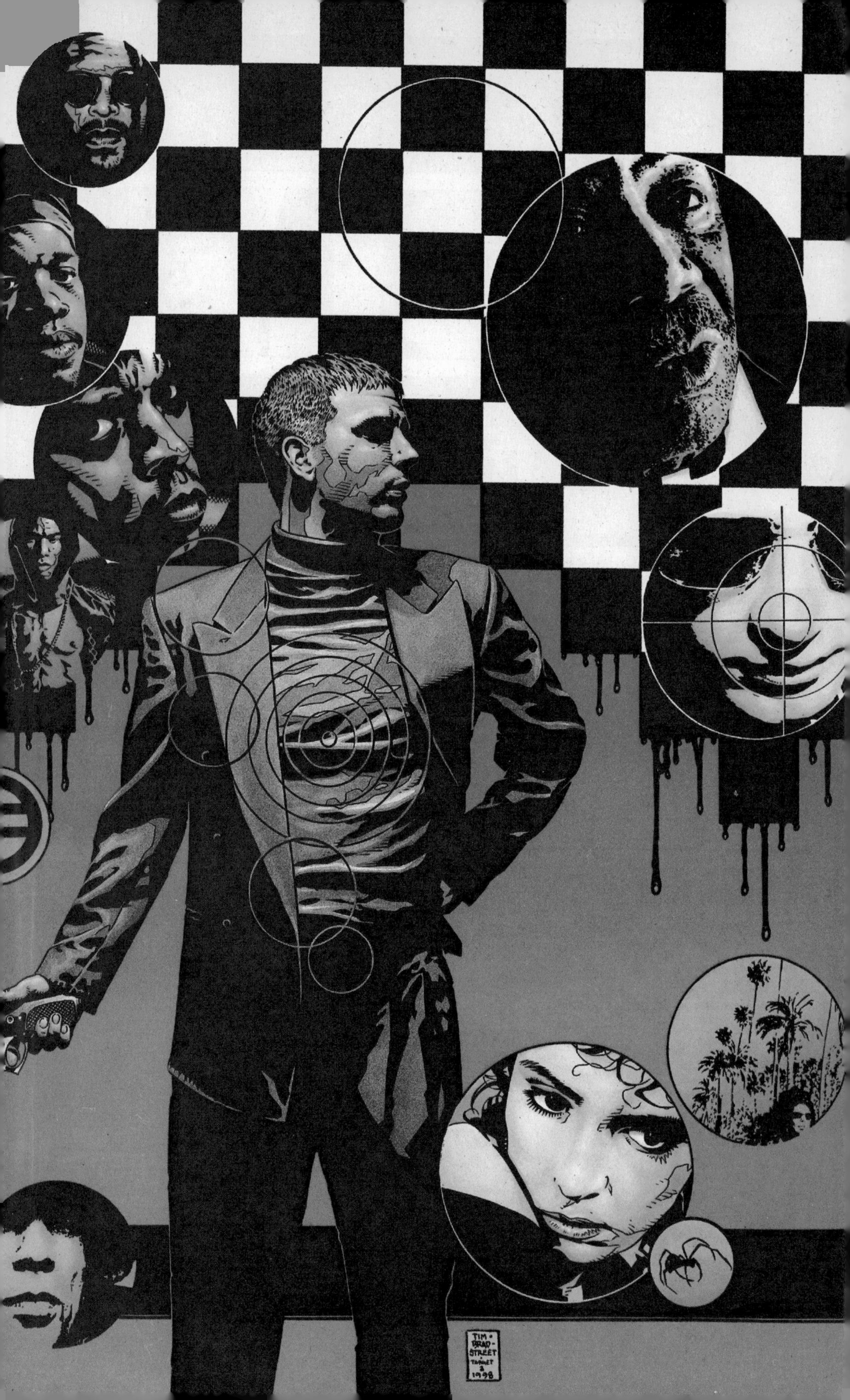
TIM • BRAD-
STREET
1998

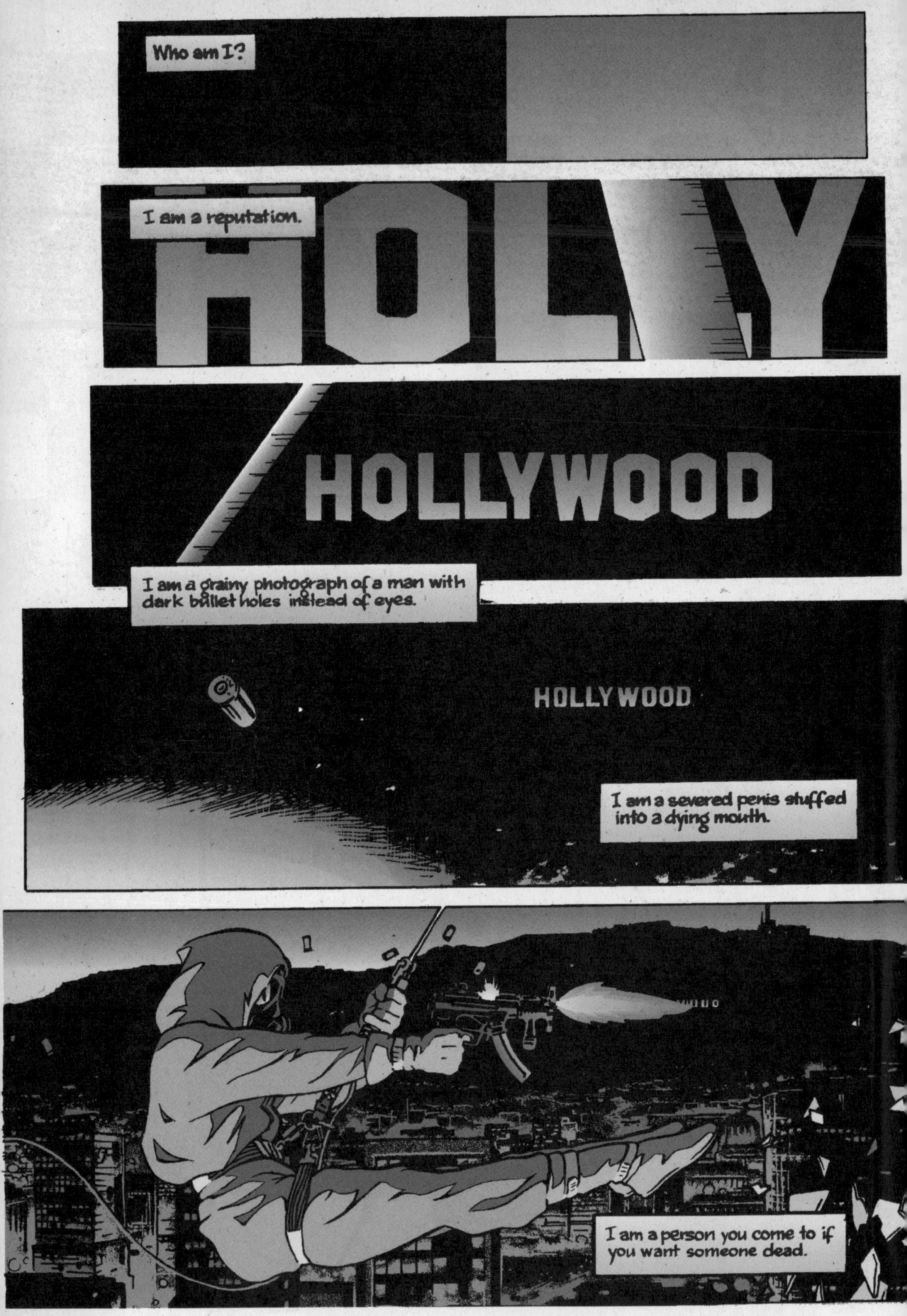
Who am I?
I am a reputation.
HOLLY
HOLLYWOOD
I am a grainy photograph of a man with dark bullet holes instead of eyes.
HOLLYWOOD
I am a severed penis stuffed into a dying mouth.
I am a person you come to if you want someone dead.

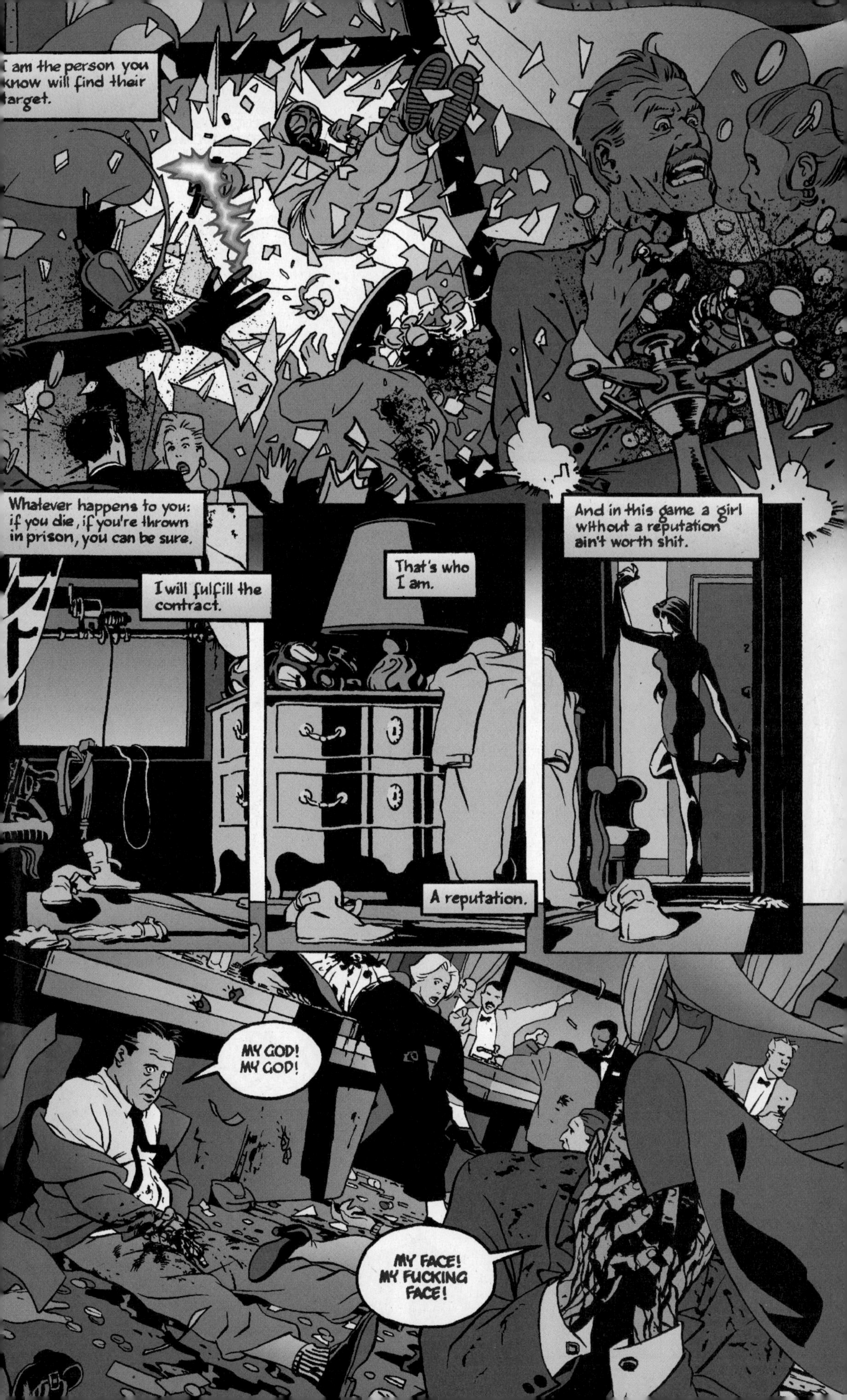
I am the person you know will find their target.
Whatever happens to you: if you die, if you're thrown in prison, you can be sure.
I will fulfill the contract.
That's who I am.
A reputation.
And in this game a girl without a reputation ain't worth shit.
MY GOD! MY GOD!
MY FACE! MY FUCKING FACE!

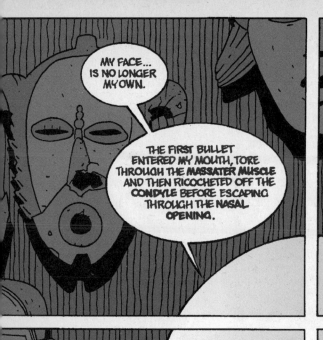

MY FACE... IS NO LONGER MY OWN.

THE FIRST BULLET ENTERED MY MOUTH, TORE THROUGH THE MASSATER MUSCLE AND THEN RICOCHETED OFF THE CONDYLE BEFORE ESCAPING THROUGH THE NASAL OPENING.

WHAT THE SECOND BULLET LACKED IN... WANDERLUST IT MADE UP FOR IN BRUTE POWER, SMASHING MY LOWER JAW.

I'M SORRY. YOU DON'T NEED TO HEAR THIS. THE POINT IS, I HAVE A TEAM OF EXCELLENT DOCTORS WHO ARE CONFIDENT THEY CAN REBUILD MY FACE.

BUT THIS WILL TAKE TIME... AND... AND THE PERSON WHO DID THIS MIGHT RETURN TO FINISH OFF THE JOB.

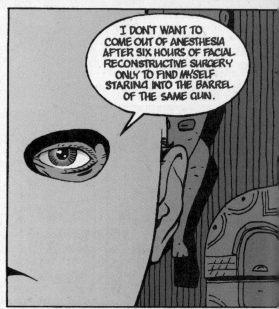

I DON'T WANT TO COME OUT OF ANESTHESIA AFTER SIX HOURS OF FACIAL RECONSTRUCTIVE SURGERY ONLY TO FIND MYSELF STARING INTO THE BARREL OF THE SAME GUN.

THAT'S WHY I NEED YOU TO BE ME. TO REALLY BE ME. TO BE A HUMAN TARGET. TO DRAW THE FIRE OF ONE WHO WISHES ME DEAD.

YOU ARE...

...I KNOW WHO I AM...

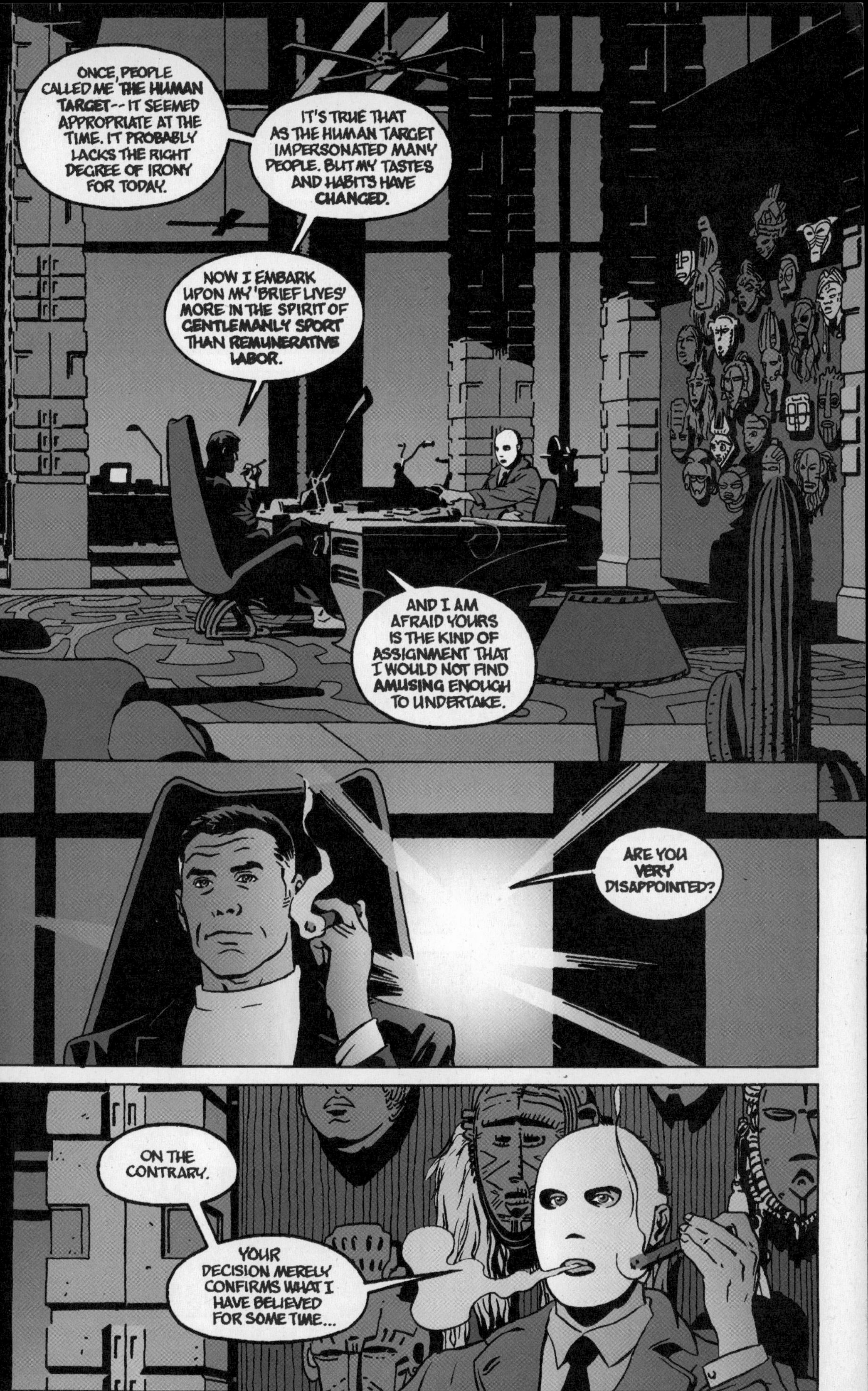
ONCE, PEOPLE CALLED ME THE HUMAN TARGET-- IT SEEMED APPROPRIATE AT THE TIME. IT PROBABLY LACKS THE RIGHT DEGREE OF IRONY FOR TODAY.
IT'S TRUE THAT AS THE HUMAN TARGET IMPERSONATED MANY PEOPLE. BUT MY TASTES AND HABITS HAVE CHANGED.
NOW I EMBARK UPON MY 'BRIEF LIVES' MORE IN THE SPIRIT OF GENTLEMANLY SPORT THAN REMUNERATIVE LABOR.
AND I AM AFRAID YOURS IS THE KIND OF ASSIGNMENT THAT I WOULD NOT FIND AMUSING ENOUGH TO UNDERTAKE.
ARE YOU VERY DISAPPOINTED?
ON THE CONTRARY.
YOUR DECISION MERELY CONFIRMS WHAT I HAVE BELIEVED FOR SOME TIME...

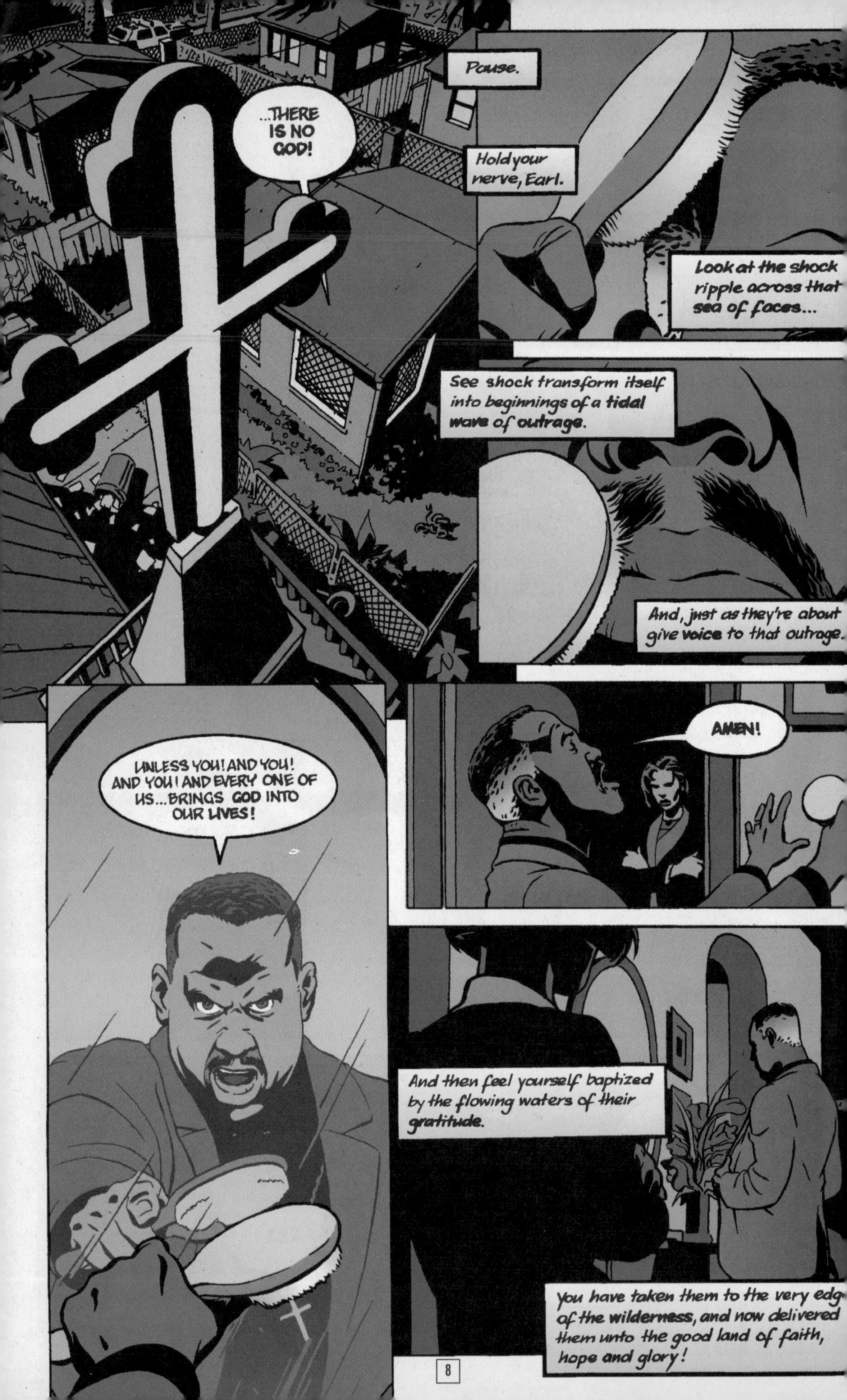
...THERE IS NO GOD!
Pause.
Hold your nerve, Earl.
Look at the shock ripple across that sea of faces...
See shock transform itself into beginnings of a tidal wave of outrage.
And, just as they're about give voice to that outrage.
UNLESS YOU! AND YOU! AND YOU! AND EVERY ONE OF US...BRINGS GOD INTO OUR LIVES!
AMEN!
And then feel yourself baptized by the flowing waters of their gratitude.
you have taken them to the very edg of the wilderness, and now delivered them unto the good land of faith, hope and glory!

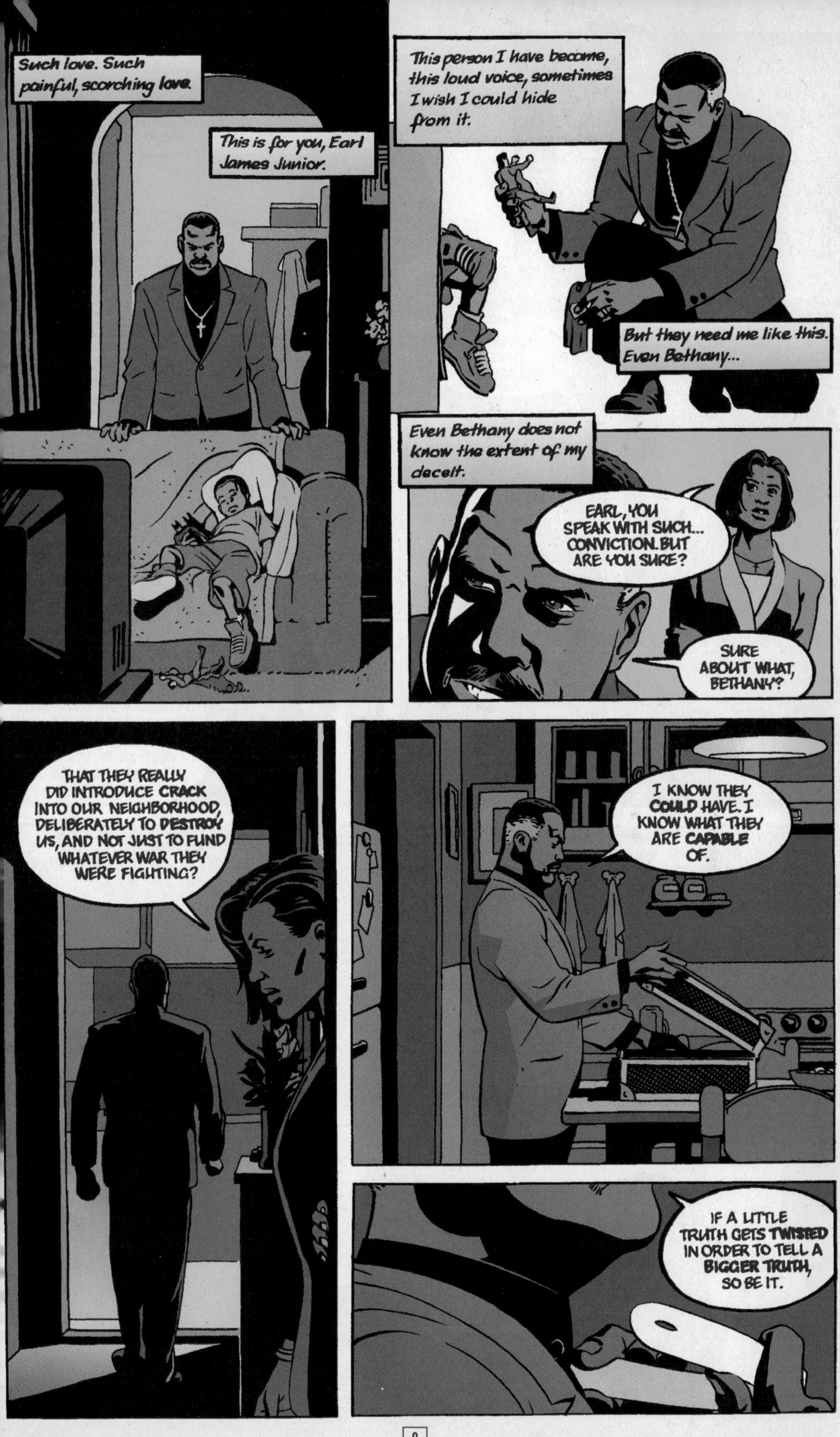

Such love. Such painful, scorching love.
This is for you, Earl James Junior.
This person I have become, this loud voice, sometimes I wish I could hide from it.
But they need me like this. Even Bethany...
Even Bethany does not know the extent of my deceit.
EARL, YOU SPEAK WITH SUCH... CONVICTION. BUT ARE YOU SURE?
SURE ABOUT WHAT, BETHANY?
THAT THEY REALLY DID INTRODUCE CRACK INTO OUR NEIGHBORHOOD, DELIBERATELY TO DESTROY US, AND NOT JUST TO FUND WHATEVER WAR THEY WERE FIGHTING?
I KNOW THEY COULD HAVE. I KNOW WHAT THEY ARE CAPABLE OF.
IF A LITTLE TRUTH GETS TWISTED IN ORDER TO TELL A BIGGER TRUTH, SO BE IT.

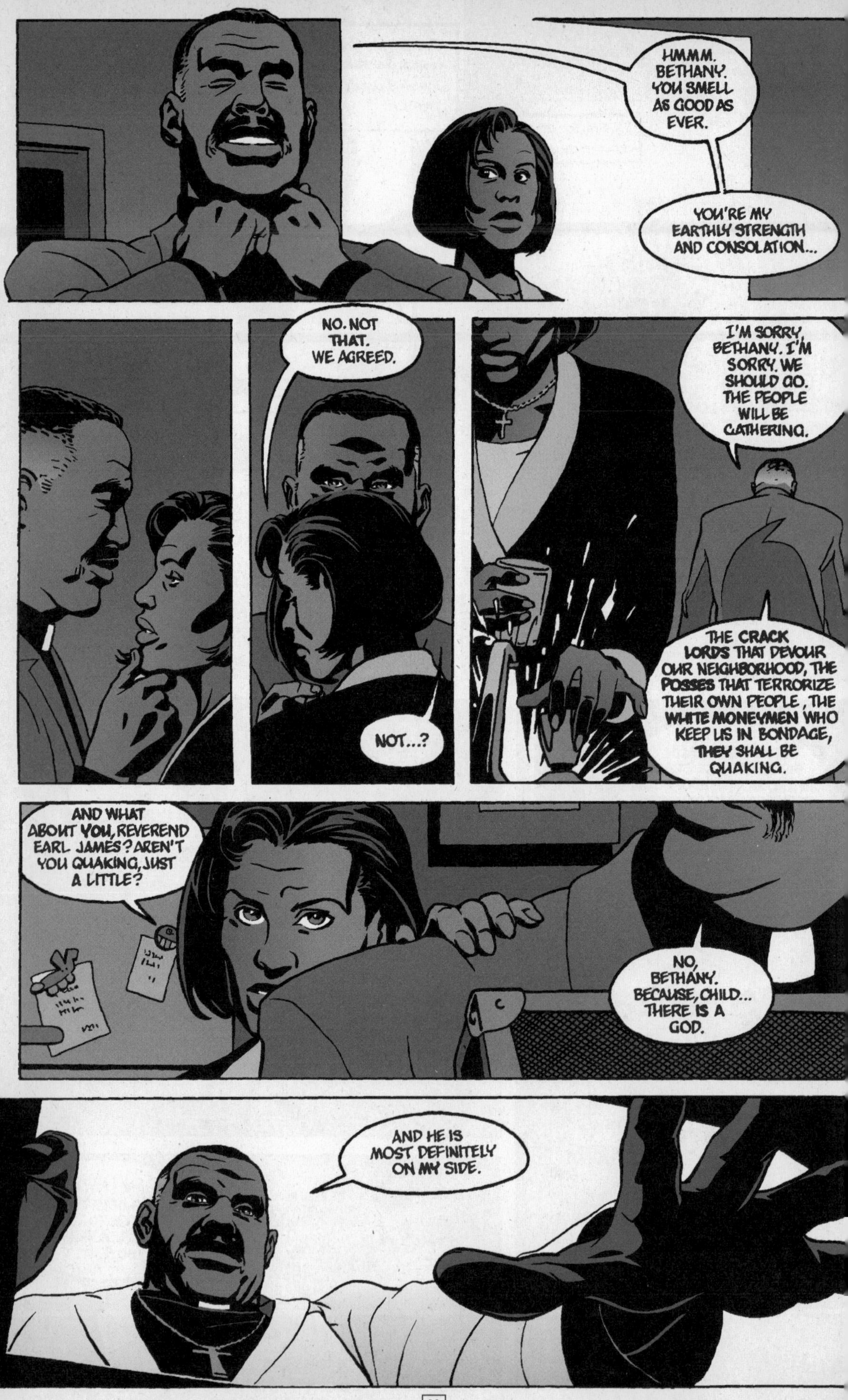
HMMM. BETHANY. YOU SMELL AS GOOD AS EVER.
YOU'RE MY EARTHLY STRENGTH AND CONSOLATION...
NO. NOT THAT. WE AGREED.
NOT...?
I'M SORRY, BETHANY. I'M SORRY. WE SHOULD GO. THE PEOPLE WILL BE GATHERING.
THE CRACK LORDS THAT DEVOUR OUR NEIGHBORHOOD, THE POSSES THAT TERRORIZE THEIR OWN PEOPLE, THE WHITE MONEYMEN WHO KEEP US IN BONDAGE, THEY SHALL BE QUAKING.
AND WHAT ABOUT YOU, REVEREND EARL JAMES? AREN'T YOU QUAKING, JUST A LITTLE?
NO, BETHANY. BECAUSE, CHILD... THERE IS A GOD.
AND HE IS MOST DEFINITELY ON MY SIDE.

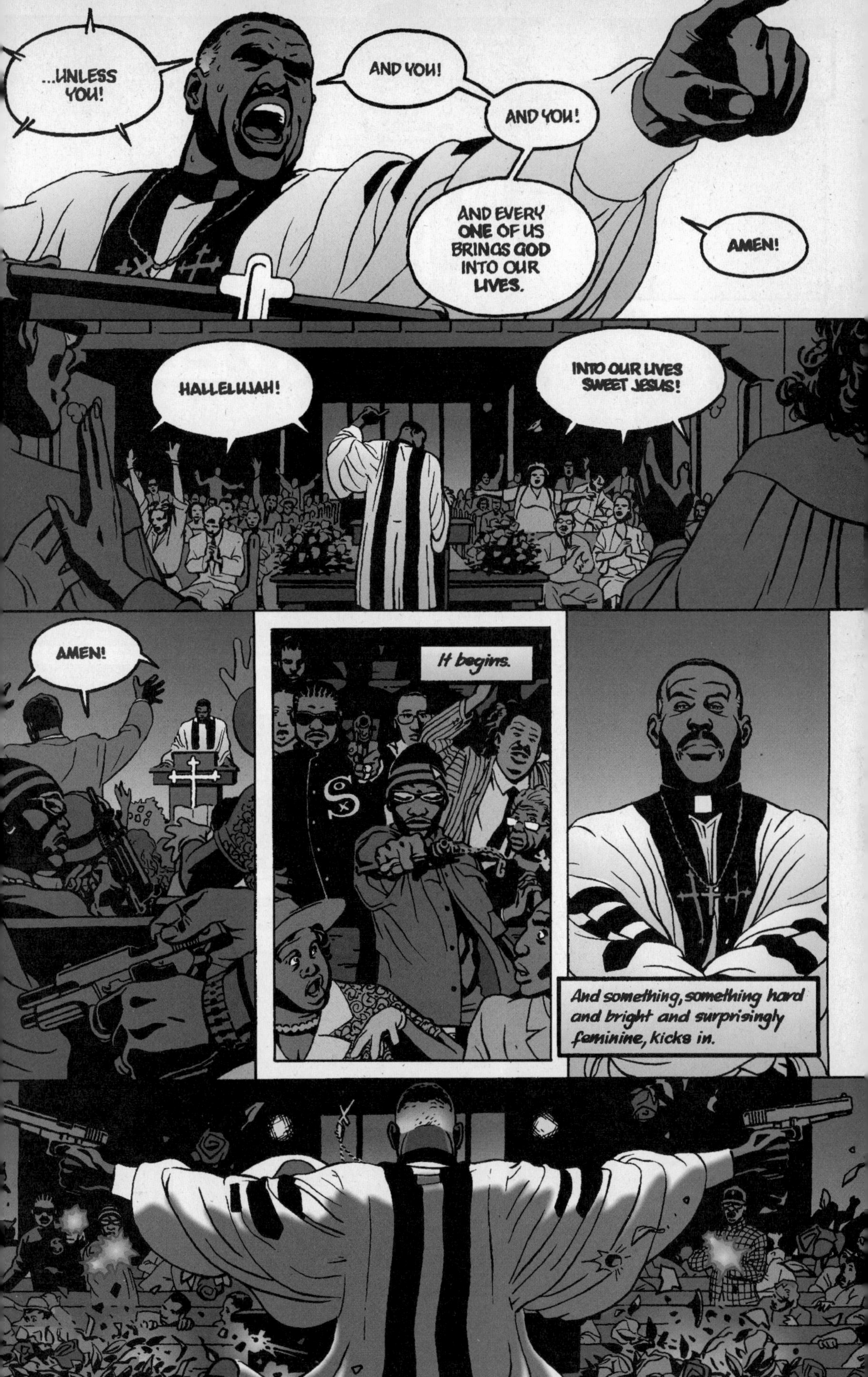

...UNLESS YOU!
AND YOU!
AND YOU!
AND EVERY ONE OF US BRINGS GOD INTO OUR LIVES.
AMEN!
HALLELUJAH!
INTO OUR LIVES SWEET JESUS!
AMEN!
It begins.
And something, something hard and bright and surprisingly feminine, kicks in.

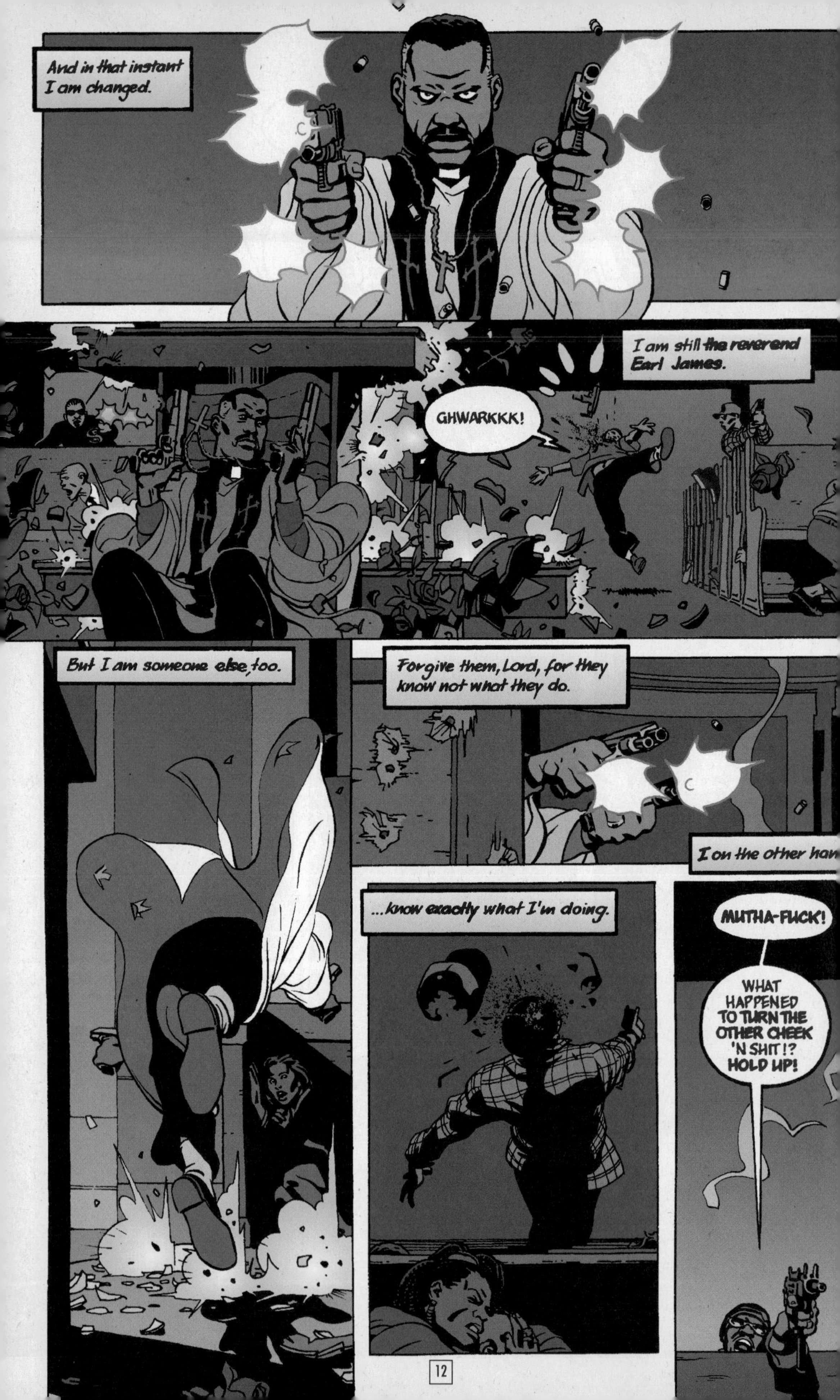

And in that instant I am changed.
I am still the reverend Earl James.
GHWARKKK!
But I am someone else, too.
Forgive them, Lord, for they know not what they do.
I on the other han
...know exactly what I'm doing.
MUTHA-FUCK!
WHAT HAPPENED TO TURN THE OTHER CHEEK 'N SHIT!? HOLD UP!

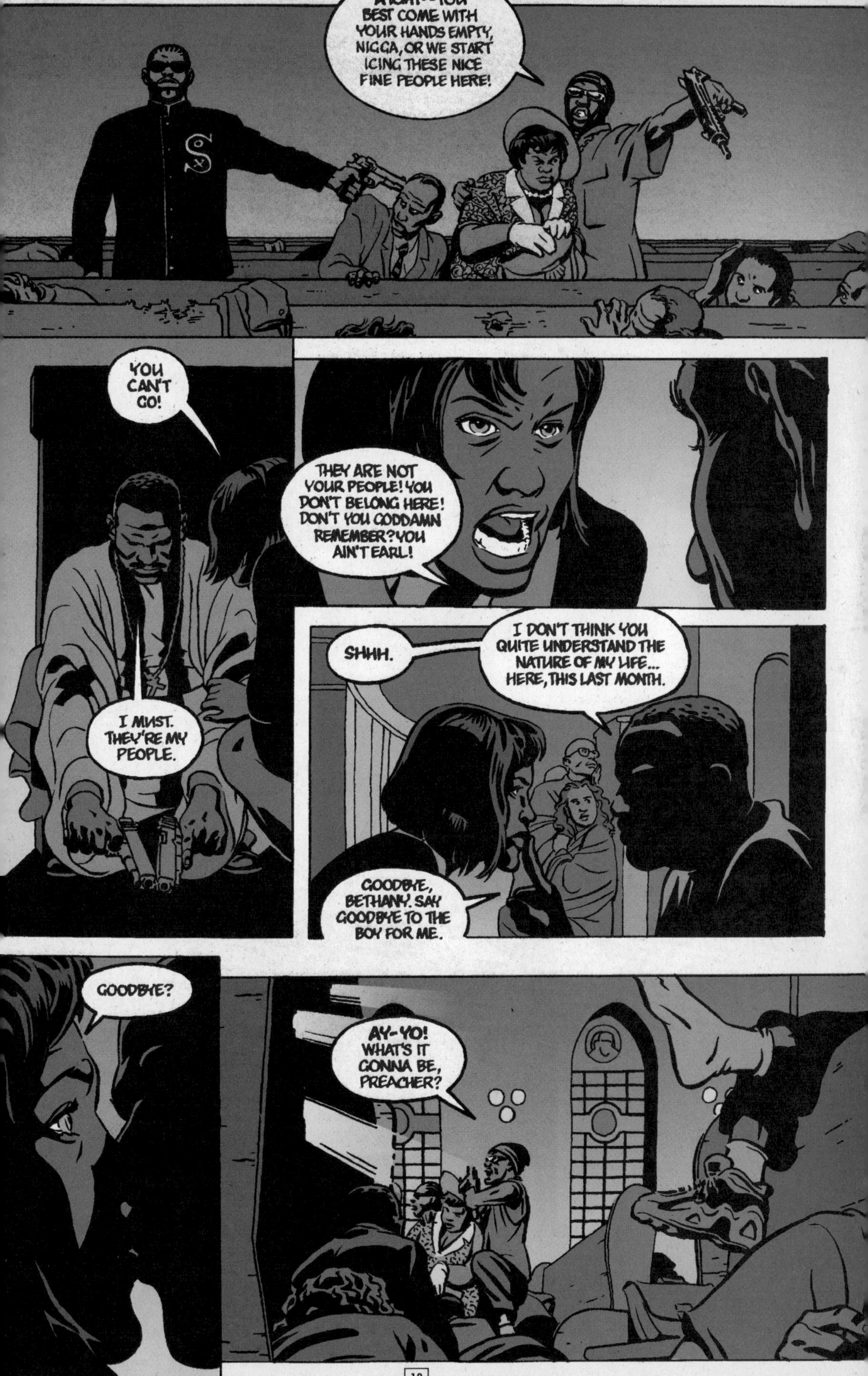
A'IGHT--YOU BEST COME WITH YOUR HANDS EMPTY, NIGGA, OR WE START ICING THESE NICE FINE PEOPLE HERE!
YOU CAN'T GO!
THEY ARE NOT YOUR PEOPLE! YOU DON'T BELONG HERE! DON'T YOU GODDAMN REMEMBER? YOU AIN'T EARL!
I MUST. THEY'RE MY PEOPLE.
SHHH.
I DON'T THINK YOU QUITE UNDERSTAND THE NATURE OF MY LIFE... HERE, THIS LAST MONTH.
GOODBYE, BETHANY. SAY GOODBYE TO THE BOY FOR ME.
GOODBYE?
AY-YO! WHAT'S IT GONNA BE, PREACHER?

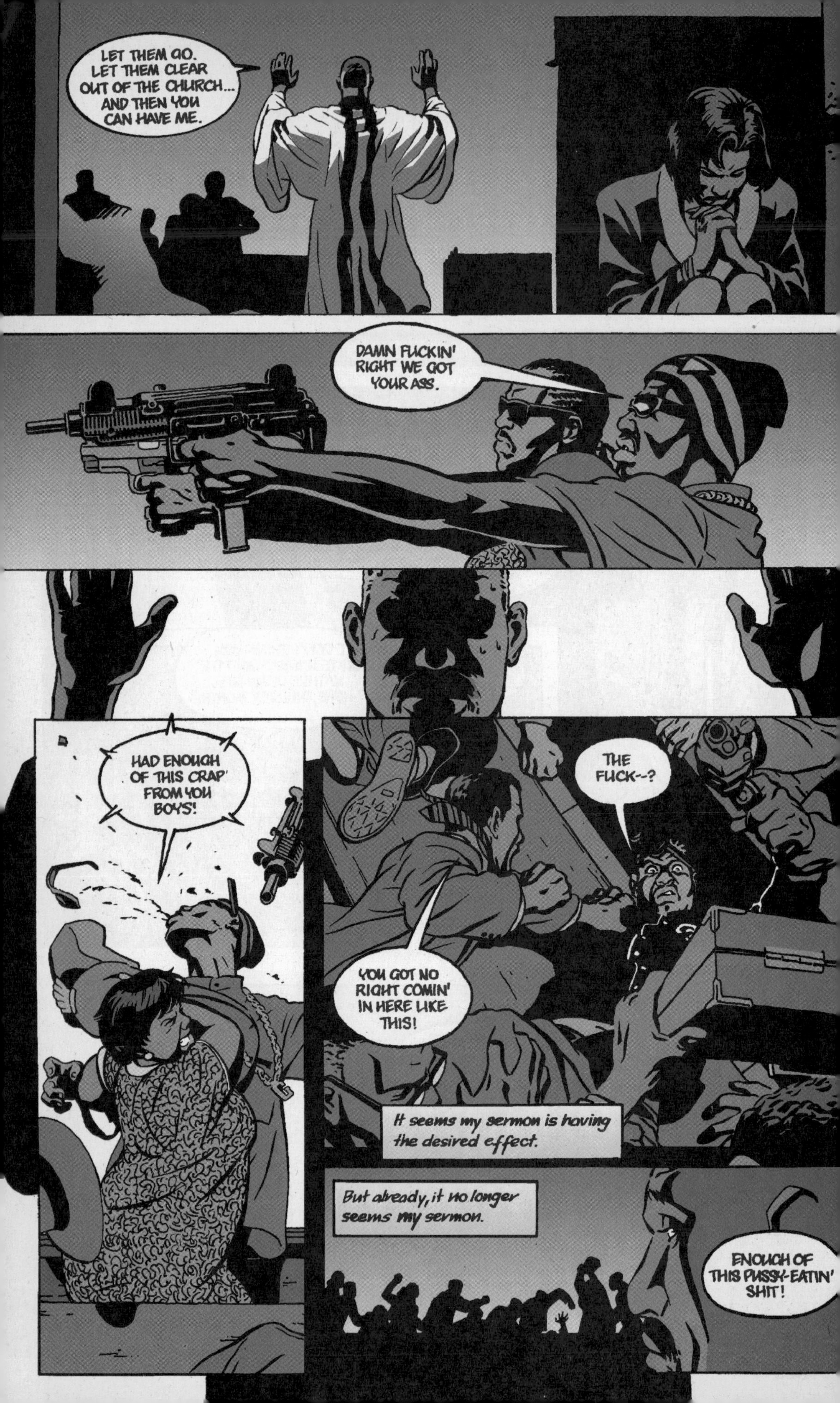
LET THEM GO. LET THEM CLEAR OUT OF THE CHURCH... AND THEN YOU CAN HAVE ME.
DAMN FUCKIN' RIGHT WE GOT YOUR ASS.
HAD ENOUGH OF THIS CRAP FROM YOU BOYS!
THE FUCK--?
YOU GOT NO RIGHT COMIN' IN HERE LIKE THIS!
It seems my sermon is having the desired effect.
But already, it no longer seems my sermon.
ENOUGH OF THIS PUSSY-EATIN' SHIT!

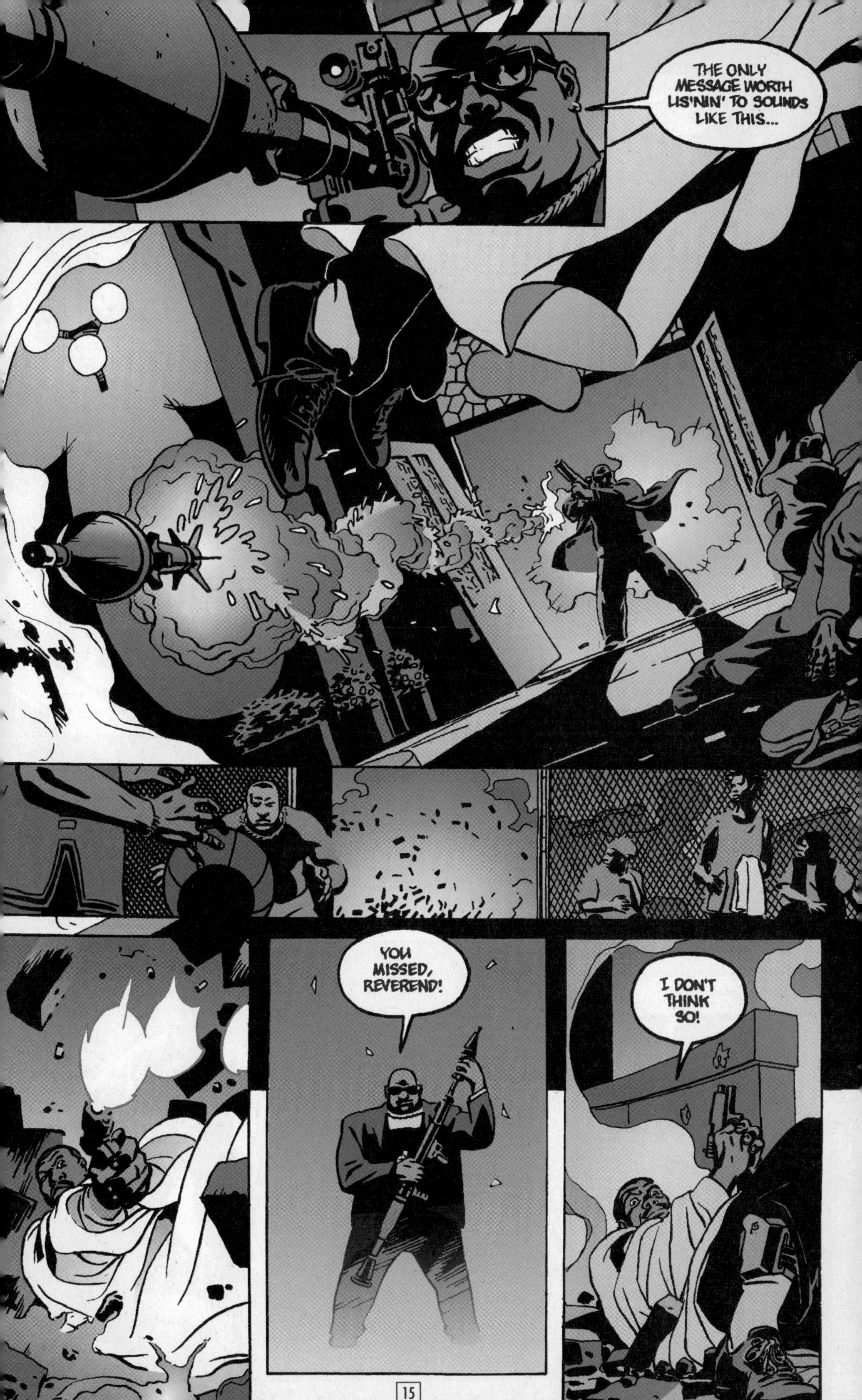
THE ONLY MESSAGE WORTH LIS'NIN' TO SOUNDS LIKE THIS...
YOU MISSED, REVEREND!
I DON'T THINK SO!

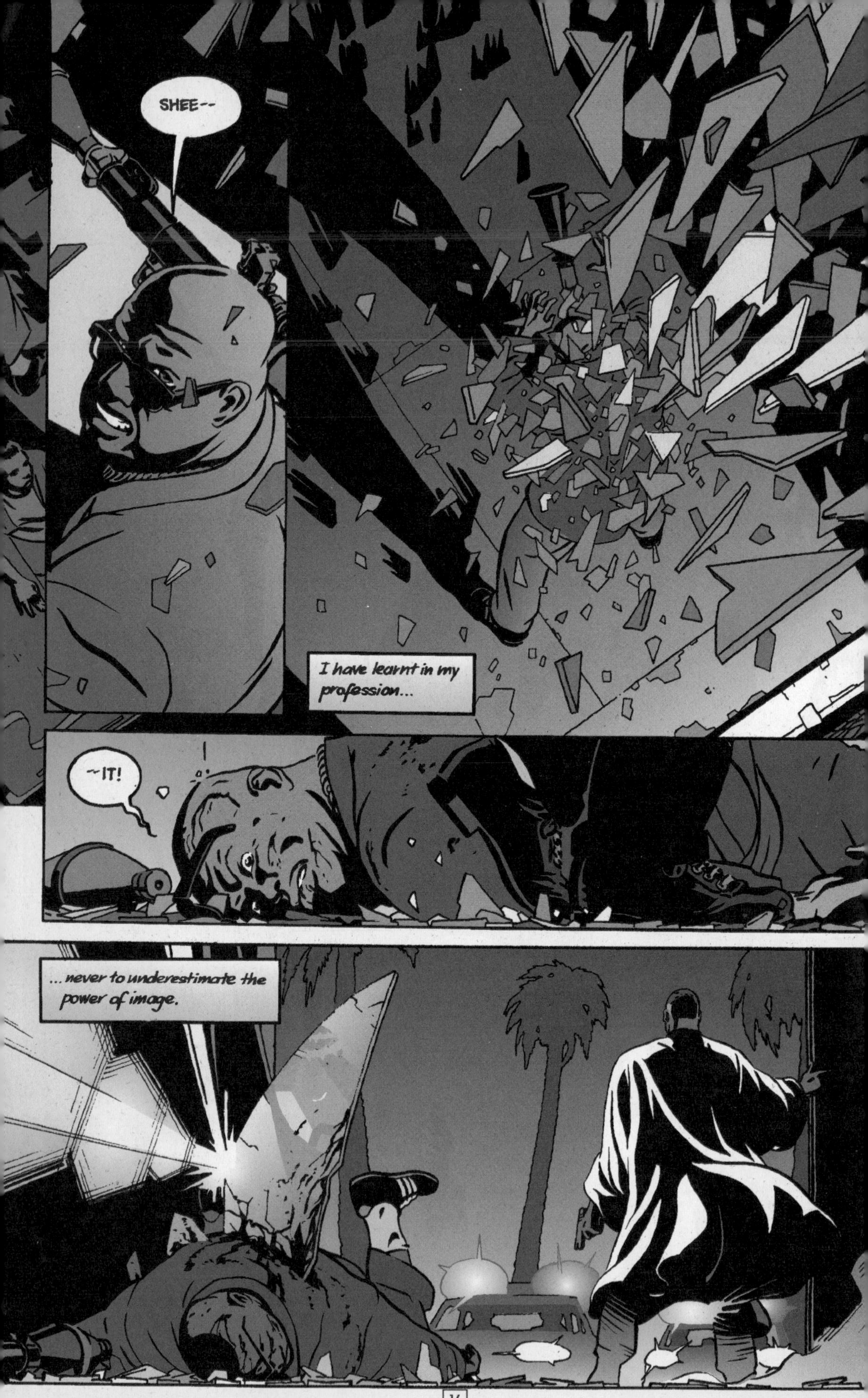
SHEE--
I have learnt in my profession...
--IT!
...never to underestimate the power of image.

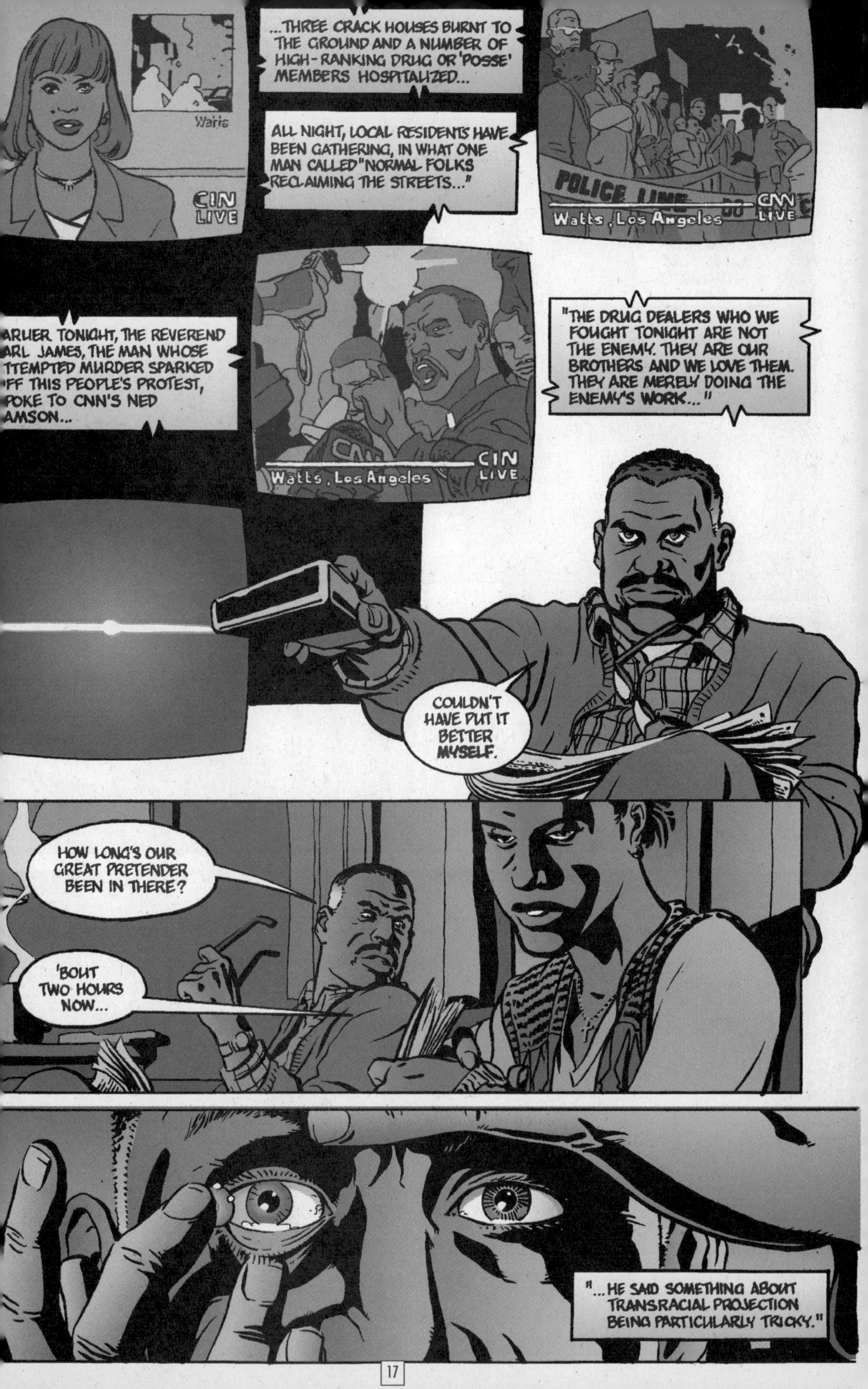
Watts
CIN LIVE
...THREE CRACK HOUSES BURNT TO THE GROUND AND A NUMBER OF HIGH-RANKING DRUG OR 'POSSE' MEMBERS HOSPITALIZED...
ALL NIGHT, LOCAL RESIDENTS HAVE BEEN GATHERING, IN WHAT ONE MAN CALLED "NORMAL FOLKS RECLAIMING THE STREETS..."
POLICE LINE
Watts, Los Angeles
CNN LIVE
ARLIER TONIGHT, THE REVEREND ARL JAMES, THE MAN WHOSE TTEMPTED MURDER SPARKED FF THIS PEOPLE'S PROTEST, POKE TO CNN'S NED AMSON...
Watts, Los Angeles
CIN LIVE
"THE DRUG DEALERS WHO WE FOUGHT TONIGHT ARE NOT THE ENEMY. THEY ARE OUR BROTHERS AND WE LOVE THEM. THEY ARE MERELY DOING THE ENEMY'S WORK..."
COULDN'T HAVE PUT IT BETTER MYSELF.
HOW LONG'S OUR GREAT PRETENDER BEEN IN THERE?
'BOUT TWO HOURS NOW...
"...HE SAID SOMETHING ABOUT TRANSRACIAL PROJECTION BEING PARTICULARLY TRICKY."

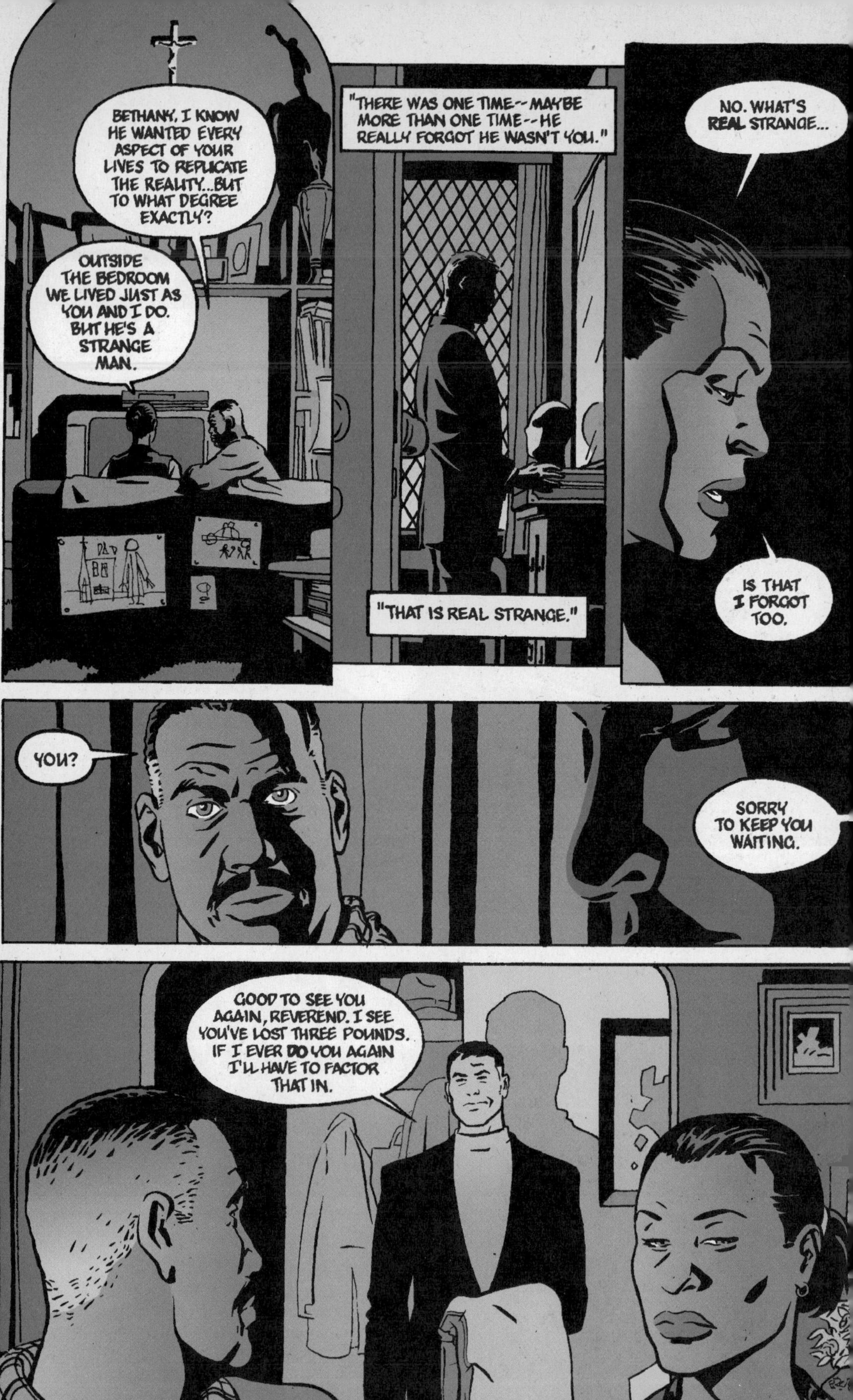

BETHANY, I KNOW HE WANTED EVERY ASPECT OF YOUR LIVES TO REPLICATE THE REALITY...BUT TO WHAT DEGREE EXACTLY?
OUTSIDE THE BEDROOM WE LIVED JUST AS YOU AND I DO. BUT HE'S A STRANGE MAN.
DAD
"THERE WAS ONE TIME--MAYBE MORE THAN ONE TIME--HE REALLY FORGOT HE WASN'T YOU."
"THAT IS REAL STRANGE."
NO. WHAT'S REAL STRANGE...
IS THAT I FORGOT TOO.
YOU?
SORRY TO KEEP YOU WAITING.
GOOD TO SEE YOU AGAIN, REVEREND. I SEE YOU'VE LOST THREE POUNDS. IF I EVER DO YOU AGAIN I'LL HAVE TO FACTOR THAT IN.

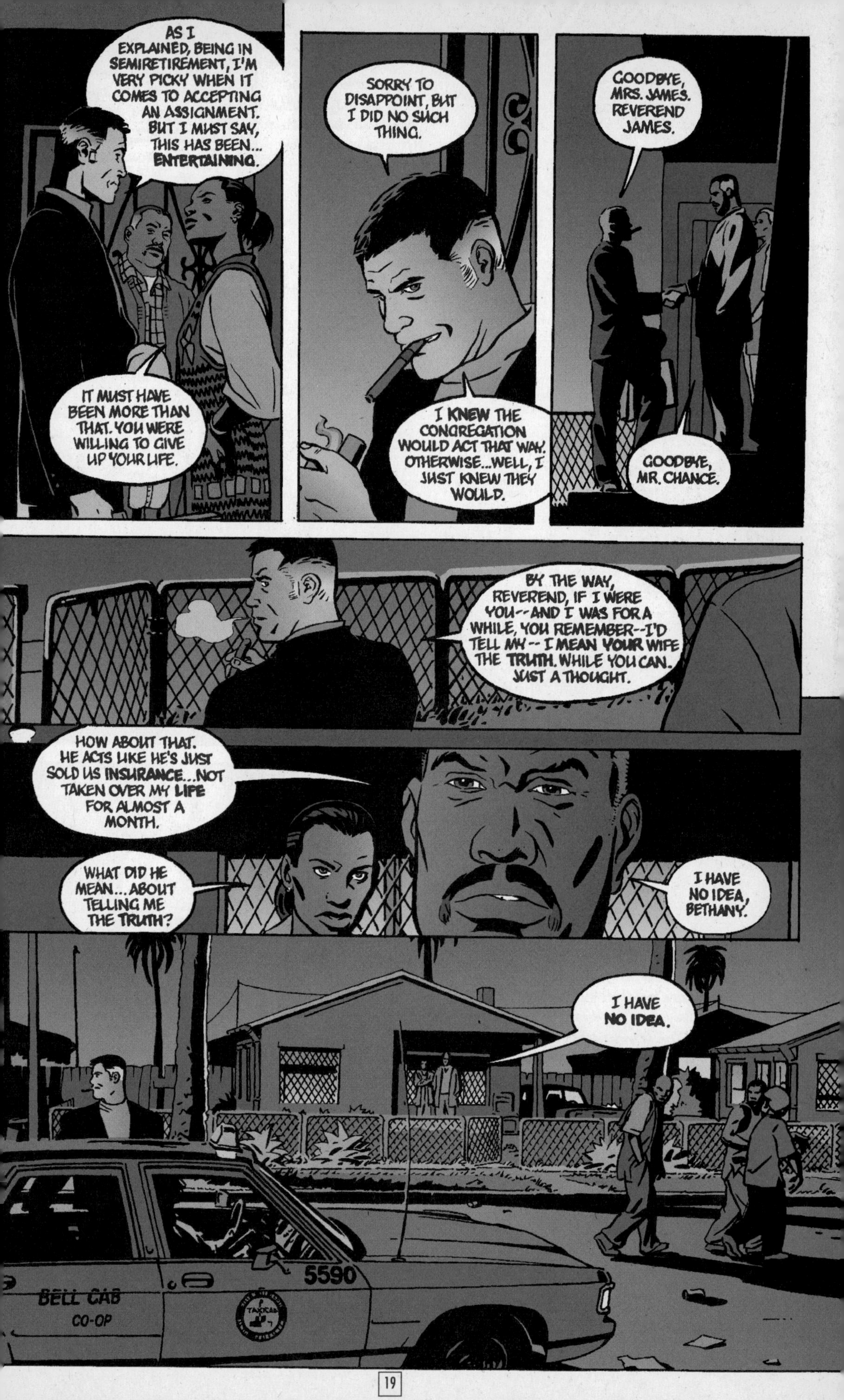
AS I EXPLAINED, BEING IN SEMIRETIREMENT, I'M VERY PICKY WHEN IT COMES TO ACCEPTING AN ASSIGNMENT. BUT I MUST SAY, THIS HAS BEEN... ENTERTAINING.
IT MUST HAVE BEEN MORE THAN THAT. YOU WERE WILLING TO GIVE UP YOUR LIFE.
SORRY TO DISAPPOINT, BUT I DID NO SUCH THING.
I KNEW THE CONGREGATION WOULD ACT THAT WAY. OTHERWISE...WELL, I JUST KNEW THEY WOULD.
GOODBYE, MRS. JAMES. REVEREND JAMES.
GOODBYE, MR. CHANCE.
BY THE WAY, REVEREND, IF I WERE YOU--AND I WAS FOR A WHILE, YOU REMEMBER--I'D TELL MY -- I MEAN YOUR WIFE THE TRUTH. WHILE YOU CAN. JUST A THOUGHT.
HOW ABOUT THAT. HE ACTS LIKE HE'S JUST SOLD US INSURANCE...NOT TAKEN OVER MY LIFE FOR ALMOST A MONTH.
WHAT DID HE MEAN... ABOUT TELLING ME THE TRUTH?
I HAVE NO IDEA, BETHANY.
I HAVE NO IDEA.
5590
BELL CAB
CO-OP

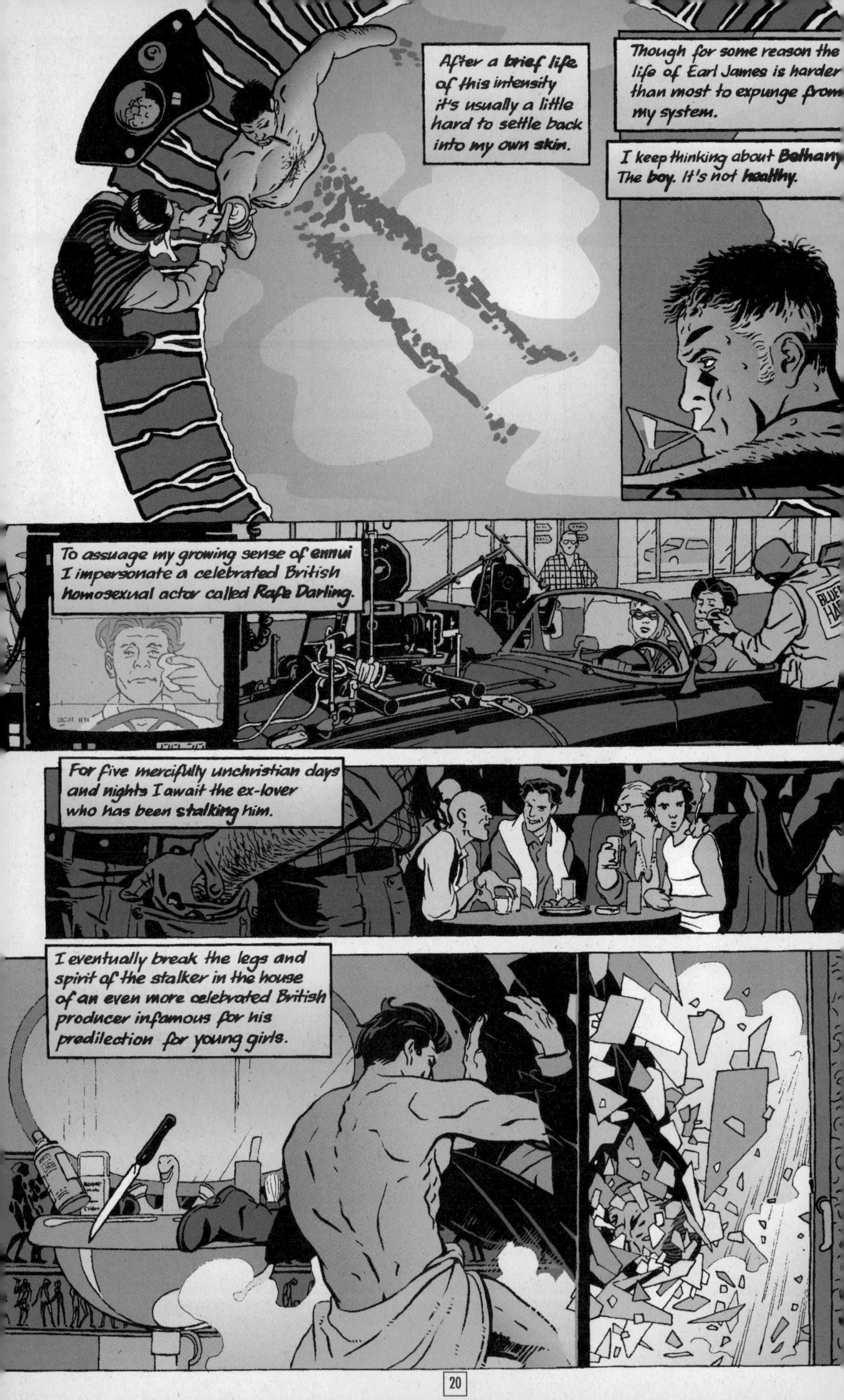

After a brief life of this intensity it's usually a little hard to settle back into my own skin.
Though for some reason the life of Earl James is harder than most to expunge from my system.
I keep thinking about Bethany. The boy. It's not healthy.
To assuage my growing sense of ennui I impersonate a celebrated British homosexual actor called Rafe Darling.
For five mercifully unchristian days and nights I await the ex-lover who has been stalking him.
I eventually break the legs and spirit of the stalker in the house of an even more celebrated British producer infamous for his predilection for young girls.

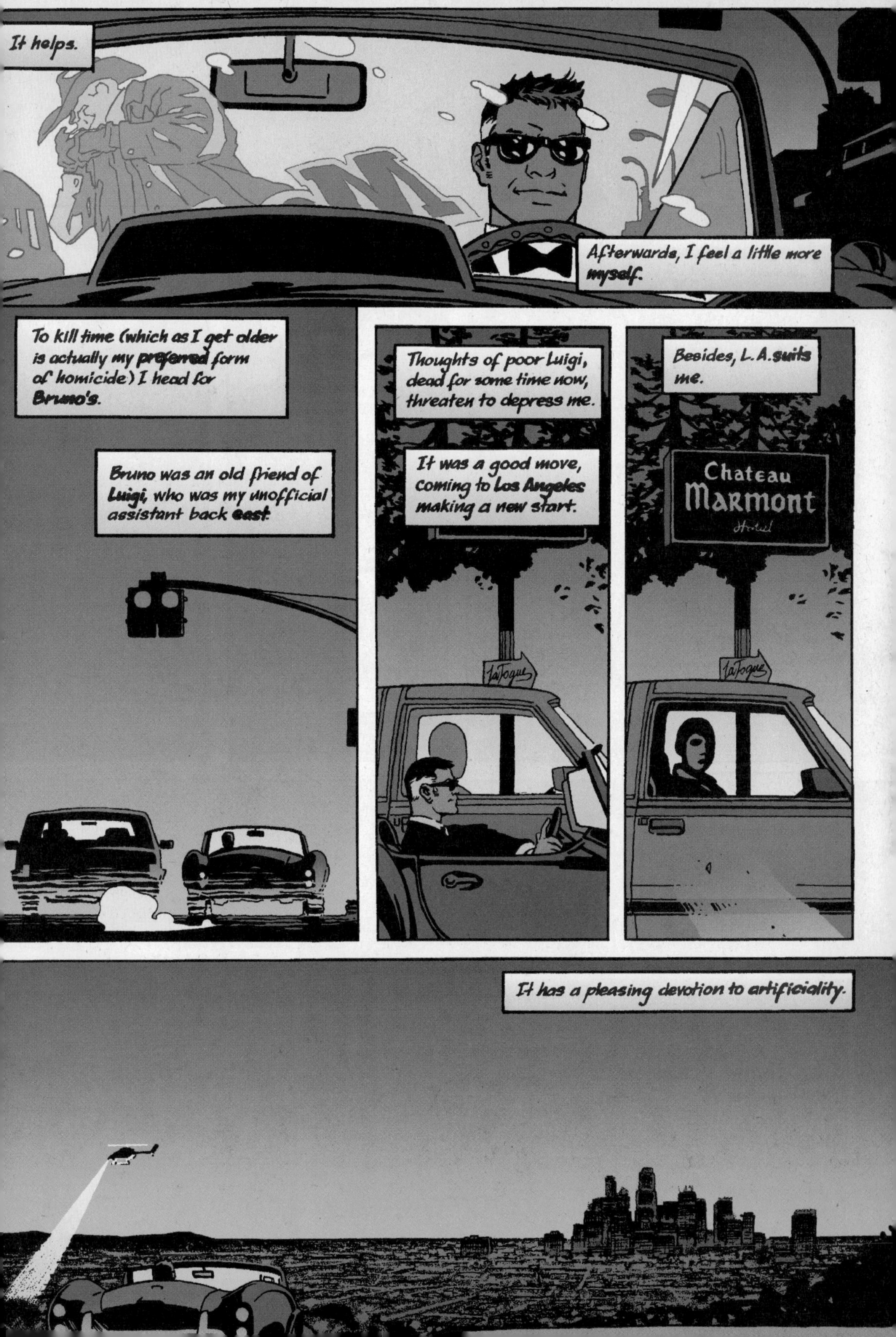

It helps.
Afterwards, I feel a little more myself.
To kill time (which as I get older is actually my preferred form of homicide) I head for Bruno's.
Bruno was an old friend of Luigi, who was my unofficial assistant back east.
Thoughts of poor Luigi, dead for some time now, threaten to depress me.
It was a good move, coming to Los Angeles making a new start.
Besides, L.A. suits me.
Chateau Marmont Hotel
It has a pleasing devotion to artificiality.

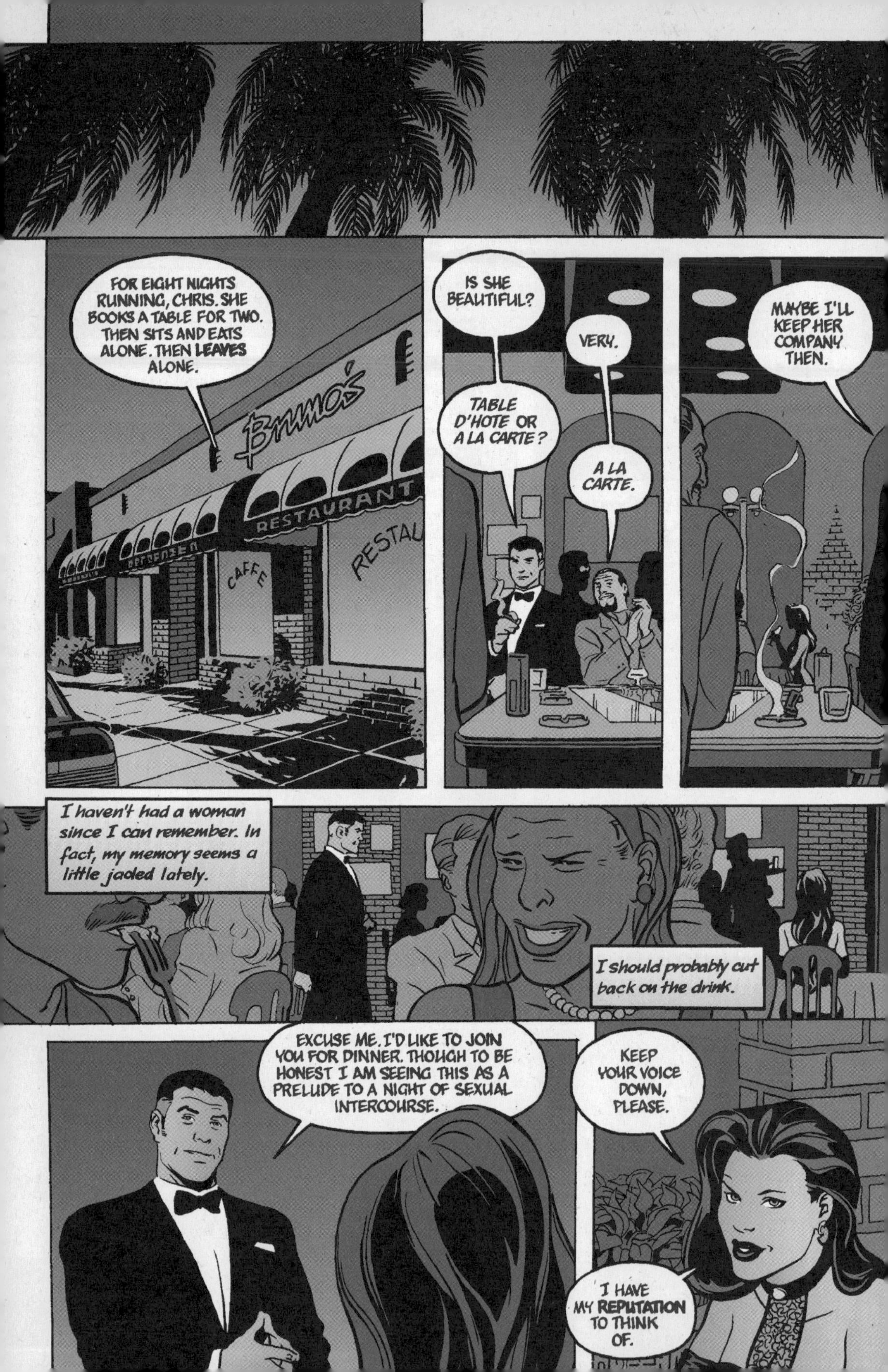
FOR EIGHT NIGHTS RUNNING, CHRIS. SHE BOOKS A TABLE FOR TWO. THEN SITS AND EATS ALONE. THEN LEAVES ALONE.
Bruno's
RESTAURANT
CAFFE
RESTAU
IS SHE BEAUTIFUL?
VERY.
TABLE D'HOTE OR A LA CARTE?
A LA CARTE.
MAYBE I'LL KEEP HER COMPANY THEN.
I haven't had a woman since I can remember. In fact, my memory seems a little jaded lately.
I should probably cut back on the drink.
EXCUSE ME. I'D LIKE TO JOIN YOU FOR DINNER. THOUGH TO BE HONEST I AM SEEING THIS AS A PRELUDE TO A NIGHT OF SEXUAL INTERCOURSE.
KEEP YOUR VOICE DOWN, PLEASE.
I HAVE MY REPUTATION TO THINK OF.

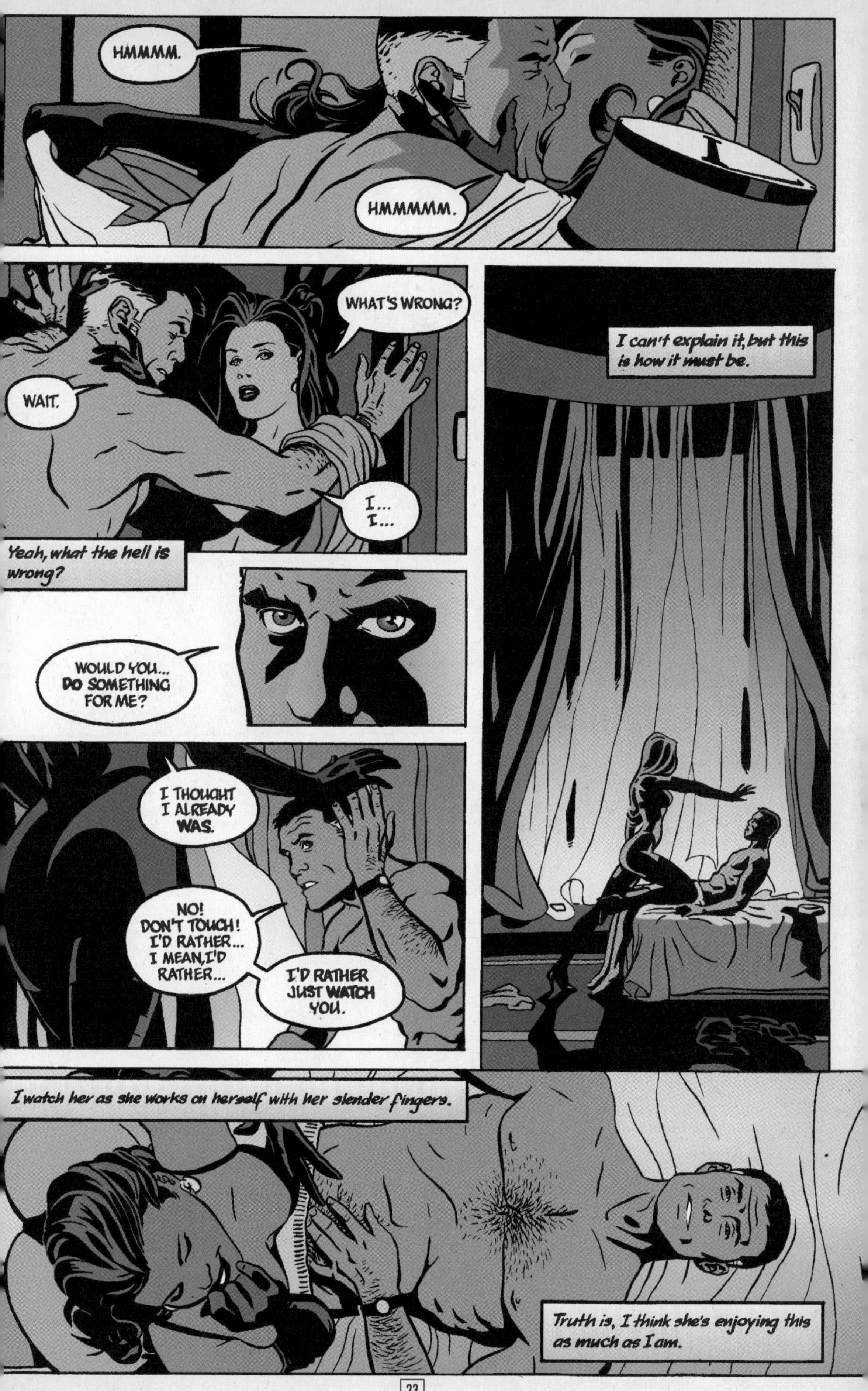
HMMMM.
HMMMMM.
WHAT'S WRONG?
WAIT.
I... I...
Yeah, what the hell is wrong?
I can't explain it, but this is how it must be.
WOULD YOU... DO SOMETHING FOR ME?
I THOUGHT I ALREADY WAS.
NO! DON'T TOUCH! I'D RATHER... I MEAN, I'D RATHER...
I'D RATHER JUST WATCH YOU.
I watch her as she works on herself with her slender fingers.
Truth is, I think she's enjoying this as much as I am.

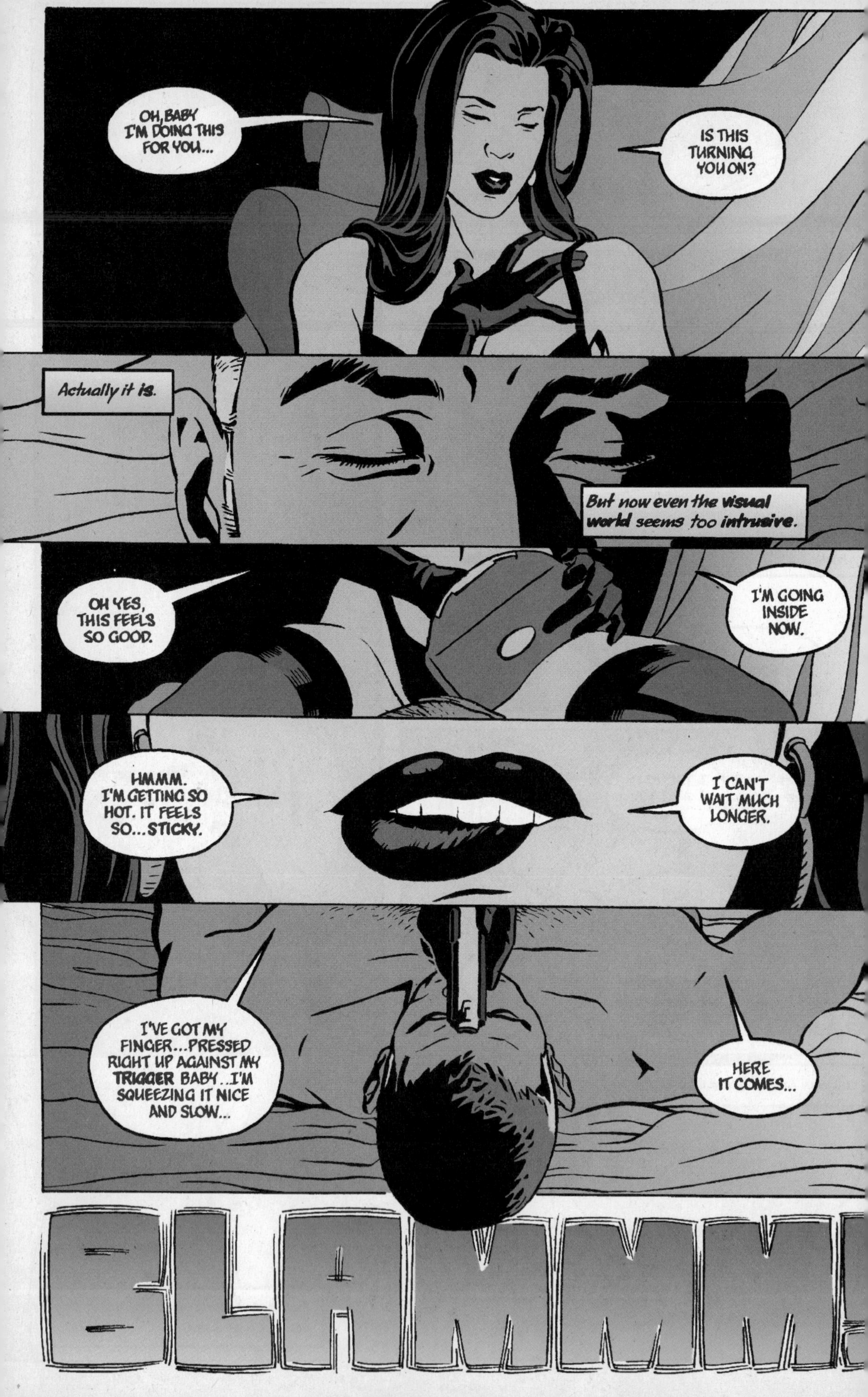

OH, BABY I'M DOING THIS FOR YOU...
IS THIS TURNING YOU ON?
Actually it is.
But now even the visual world seems too intrusive.
OH YES, THIS FEELS SO GOOD.
I'M GOING INSIDE NOW.
HMMM. I'M GETTING SO HOT. IT FEELS SO...STICKY.
I CAN'T WAIT MUCH LONGER.
I'VE GOT MY FINGER...PRESSED RIGHT UP AGAINST MY TRIGGER BABY...I'M SQUEEZING IT NICE AND SLOW...
HERE IT COMES...

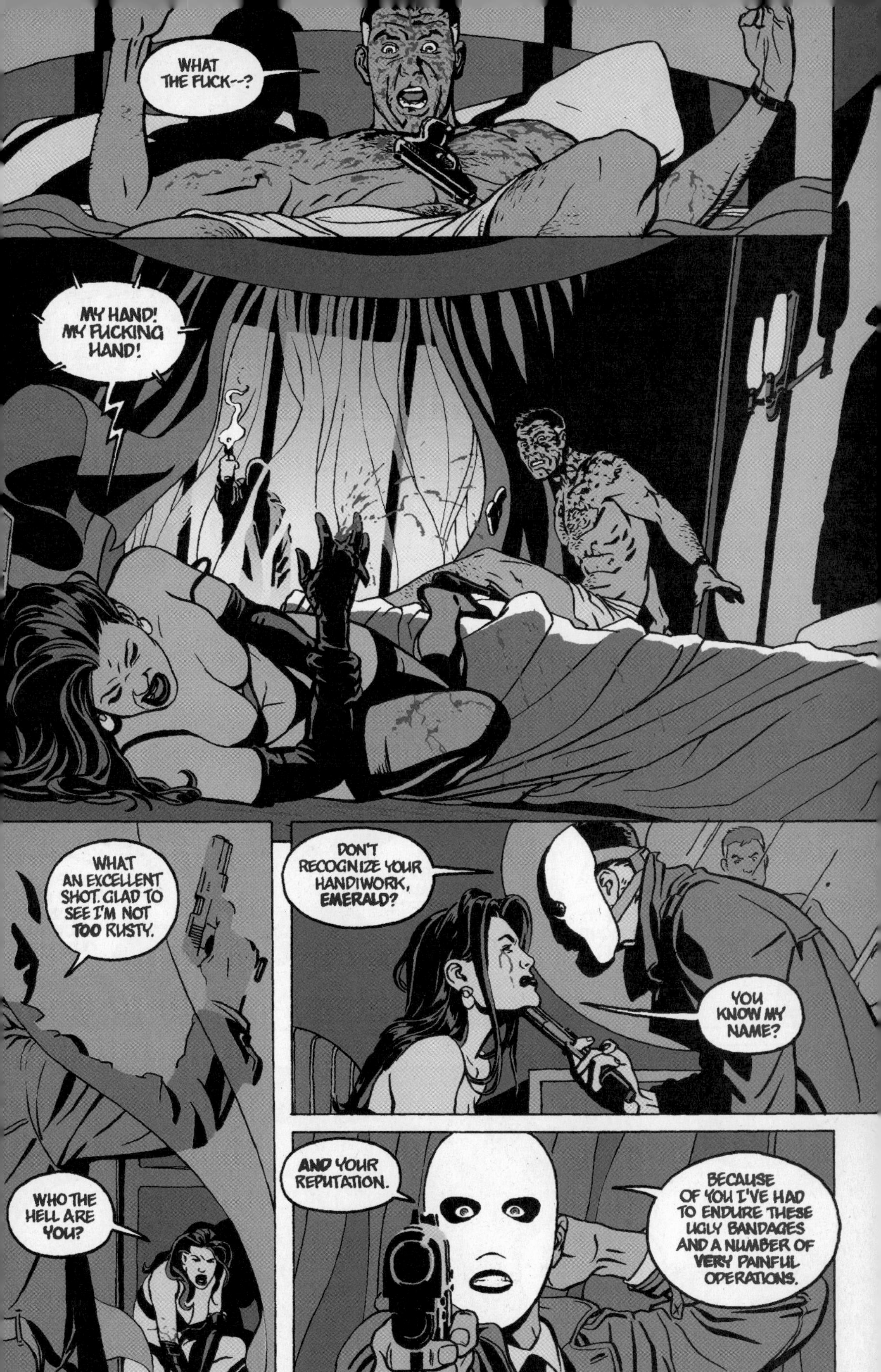
WHAT THE FUCK--?
MY HAND! MY FUCKING HAND!
WHAT AN EXCELLENT SHOT. GLAD TO SEE I'M NOT TOO RUSTY.
WHO THE HELL ARE YOU?
DON'T RECOGNIZE YOUR HANDIWORK, EMERALD?
YOU KNOW MY NAME?
AND YOUR REPUTATION.
BECAUSE OF YOU I'VE HAD TO ENDURE THESE UGLY BANDAGES AND A NUMBER OF VERY PAINFUL OPERATIONS.

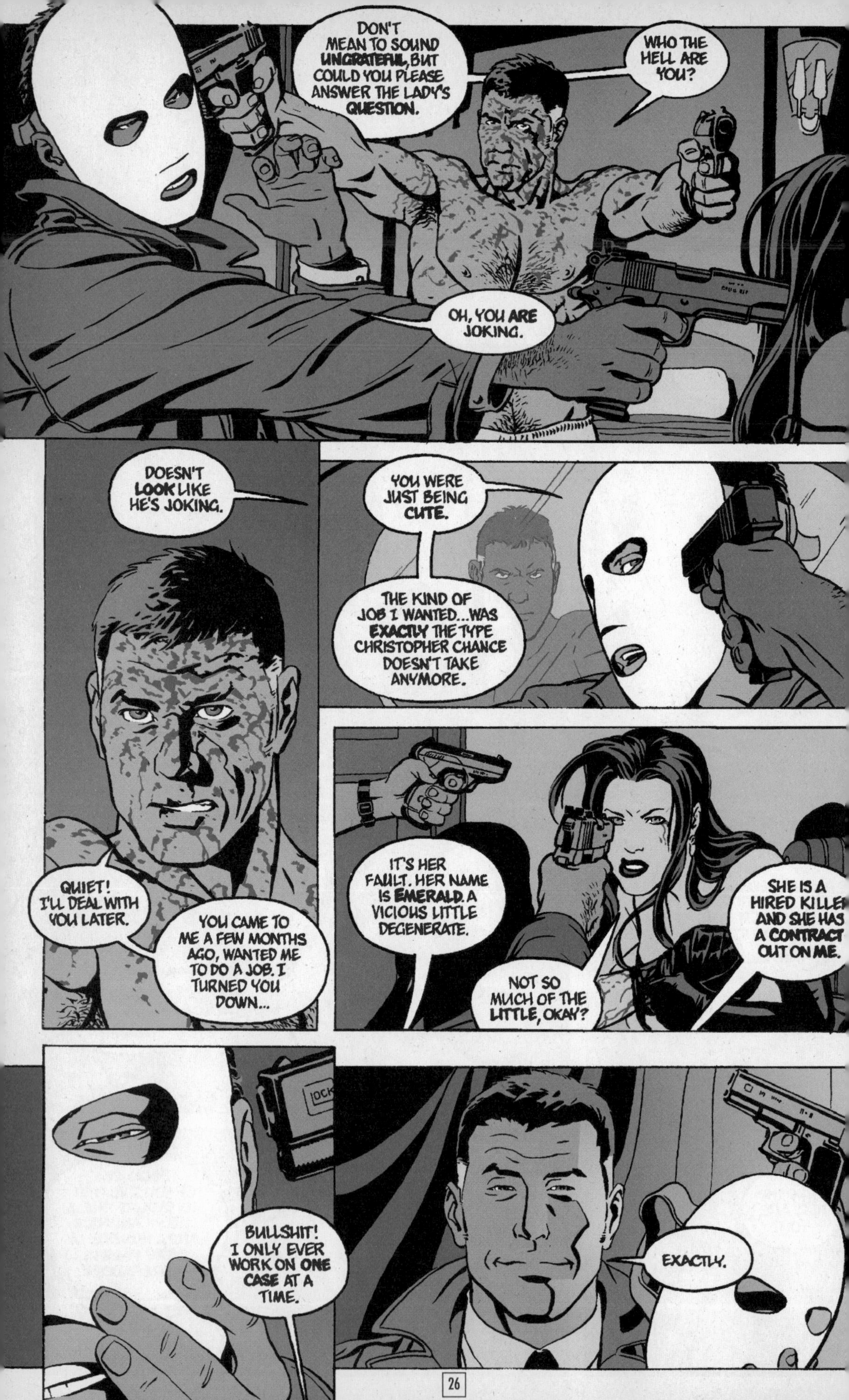
DON'T MEAN TO SOUND UNGRATEFUL, BUT COULD YOU PLEASE ANSWER THE LADY'S QUESTION.
WHO THE HELL ARE YOU?
OH, YOU ARE JOKING.
DOESN'T LOOK LIKE HE'S JOKING.
QUIET! I'LL DEAL WITH YOU LATER.
YOU CAME TO ME A FEW MONTHS AGO, WANTED ME TO DO A JOB. I TURNED YOU DOWN...
YOU WERE JUST BEING CUTE.
THE KIND OF JOB I WANTED...WAS EXACTLY THE TYPE CHRISTOPHER CHANCE DOESN'T TAKE ANYMORE.
IT'S HER FAULT. HER NAME IS EMERALD. A VICIOUS LITTLE DEGENERATE.
NOT SO MUCH OF THE LITTLE, OKAY?
SHE IS A HIRED KILLE[R] AND SHE HAS A CONTRACT OUT ON ME.
BULLSHIT! I ONLY EVER WORK ON ONE CASE AT A TIME.
EXACTLY.

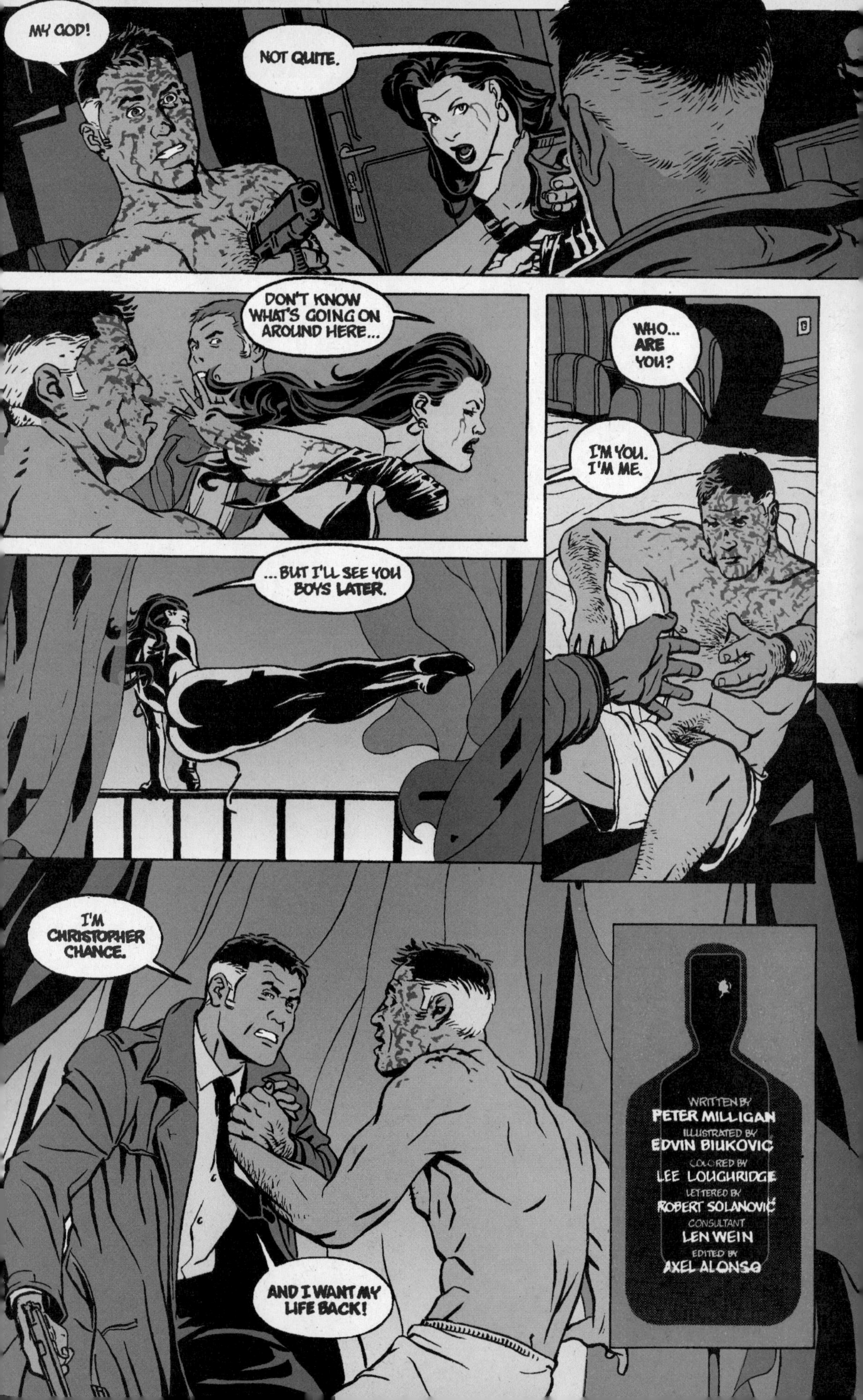
MY GOD!
NOT QUITE.
DON'T KNOW WHAT'S GOING ON AROUND HERE...
...BUT I'LL SEE YOU BOYS LATER.
13
WHO... ARE YOU?
I'M YOU. I'M ME.
I'M CHRISTOPHER CHANCE.
AND I WANT MY LIFE BACK!
WRITTEN BY
PETER MILLIGAN
ILLUSTRATED BY
EDVIN BIUKOVIC
COLORED BY
LEE LOUGHRIDGE
LETTERED BY
ROBERT SOLANOVIĆ
CONSULTANT
LEN WEIN
EDITED BY
AXEL ALONSO

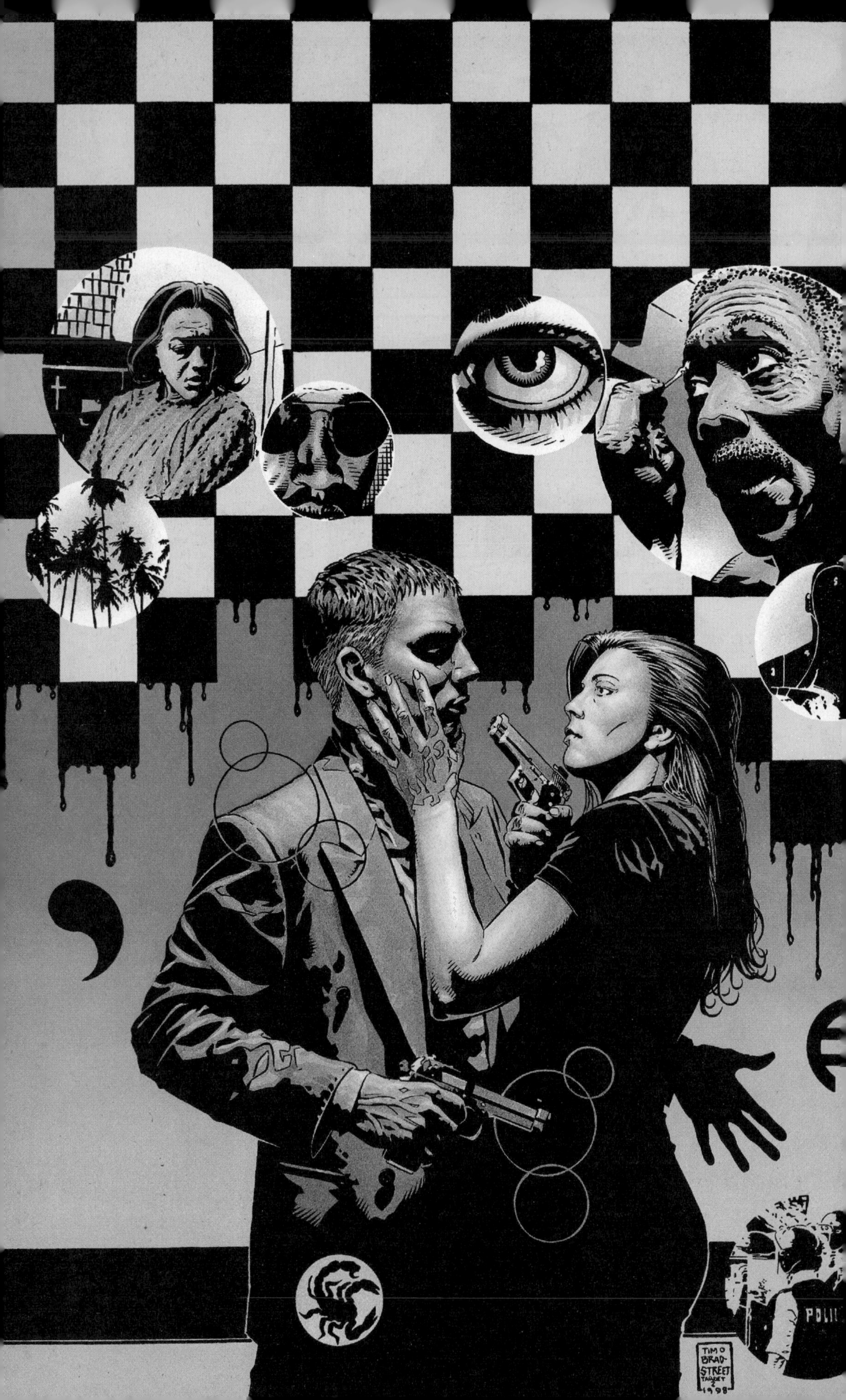
POLI
TIM O BRAD-STREET TARGET 2 1998

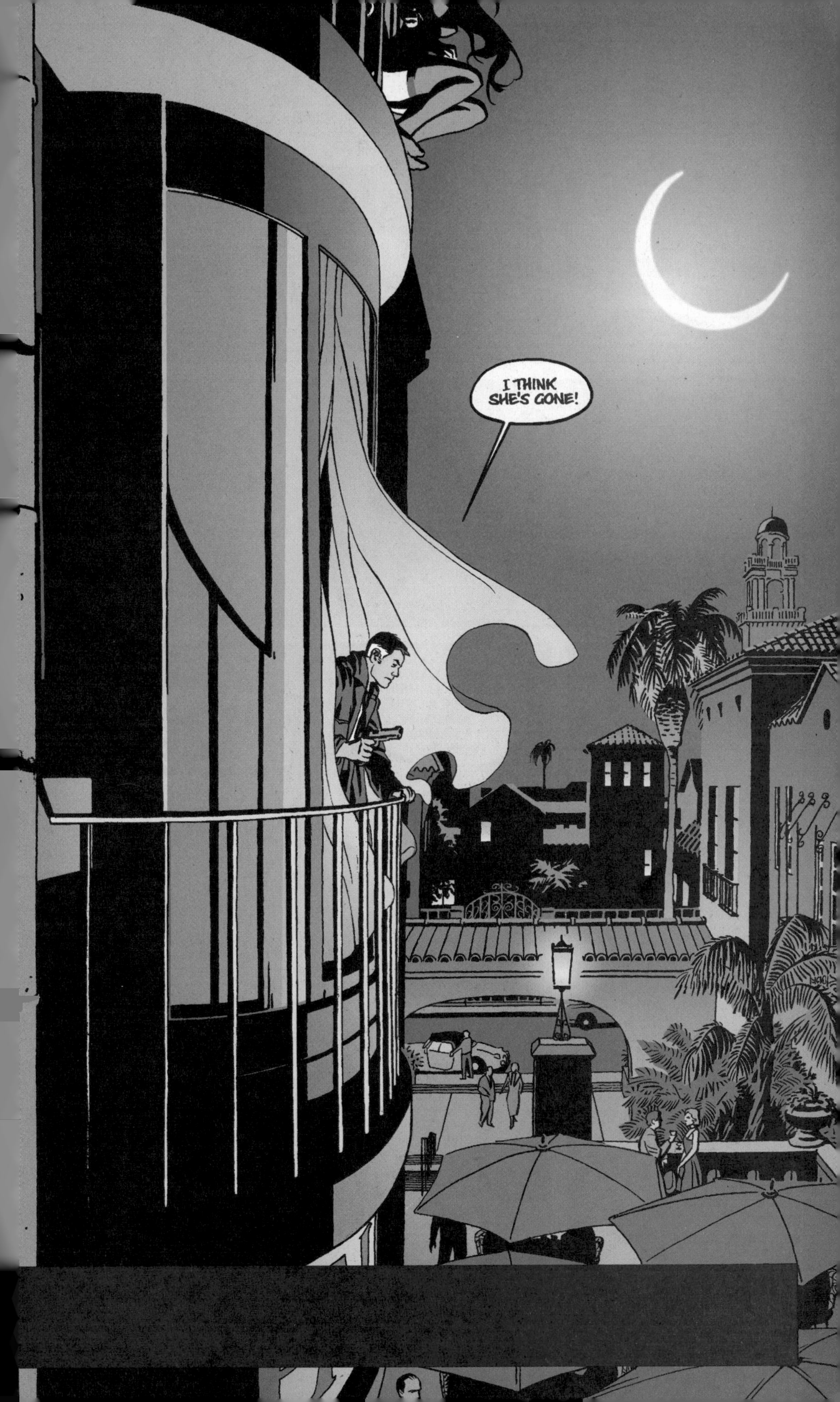
I THINK SHE'S GONE!

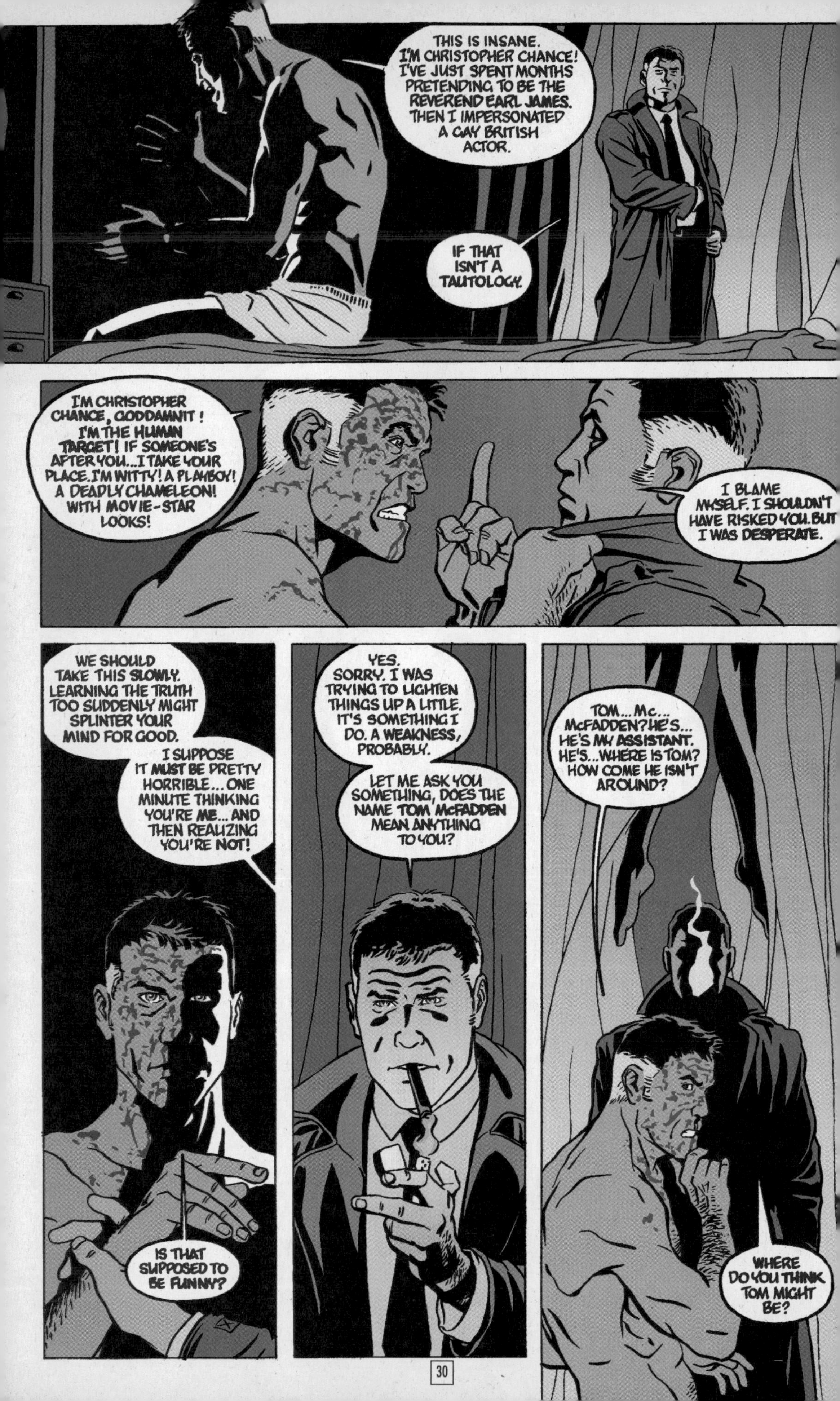
THIS IS INSANE. I'M CHRISTOPHER CHANCE! I'VE JUST SPENT MONTHS PRETENDING TO BE THE REVEREND EARL JAMES. THEN I IMPERSONATED A GAY BRITISH ACTOR.
IF THAT ISN'T A TAUTOLOGY.
I'M CHRISTOPHER CHANCE, GODDAMNIT! I'M THE HUMAN TARGET! IF SOMEONE'S AFTER YOU...I TAKE YOUR PLACE. I'M WITTY! A PLAYBOY! A DEADLY CHAMELEON! WITH MOVIE-STAR LOOKS!
I BLAME MYSELF. I SHOULDN'T HAVE RISKED YOU. BUT I WAS DESPERATE.
WE SHOULD TAKE THIS SLOWLY. LEARNING THE TRUTH TOO SUDDENLY MIGHT SPLINTER YOUR MIND FOR GOOD.
I SUPPOSE IT MUST BE PRETTY HORRIBLE... ONE MINUTE THINKING YOU'RE ME... AND THEN REALIZING YOU'RE NOT!
IS THAT SUPPOSED TO BE FUNNY?
YES. SORRY. I WAS TRYING TO LIGHTEN THINGS UP A LITTLE. IT'S SOMETHING I DO. A WEAKNESS, PROBABLY.
LET ME ASK YOU SOMETHING, DOES THE NAME TOM McFADDEN MEAN ANYTHING TO YOU?
TOM... Mc... McFADDEN? HE'S... HE'S MY ASSISTANT. HE'S...WHERE IS TOM? HOW COME HE ISN'T AROUND?
WHERE DO YOU THINK TOM MIGHT BE?

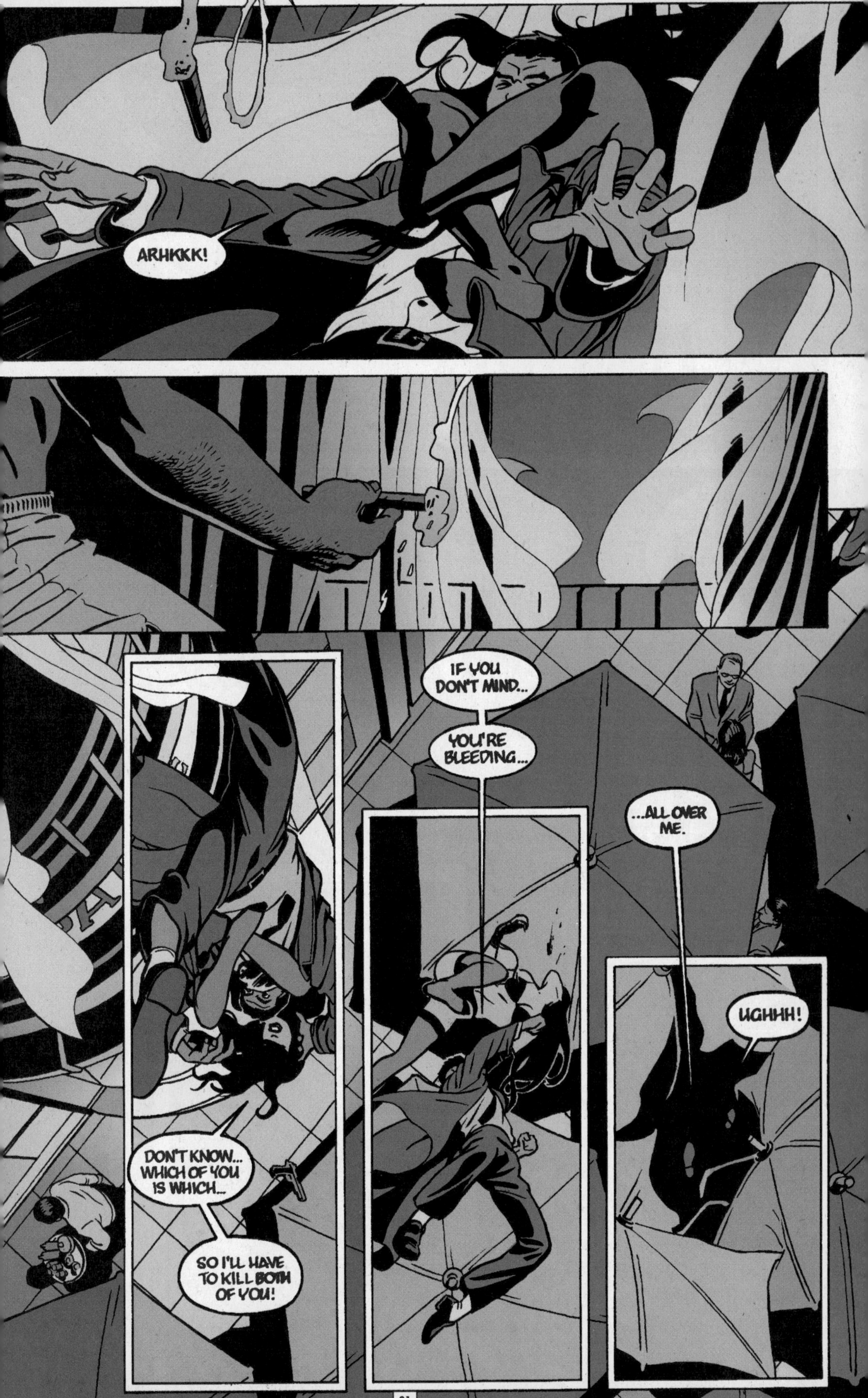
ARHKKK!
IF YOU DON'T MIND...
YOU'RE BLEEDING...
...ALL OVER ME.
DON'T KNOW... WHICH OF YOU IS WHICH...
SO I'LL HAVE TO KILL BOTH OF YOU!
UGHHH!

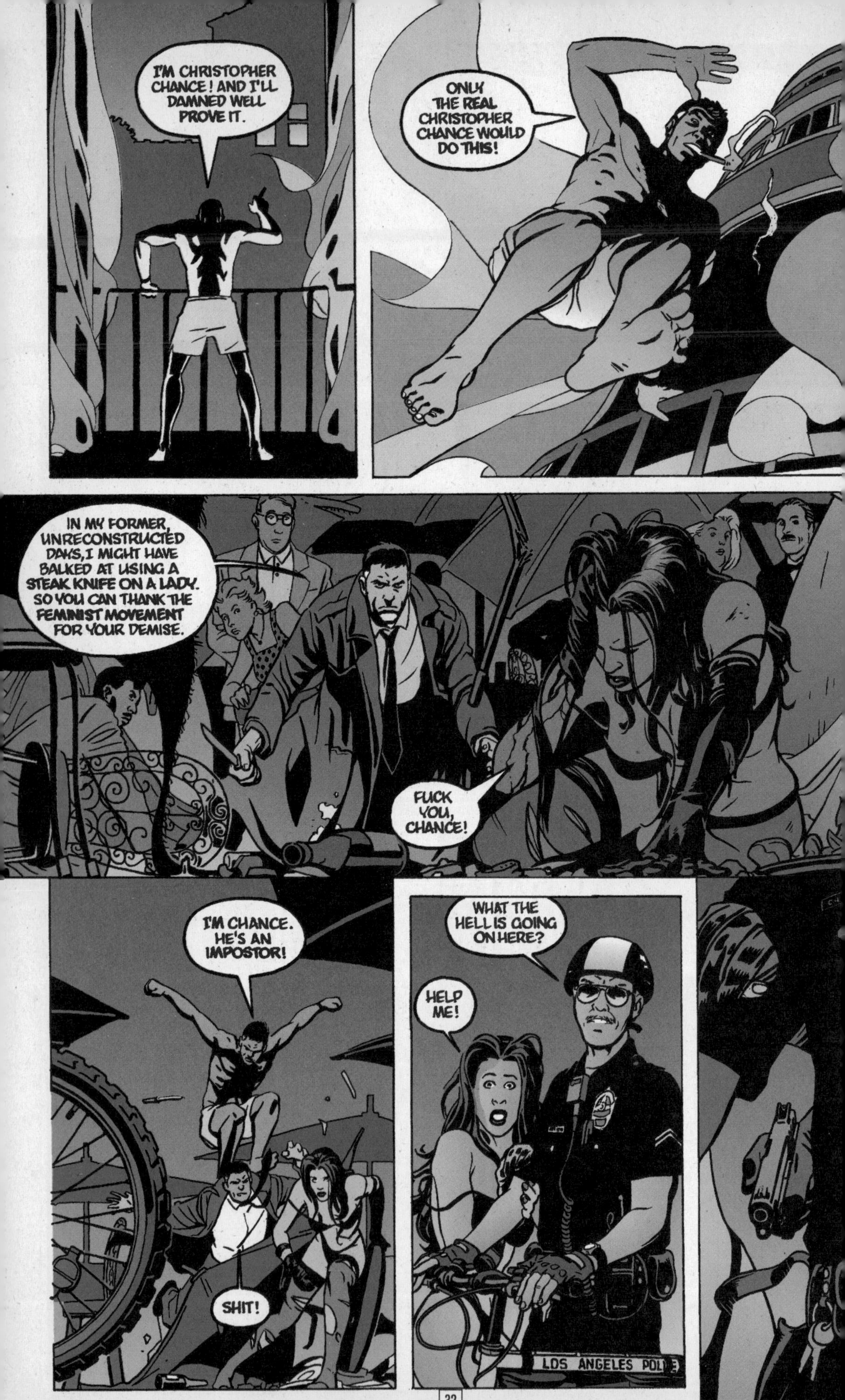
I'M CHRISTOPHER CHANCE! AND I'LL DAMNED WELL PROVE IT.
ONLY THE REAL CHRISTOPHER CHANCE WOULD DO THIS!
IN MY FORMER, UNRECONSTRUCTED DAYS, I MIGHT HAVE BALKED AT USING A STEAK KNIFE ON A LADY. SO YOU CAN THANK THE FEMINIST MOVEMENT FOR YOUR DEMISE.
FUCK YOU, CHANCE!
I'M CHANCE. HE'S AN IMPOSTOR!
SHIT!
WHAT THE HELL IS GOING ON HERE?
HELP ME!
LOS ANGELES POL

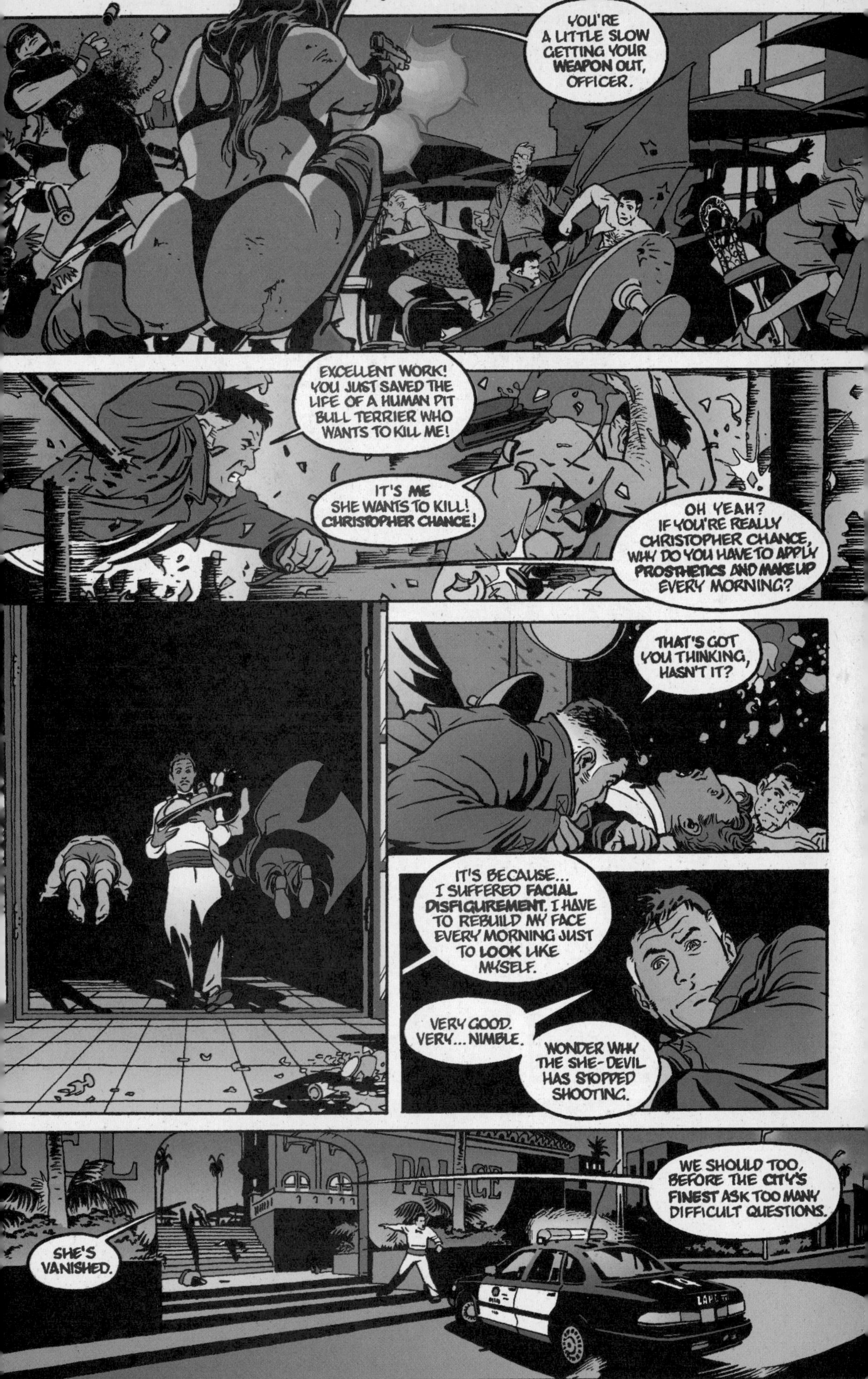
YOU'RE A LITTLE SLOW GETTING YOUR WEAPON OUT, OFFICER.
EXCELLENT WORK! YOU JUST SAVED THE LIFE OF A HUMAN PIT BULL TERRIER WHO WANTS TO KILL ME!
IT'S ME SHE WANTS TO KILL! CHRISTOPHER CHANCE!
OH YEAH? IF YOU'RE REALLY CHRISTOPHER CHANCE, WHY DO YOU HAVE TO APPLY PROSTHETICS AND MAKE UP EVERY MORNING?
THAT'S GOT YOU THINKING, HASN'T IT?
IT'S BECAUSE... I SUFFERED FACIAL DISFIGUREMENT. I HAVE TO REBUILD MY FACE EVERY MORNING JUST TO LOOK LIKE MYSELF.
VERY GOOD. VERY... NIMBLE.
WONDER WHY THE SHE-DEVIL HAS STOPPED SHOOTING.
SHE'S VANISHED.
WE SHOULD TOO, BEFORE THE CITY'S FINEST ASK TOO MANY DIFFICULT QUESTIONS.

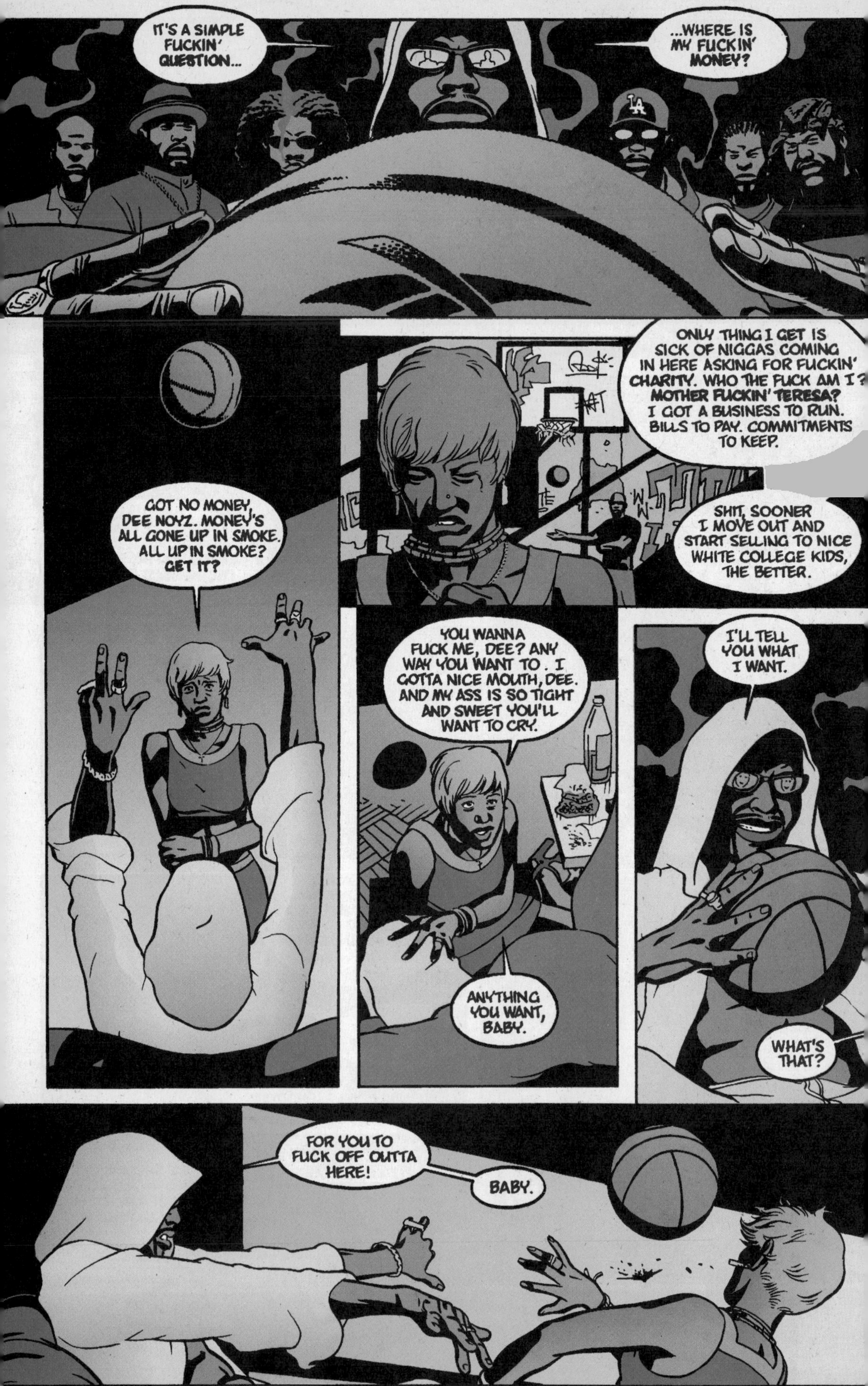
IT'S A SIMPLE FUCKIN' QUESTION...
...WHERE IS MY FUCKIN' MONEY?
GOT NO MONEY, DEE NOYZ. MONEY'S ALL GONE UP IN SMOKE. ALL UP IN SMOKE? GET IT?
ONLY THING I GET IS SICK OF NIGGAS COMING IN HERE ASKING FOR FUCKIN' CHARITY. WHO THE FUCK AM I? MOTHER FUCKIN' TERESA? I GOT A BUSINESS TO RUN. BILLS TO PAY. COMMITMENTS TO KEEP.
SHIT, SOONER I MOVE OUT AND START SELLING TO NICE WHITE COLLEGE KIDS, THE BETTER.
YOU WANNA FUCK ME, DEE? ANY WAY YOU WANT TO. I GOTTA NICE MOUTH, DEE. AND MY ASS IS SO TIGHT AND SWEET YOU'LL WANT TO CRY.
ANYTHING YOU WANT, BABY.
I'LL TELL YOU WHAT I WANT.
WHAT'S THAT?
FOR YOU TO FUCK OFF OUTTA HERE!
BABY.

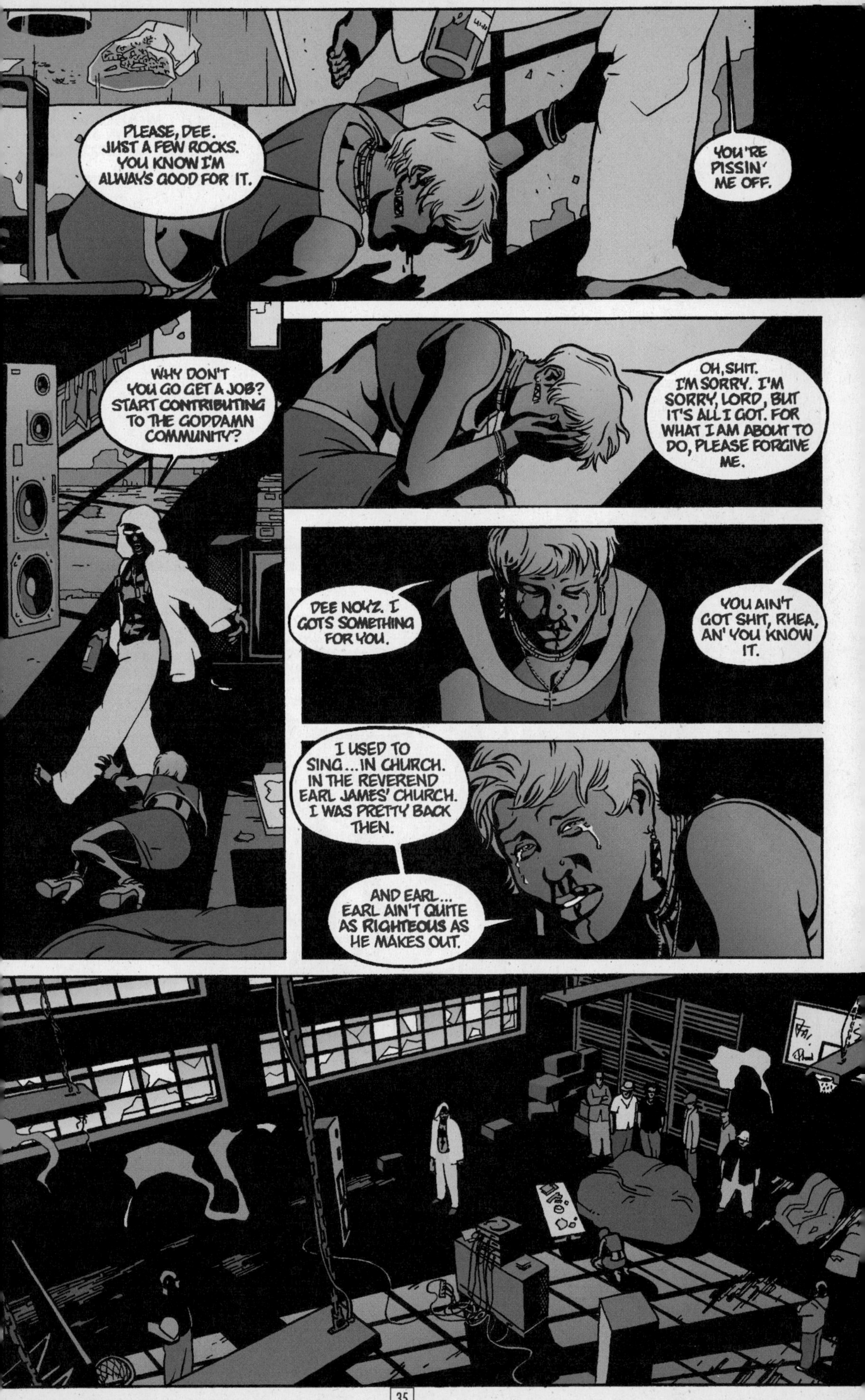
PLEASE, DEE. JUST A FEW ROCKS. YOU KNOW I'M ALWAYS GOOD FOR IT.
YOU'RE PISSIN' ME OFF.
WHY DON'T YOU GO GET A JOB? START CONTRIBUTING TO THE GODDAMN COMMUNITY?
OH, SHIT. I'M SORRY. I'M SORRY, LORD, BUT IT'S ALL I GOT. FOR WHAT I AM ABOUT TO DO, PLEASE FORGIVE ME.
DEE NOY'Z. I GOTS SOMETHING FOR YOU.
YOU AIN'T GOT SHIT, RHEA, AN' YOU KNOW IT.
I USED TO SING... IN CHURCH. IN THE REVEREND EARL JAMES' CHURCH. I WAS PRETTY BACK THEN.
AND EARL... EARL AIN'T QUITE AS RIGHTEOUS AS HE MAKES OUT.

YOU'RE NOT WHO YOU THINK YOU ARE.

OR THOUGHT YOU WERE. YOU'RE MY ASSISTANT. MORE THAN MY ASSISTANT, MY SUCCESSOR.

I'M TOM McFADDEN.

EXACTLY. TOM McFADDEN. GOOD OLD TOM. GOOD OLD MAC. DO YOU REMEMBER?

YOU...YOU SET UP AN AGENCY HERE, IN L.A.. BUT WHEN YOU STARTED TO FEEL... BURNOUT COMING ON... YOU HIRED AN ASSISTANT. ME. YOU TAUGHT ME. TAUGHT ME HOW TO WORK AS A HUMAN TARGET.

YOU WERE A NATURAL. BETTER THAN I EVER WAS. YOU COULD TOTALLY IMMERSE YOURSELF, TOTALLY LOSE YOURSELF IN A CLIENT'S PERSONALITY. YOU'RE GOOD.

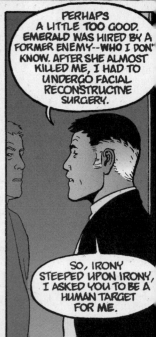

PERHAPS A LITTLE TOO GOOD. EMERALD WAS HIRED BY A FORMER ENEMY--WHO I DON' KNOW. AFTER SHE ALMOST KILLED ME, I HAD TO UNDERGO FACIAL RECONSTRUCTIVE SURGERY.

SO, IRONY STEEPED UPON IRONY, I ASKED YOU TO BE A HUMAN TARGET FOR ME.

BUT THAT'S NO LONGER YOUR CONCERN.

TAKE MY ADVICE, TOM, QUIT NOW. TAKE A VACATION. FIND YOURSELF AGAIN.

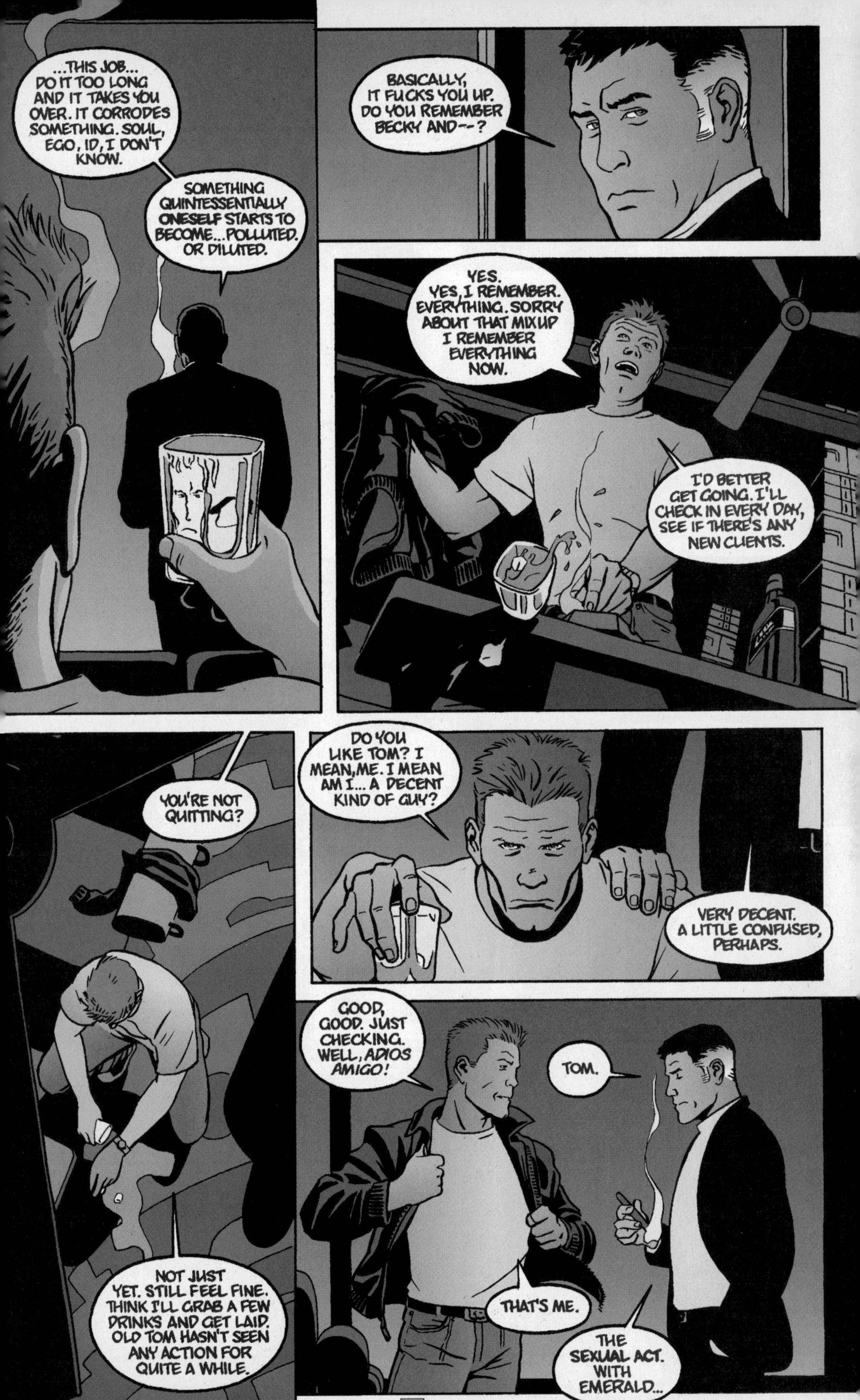
...THIS JOB... DO IT TOO LONG AND IT TAKES YOU OVER. IT CORRODES SOMETHING. SOUL, EGO, ID, I DON'T KNOW.
SOMETHING QUINTESSENTIALLY ONESELF STARTS TO BECOME... POLLUTED. OR DILUTED.
BASICALLY, IT FUCKS YOU UP. DO YOU REMEMBER BECKY AND--?
YES. YES, I REMEMBER. EVERYTHING. SORRY ABOUT THAT MIXUP I REMEMBER EVERYTHING NOW.
I'D BETTER GET GOING. I'LL CHECK IN EVERY DAY, SEE IF THERE'S ANY NEW CLIENTS.
YOU'RE NOT QUITTING?
NOT JUST YET. STILL FEEL FINE. THINK I'LL GRAB A FEW DRINKS AND GET LAID. OLD TOM HASN'T SEEN ANY ACTION FOR QUITE A WHILE.
DO YOU LIKE TOM? I MEAN, ME. I MEAN AM I... A DECENT KIND OF GUY?
VERY DECENT. A LITTLE CONFUSED, PERHAPS.
GOOD, GOOD. JUST CHECKING. WELL, ADIOS AMIGO!
TOM.
THAT'S ME.
THE SEXUAL ACT. WITH EMERALD...

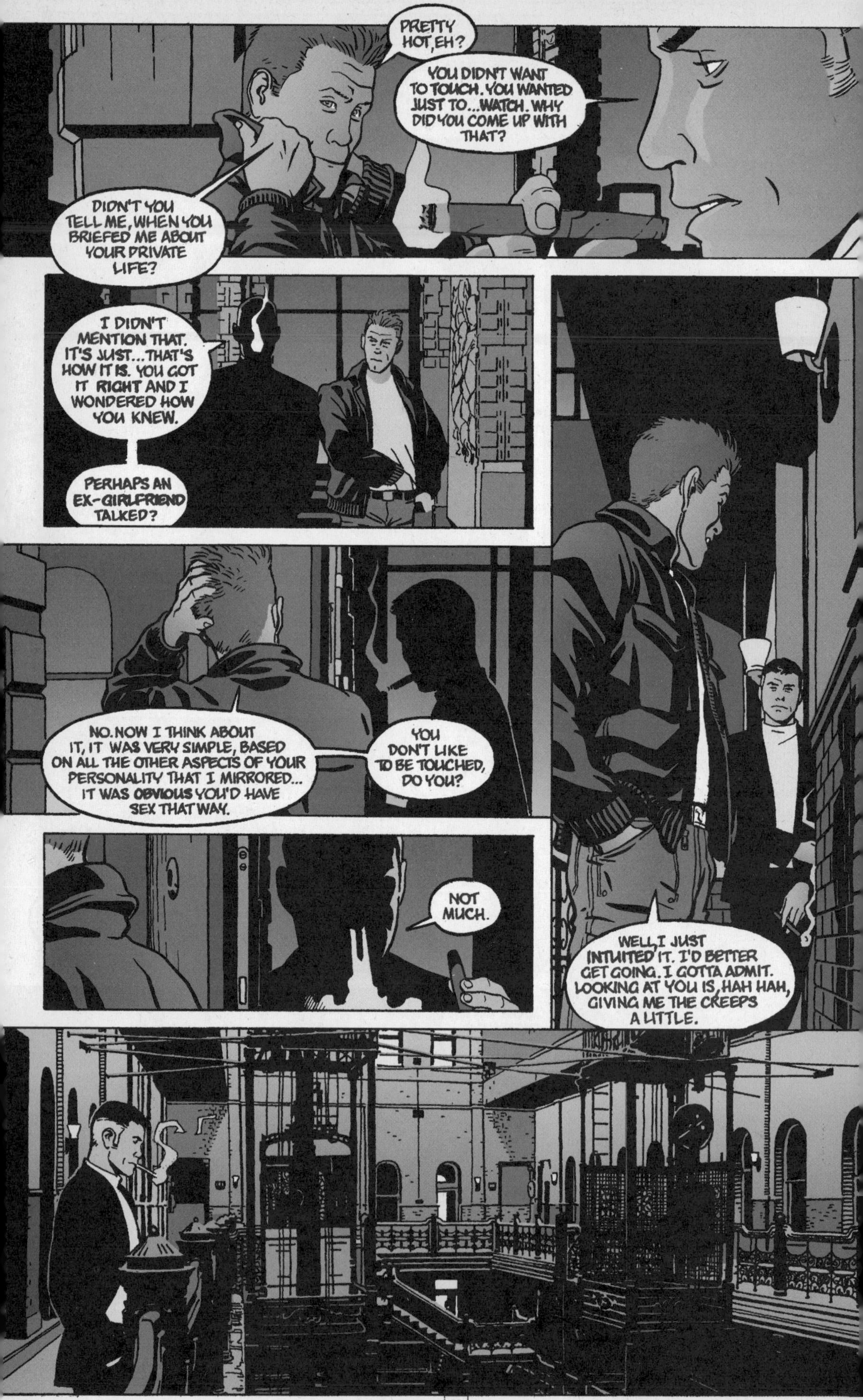
PRETTY HOT, EH?
YOU DIDN'T WANT TO TOUCH. YOU WANTED JUST TO...WATCH. WHY DID YOU COME UP WITH THAT?
DIDN'T YOU TELL ME, WHEN YOU BRIEFED ME ABOUT YOUR PRIVATE LIFE?
I DIDN'T MENTION THAT. IT'S JUST...THAT'S HOW IT IS. YOU GOT IT RIGHT AND I WONDERED HOW YOU KNEW.
PERHAPS AN EX-GIRLFRIEND TALKED?
NO. NOW I THINK ABOUT IT, IT WAS VERY SIMPLE, BASED ON ALL THE OTHER ASPECTS OF YOUR PERSONALITY THAT I MIRRORED... IT WAS OBVIOUS YOU'D HAVE SEX THAT WAY.
YOU DON'T LIKE TO BE TOUCHED, DO YOU?
NOT MUCH.
WELL, I JUST INTUITED IT. I'D BETTER GET GOING. I GOTTA ADMIT. LOOKING AT YOU IS, HAH HAH, GIVING ME THE CREEPS A LITTLE.

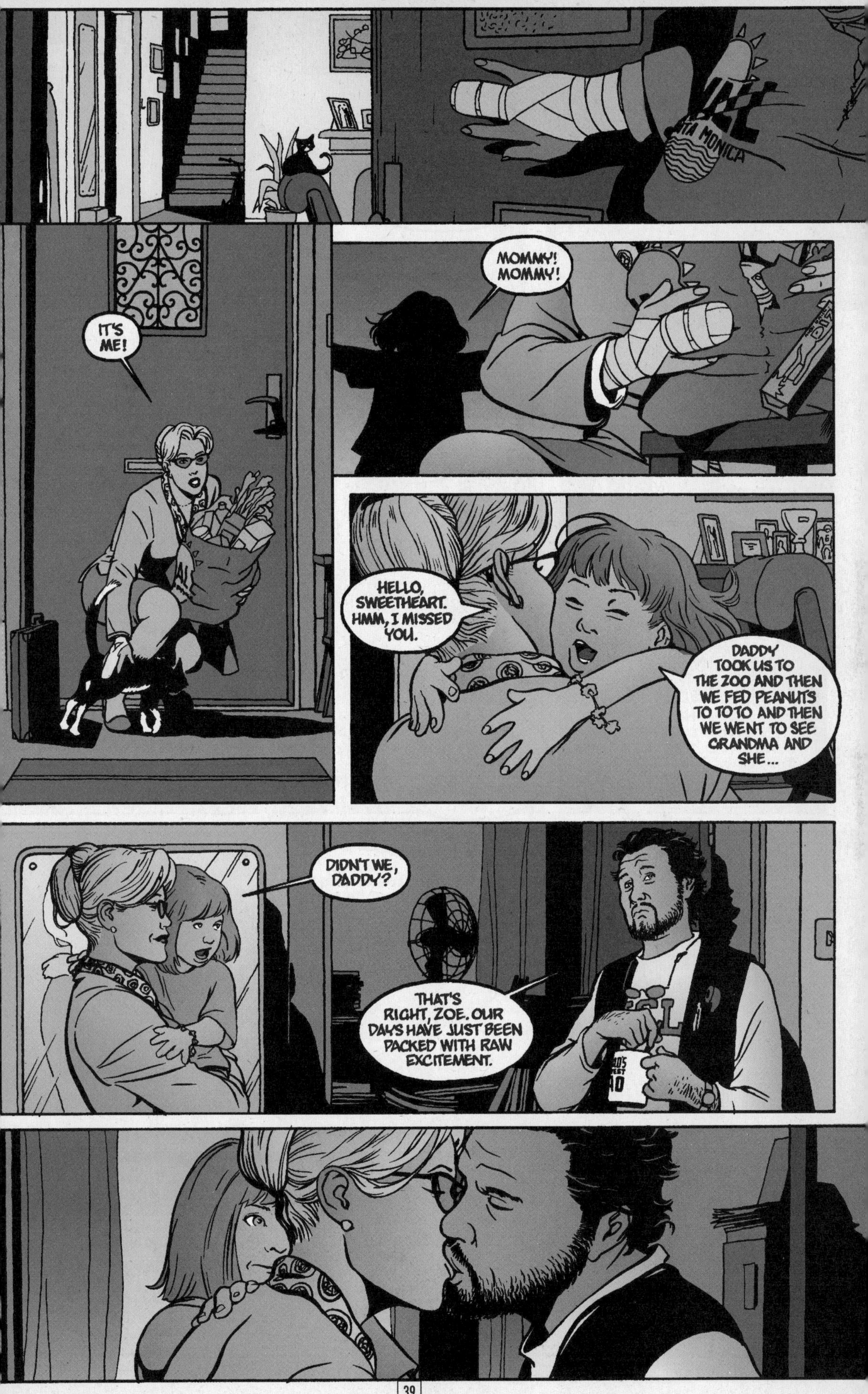

IT'S ME!
MOMMY! MOMMY!
HELLO, SWEETHEART. HMM, I MISSED YOU.
DADDY TOOK US TO THE ZOO AND THEN WE FED PEANUTS TO TOTO AND THEN WE WENT TO SEE GRANDMA AND SHE...
DIDN'T WE, DADDY?
THAT'S RIGHT, ZOE. OUR DAYS HAVE JUST BEEN PACKED WITH RAW EXCITEMENT.

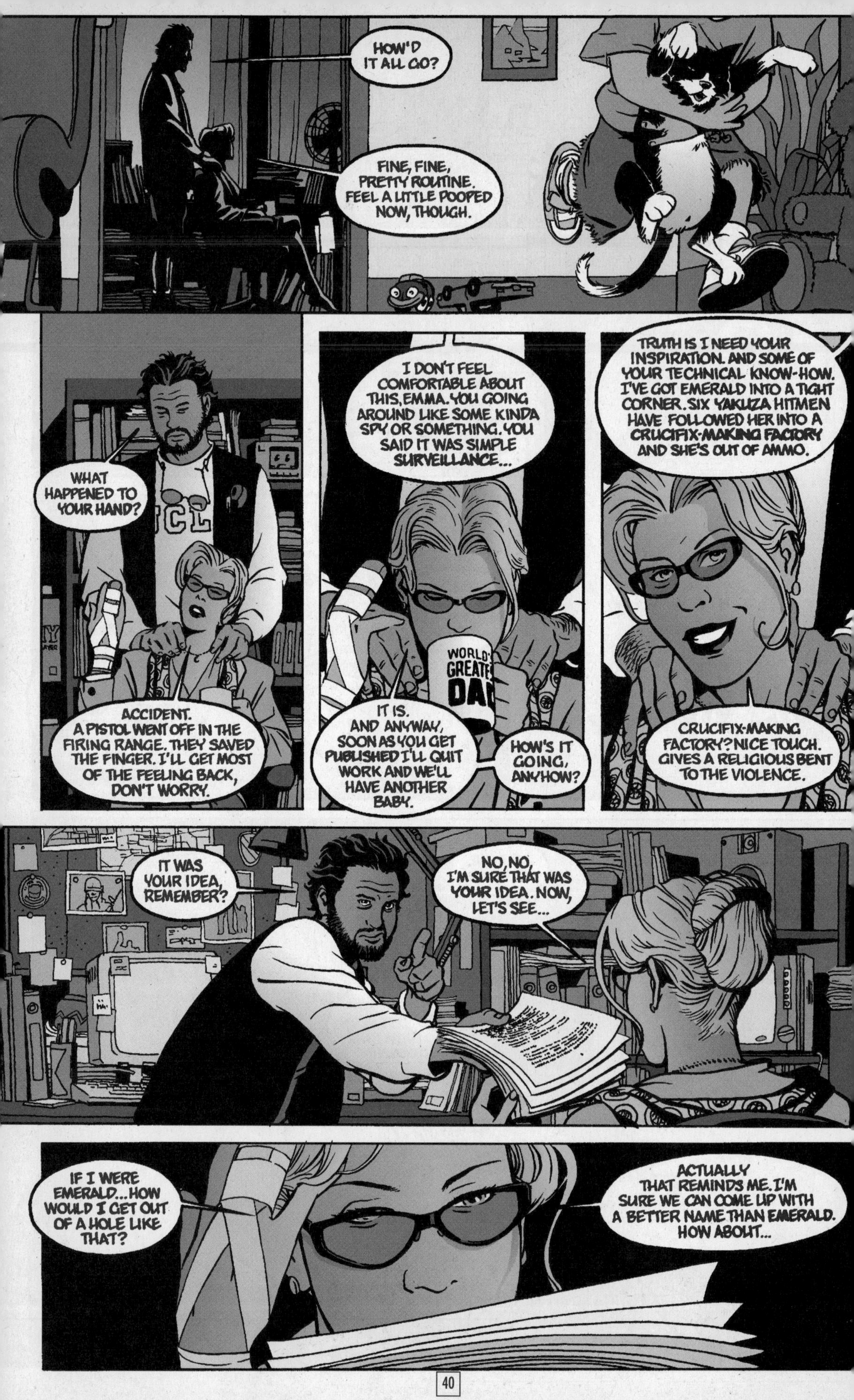
HOW'D IT ALL GO?
FINE, FINE, PRETTY ROUTINE. FEEL A LITTLE POOPED NOW, THOUGH.
WHAT HAPPENED TO YOUR HAND?
ACCIDENT. A PISTOL WENT OFF IN THE FIRING RANGE. THEY SAVED THE FINGER. I'LL GET MOST OF THE FEELING BACK, DON'T WORRY.
I DON'T FEEL COMFORTABLE ABOUT THIS, EMMA. YOU GOING AROUND LIKE SOME KINDA SPY OR SOMETHING. YOU SAID IT WAS SIMPLE SURVEILLANCE...
IT IS. AND ANYWAY, SOON AS YOU GET PUBLISHED I'LL QUIT WORK AND WE'LL HAVE ANOTHER BABY.
HOW'S IT GOING, ANYHOW?
TRUTH IS I NEED YOUR INSPIRATION. AND SOME OF YOUR TECHNICAL KNOW-HOW. I'VE GOT EMERALD INTO A TIGHT CORNER. SIX YAKUZA HITMEN HAVE FOLLOWED HER INTO A CRUCIFIX-MAKING FACTORY AND SHE'S OUT OF AMMO.
CRUCIFIX-MAKING FACTORY? NICE TOUCH. GIVES A RELIGIOUS BENT TO THE VIOLENCE.
IT WAS YOUR IDEA, REMEMBER?
NO, NO, I'M SURE THAT WAS YOUR IDEA. NOW, LET'S SEE...
IF I WERE EMERALD... HOW WOULD I GET OUT OF A HOLE LIKE THAT?
ACTUALLY THAT REMINDS ME. I'M SURE WE CAN COME UP WITH A BETTER NAME THAN EMERALD. HOW ABOUT...

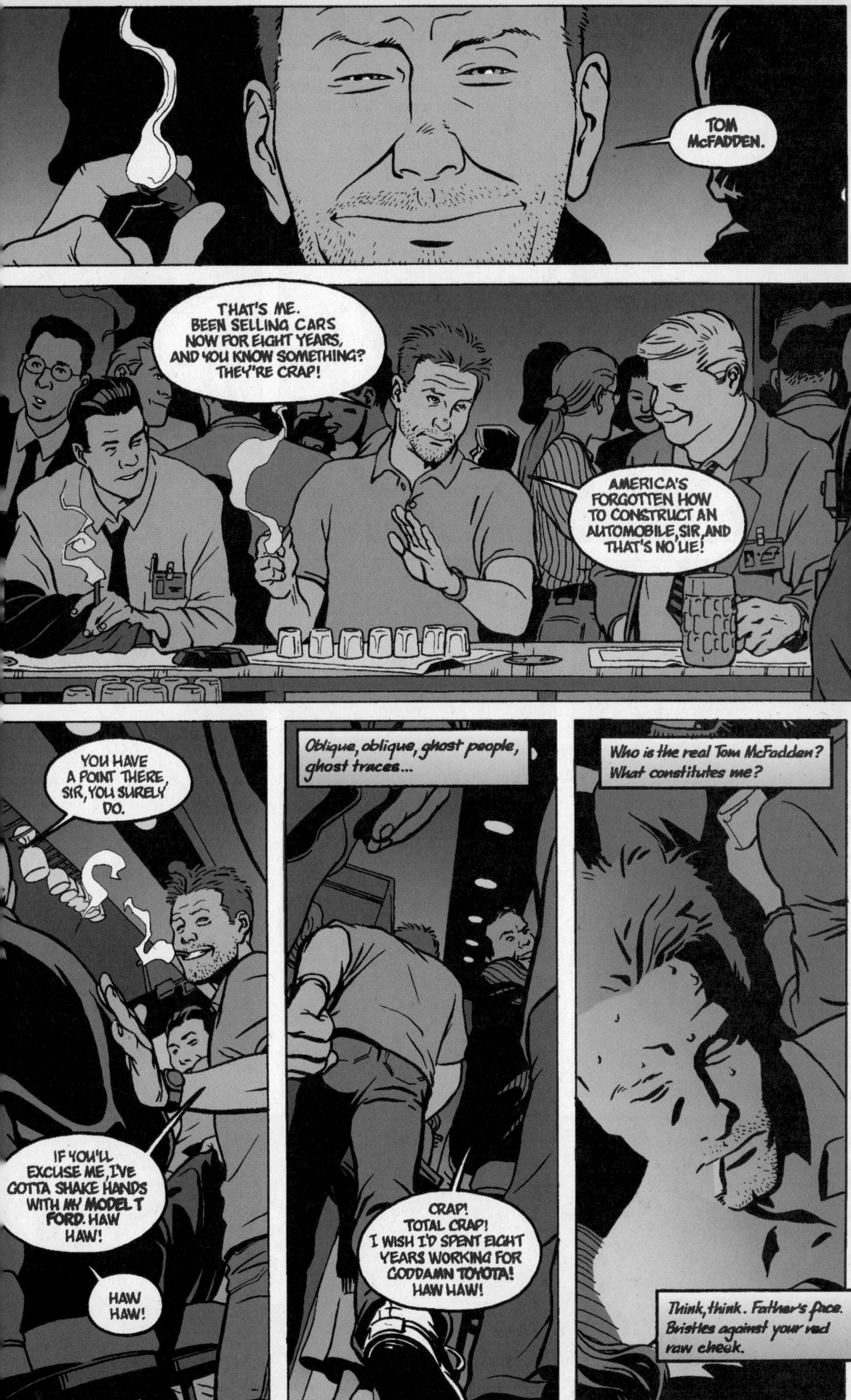
TOM McFADDEN.
THAT'S ME. BEEN SELLING CARS NOW FOR EIGHT YEARS, AND YOU KNOW SOMETHING? THEY'RE CRAP!
AMERICA'S FORGOTTEN HOW TO CONSTRUCT AN AUTOMOBILE, SIR, AND THAT'S NO LIE!
YOU HAVE A POINT THERE, SIR, YOU SURELY DO.
IF YOU'LL EXCUSE ME, I'VE GOTTA SHAKE HANDS WITH MY MODEL T FORD. HAW HAW!
HAW HAW!
Oblique, oblique, ghost people, ghost traces...
CRAP! TOTAL CRAP! I WISH I'D SPENT EIGHT YEARS WORKING FOR GODDAMN TOYOTA! HAW HAW!
Who is the real Tom McFadden? What constitutes me?
Think, think. Father's face. Bristles against your red raw cheek.

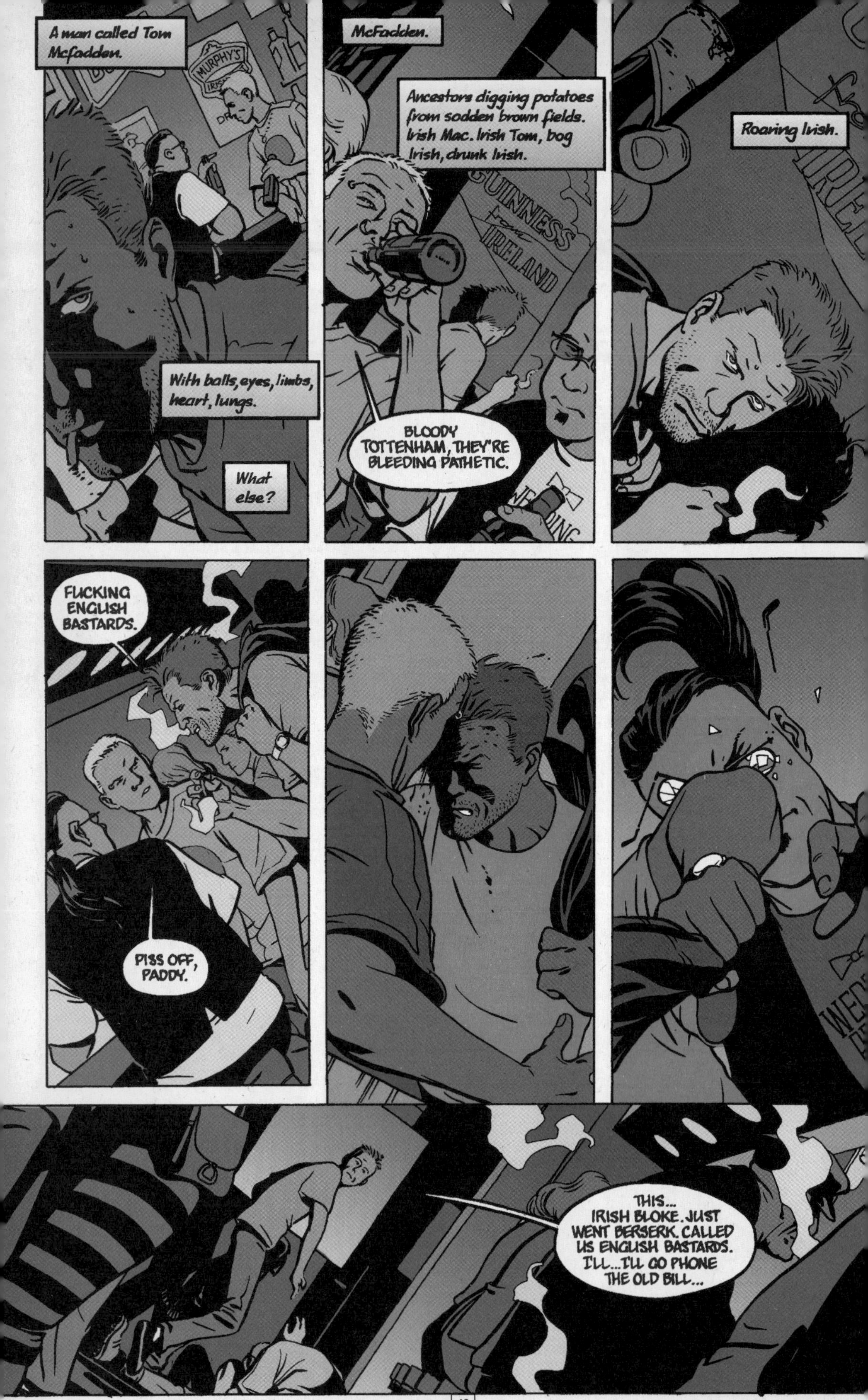
A man called Tom Mcfadden.
With balls, eyes, limbs, heart, lungs.
What else?
McFadden.
Ancestors digging potatoes from sodden brown fields. Irish Mac. Irish Tom, bog Irish, drunk Irish.
GUINNESS from IRELAND
BLOODY TOTTENHAM, THEY'RE BLEEDING PATHETIC.
Roaring Irish.
FUCKING ENGLISH BASTARDS.
PISS OFF, PADDY.
THIS... IRISH BLOKE. JUST WENT BERSERK. CALLED US ENGLISH BASTARDS. I'LL... I'LL GO PHONE THE OLD BILL...

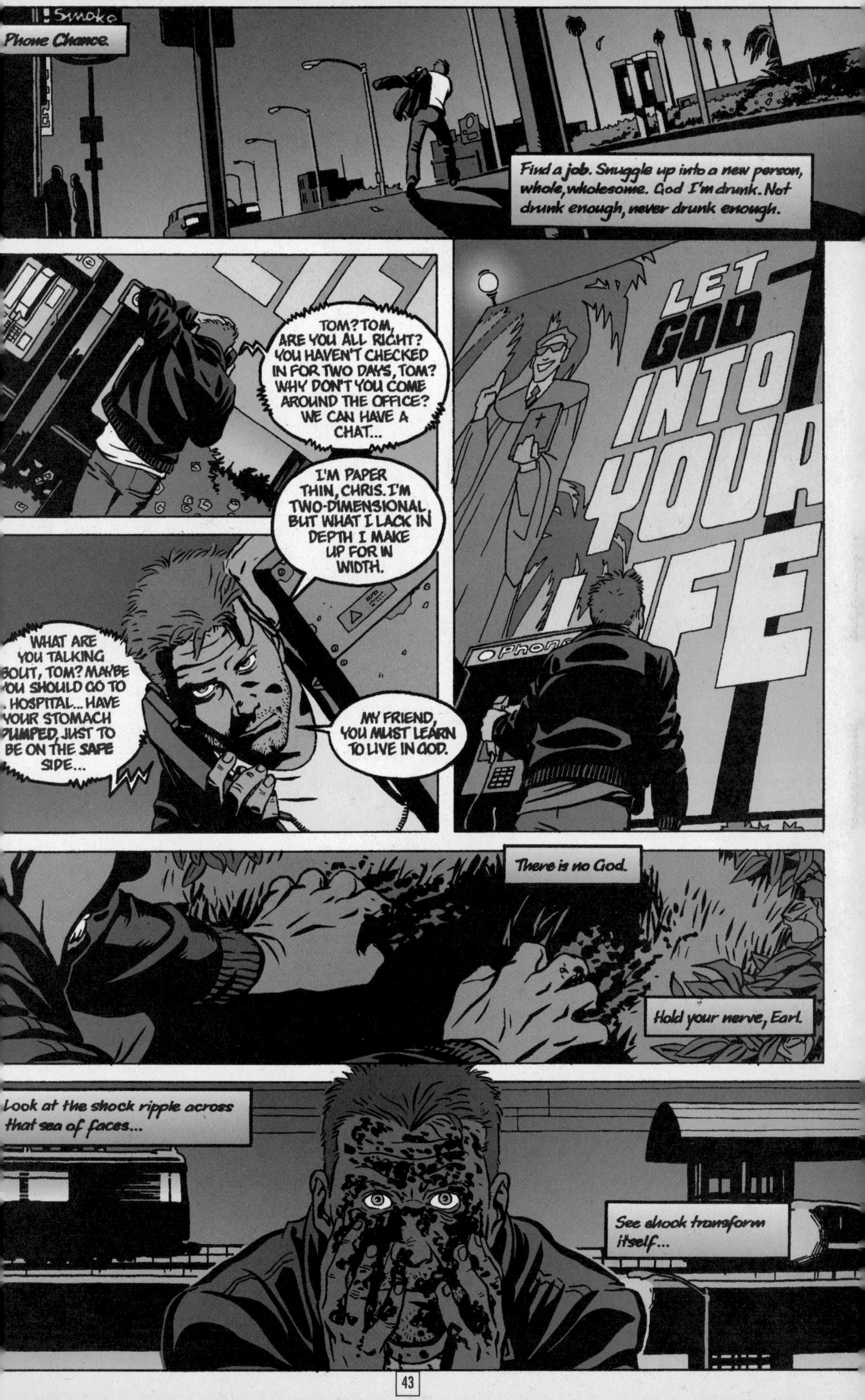
Smoko
Phone Chance.
Find a job. Snuggle up into a new person, whole, wholesome. God I'm drunk. Not drunk enough, never drunk enough.
TOM? TOM, ARE YOU ALL RIGHT? YOU HAVEN'T CHECKED IN FOR TWO DAYS, TOM? WHY DON'T YOU COME AROUND THE OFFICE? WE CAN HAVE A CHAT...
I'M PAPER THIN, CHRIS. I'M TWO-DIMENSIONAL, BUT WHAT I LACK IN DEPTH I MAKE UP FOR IN WIDTH.
WHAT ARE YOU TALKING BOUT, TOM? MAYBE YOU SHOULD GO TO HOSPITAL... HAVE YOUR STOMACH PUMPED, JUST TO BE ON THE SAFE SIDE...
MY FRIEND, YOU MUST LEARN TO LIVE IN GOD.
LET GOD INTO YOUR LIFE
Phone
There is no God.
Hold your nerve, Earl.
Look at the shock ripple across that sea of faces...
See shock transform itself...

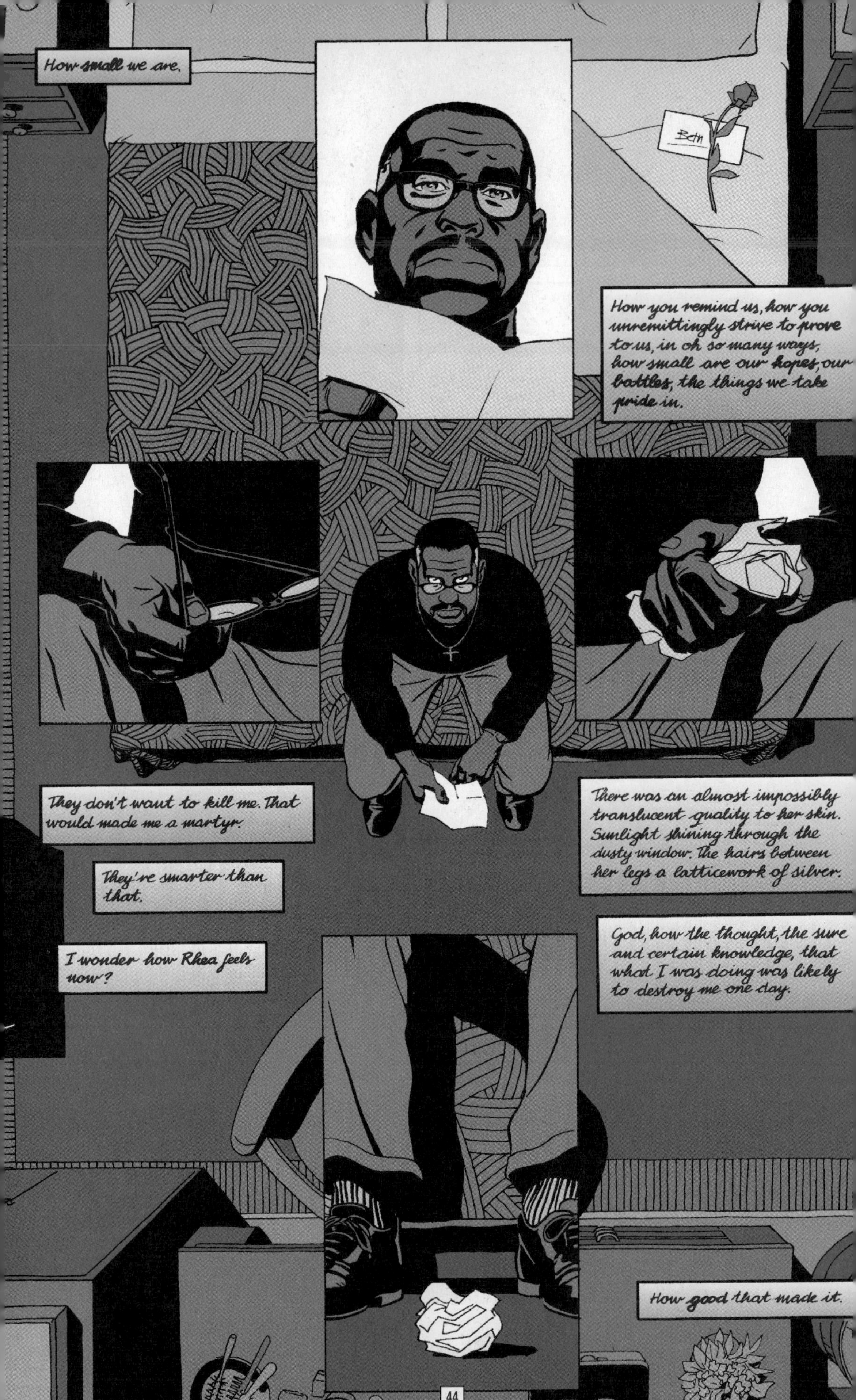
How small we are.
Beth
How you remind us, how you unremittingly strive to prove to us, in oh so many ways, how small are our hopes, our battles, the things we take pride in.
They don't want to kill me. That would made me a martyr.
They're smarter than that.
There was an almost impossibly translucent quality to her skin. Sunlight shining through the dusty window. The hairs between her legs a latticework of silver.
I wonder how Rhea feels now?
God, how the thought, the sure and certain knowledge, that what I was doing was likely to destroy me one day.
How good that made it.

I kept my guilt for you. You alone.

With Bethany... It was as though I were pure. I had not been unfaithful to her.

All bullshit. Sins wrapped in sanctimonious bullshit.

Sins? Were they sins? Of course. Of course.

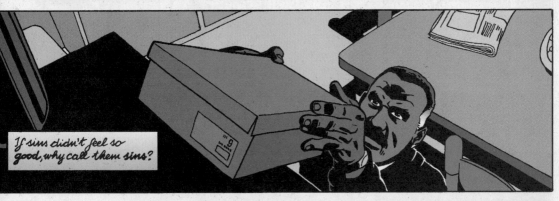

If sins didn't feel so good, why call them sins?

Why is it I can face You... But not her?

Why would I rather see your wrath than her disappointment?

Our Father...which art in heaven...

...Hallowed be name... Thy kingdom come...

Thy will be done in earth, as it

BMMMM!

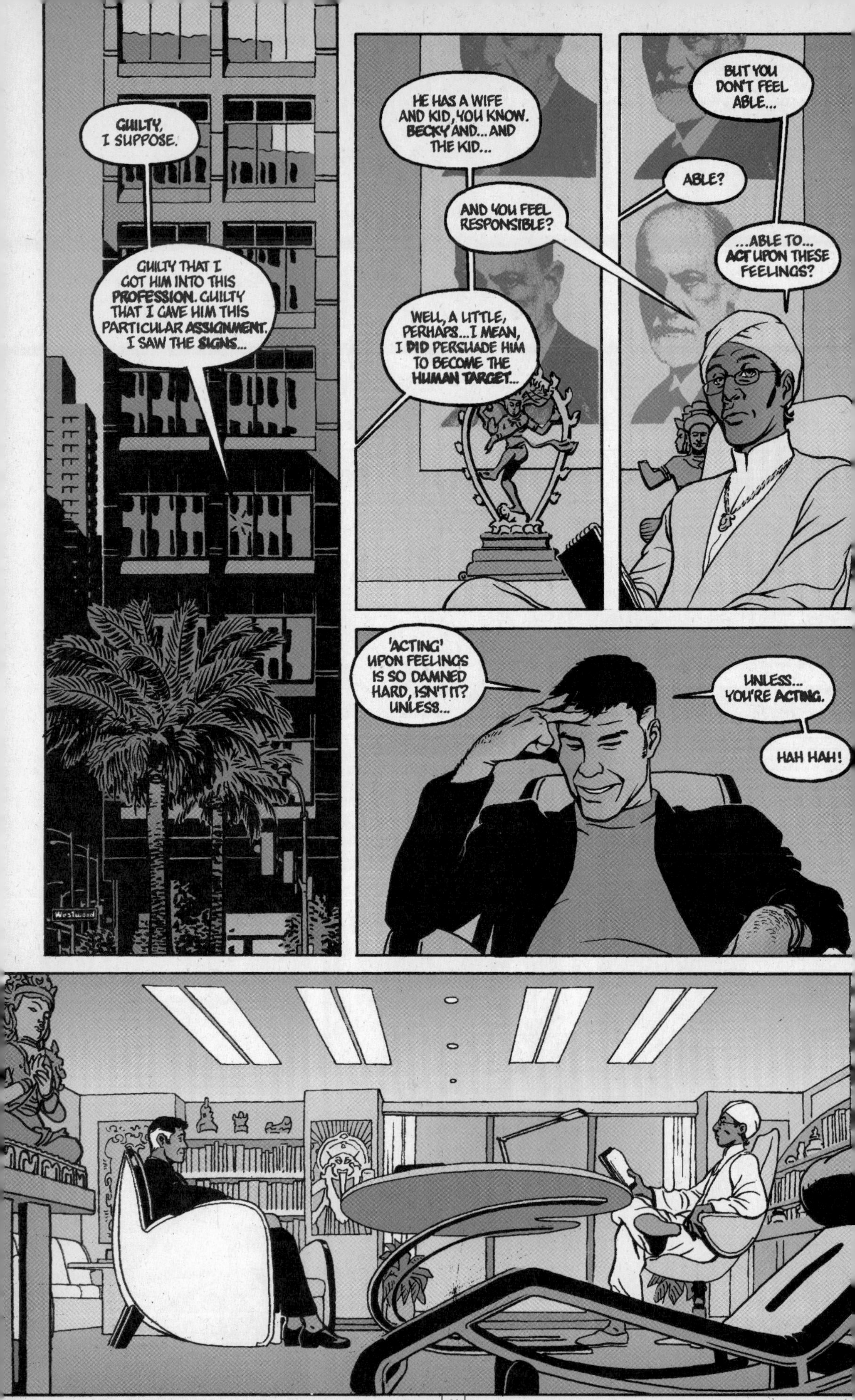
GUILTY, I SUPPOSE.
GUILTY THAT I GOT HIM INTO THIS PROFESSION. GUILTY THAT I GAVE HIM THIS PARTICULAR ASSIGNMENT. I SAW THE SIGNS...
Westwood
HE HAS A WIFE AND KID, YOU KNOW. BECKY AND... AND THE KID...
AND YOU FEEL RESPONSIBLE?
WELL, A LITTLE, PERHAPS...I MEAN, I DID PERSUADE HIM TO BECOME THE HUMAN TARGET...
BUT YOU DON'T FEEL ABLE...
ABLE?
...ABLE TO... ACT UPON THESE FEELINGS?
'ACTING' UPON FEELINGS IS SO DAMNED HARD, ISN'T IT? UNLESS...
UNLESS... YOU'RE ACTING.
HAH HAH!

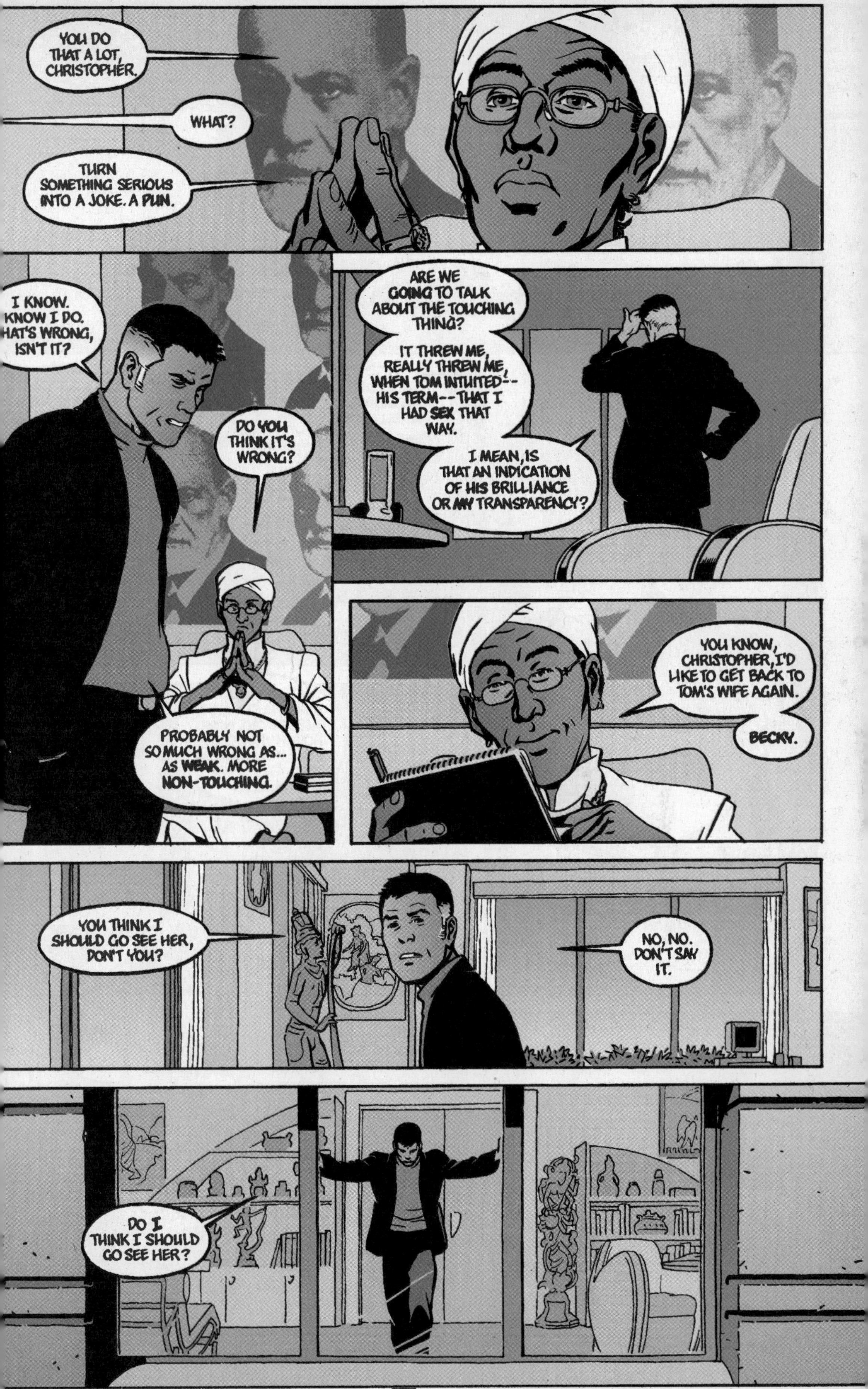
YOU DO THAT A LOT, CHRISTOPHER.
WHAT?
TURN SOMETHING SERIOUS INTO A JOKE. A PUN.
I KNOW. KNOW I DO. HAT'S WRONG, ISN'T IT?
DO YOU THINK IT'S WRONG?
PROBABLY NOT SO MUCH WRONG AS... AS WEAK. MORE NON-TOUCHING.
ARE WE GOING TO TALK ABOUT THE TOUCHING THING?
IT THREW ME, REALLY THREW ME, WHEN TOM INTUITED-- HIS TERM--THAT I HAD SEX THAT WAY.
I MEAN, IS THAT AN INDICATION OF HIS BRILLIANCE OR MY TRANSPARENCY?
YOU KNOW, CHRISTOPHER, I'D LIKE TO GET BACK TO TOM'S WIFE AGAIN.
BECKY.
YOU THINK I SHOULD GO SEE HER, DON'T YOU?
NO, NO. DON'T SAY IT.
DO I THINK I SHOULD GO SEE HER?

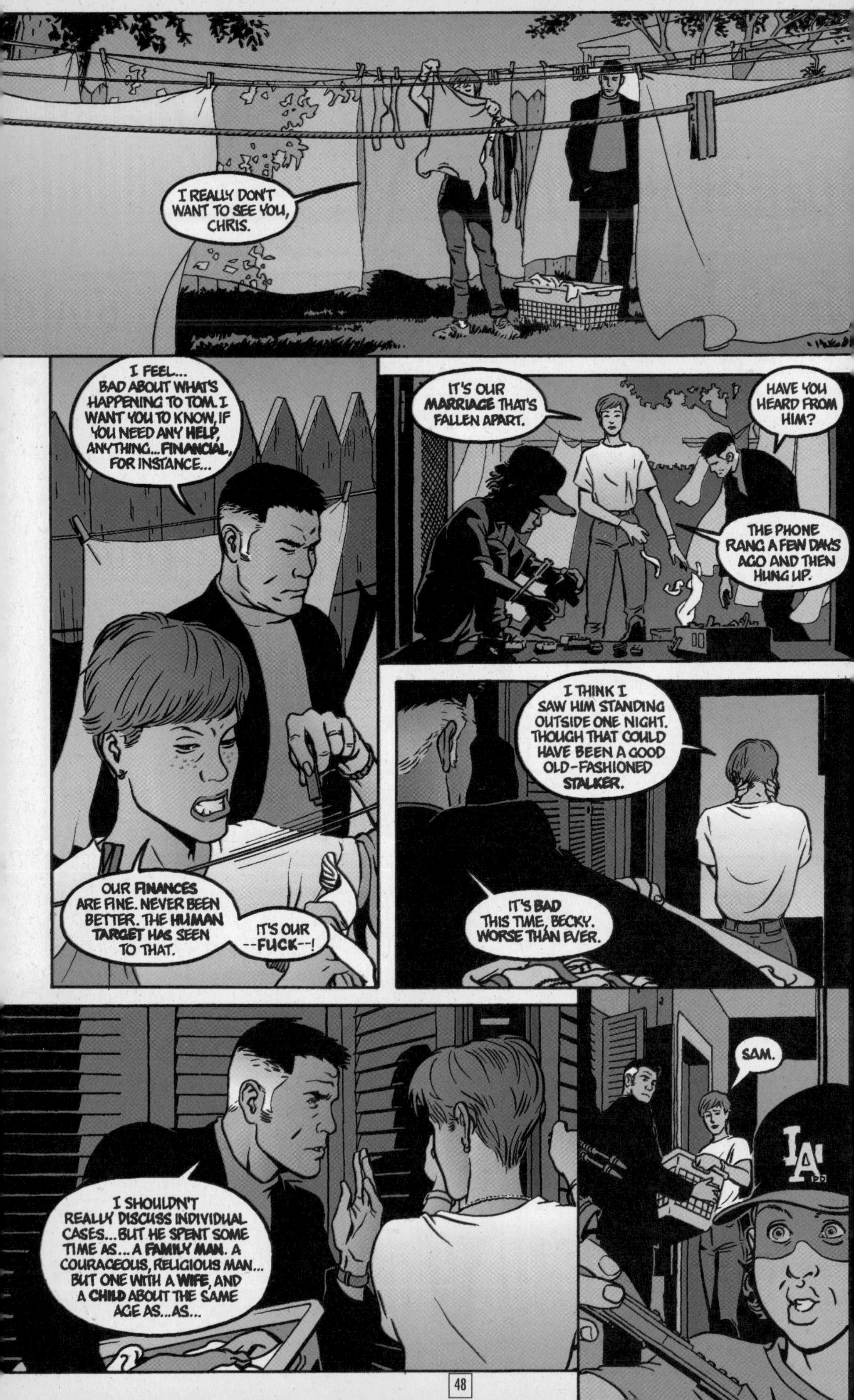

I REALLY DON'T WANT TO SEE YOU, CHRIS.
I FEEL... BAD ABOUT WHAT'S HAPPENING TO TOM. I WANT YOU TO KNOW, IF YOU NEED ANY HELP, ANYTHING... FINANCIAL, FOR INSTANCE...
OUR FINANCES ARE FINE. NEVER BEEN BETTER. THE HUMAN TARGET HAS SEEN TO THAT.
IT'S OUR --FUCK--!
IT'S OUR MARRIAGE THAT'S FALLEN APART.
HAVE YOU HEARD FROM HIM?
THE PHONE RANG A FEW DAYS AGO AND THEN HUNG UP.
I THINK I SAW HIM STANDING OUTSIDE ONE NIGHT. THOUGH THAT COULD HAVE BEEN A GOOD OLD-FASHIONED STALKER.
IT'S BAD THIS TIME, BECKY. WORSE THAN EVER.
I SHOULDN'T REALLY DISCUSS INDIVIDUAL CASES... BUT HE SPENT SOME TIME AS... A FAMILY MAN. A COURAGEOUS, RELIGIOUS MAN... BUT ONE WITH A WIFE, AND A CHILD ABOUT THE SAME AGE AS... AS...
SAM.

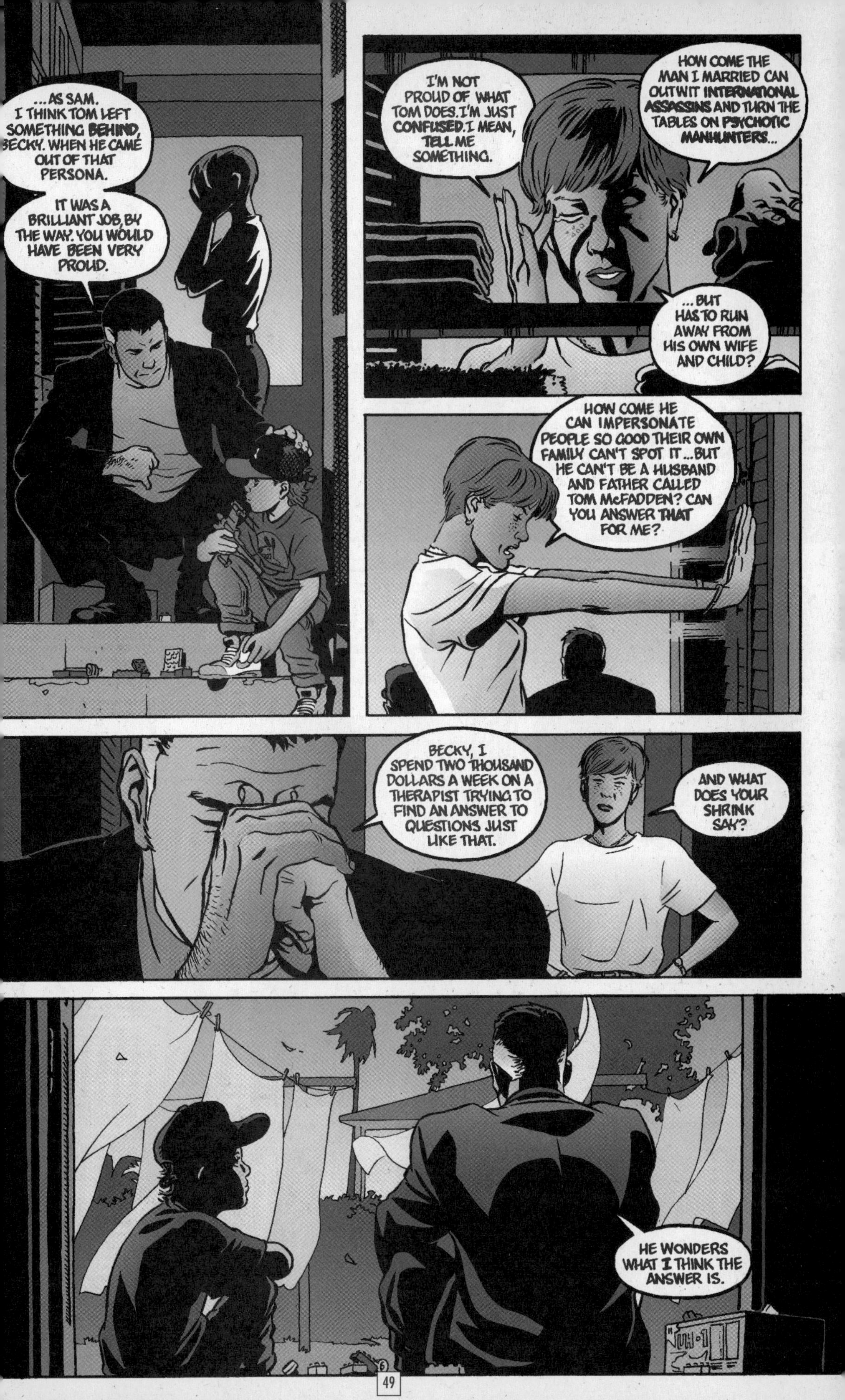
...AS SAM. I THINK TOM LEFT SOMETHING BEHIND, BECKY. WHEN HE CAME OUT OF THAT PERSONA.
IT WAS A BRILLIANT JOB, BY THE WAY. YOU WOULD HAVE BEEN VERY PROUD.
I'M NOT PROUD OF WHAT TOM DOES. I'M JUST CONFUSED. I MEAN, TELL ME SOMETHING.
HOW COME THE MAN I MARRIED CAN OUTWIT INTERNATIONAL ASSASSINS AND TURN THE TABLES ON PSYCHOTIC MANHUNTERS...
...BUT HAS TO RUN AWAY FROM HIS OWN WIFE AND CHILD?
HOW COME HE CAN IMPERSONATE PEOPLE SO GOOD THEIR OWN FAMILY CAN'T SPOT IT... BUT HE CAN'T BE A HUSBAND AND FATHER CALLED TOM McFADDEN? CAN YOU ANSWER THAT FOR ME?
BECKY, I SPEND TWO THOUSAND DOLLARS A WEEK ON A THERAPIST TRYING TO FIND AN ANSWER TO QUESTIONS JUST LIKE THAT.
AND WHAT DOES YOUR SHRINK SAY?
HE WONDERS WHAT I THINK THE ANSWER IS.

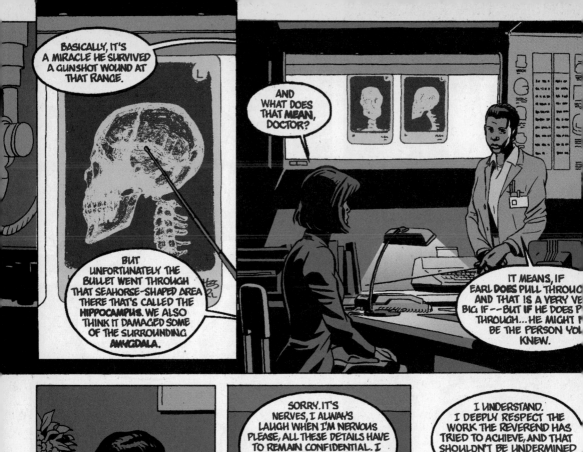

BASICALLY, IT'S A MIRACLE HE SURVIVED A GUNSHOT WOUND AT THAT RANGE.

AND WHAT DOES THAT MEAN, DOCTOR?

BUT UNFORTUNATELY THE BULLET WENT THROUGH THAT SEAHORSE-SHAPED AREA THERE THAT'S CALLED THE HIPPOCAMPUS. WE ALSO THINK IT DAMAGED SOME OF THE SURROUNDING AMYGDALA.

IT MEANS, IF EARL DOES PULL THROUGH AND THAT IS A VERY VE BIG IF-- BUT IF HE DOES P THROUGH... HE MIGHT N BE THE PERSON YOU KNEW.

SORRY. IT'S NERVES, I ALWAYS LAUGH WHEN I'M NERVOUS PLEASE, ALL THESE DETAILS HAVE TO REMAIN CONFIDENTIAL. I DON'T WANT THE OUTSIDE WORLD KNOWING THE EXTENT OF EARL'S...

I UNDERSTAND. I DEEPLY RESPECT THE WORK THE REVEREND HAS TRIED TO ACHIEVE, AND THAT SHOULDN'T BE UNDERMINED BY ANY PAST INDISCRETIONS.

HAH HAH HAH!

YOU... KNOW? ABOUT EARL AND...

ANTI-DRUG PREACHER HAD LOVER
SUICIDE ATTEMPT AFTER EX-MISTRESS REVEALS ALL

I'M AFRAID ANYONE WHO'S INTERESTED KNOWS, MRS. JAMES.

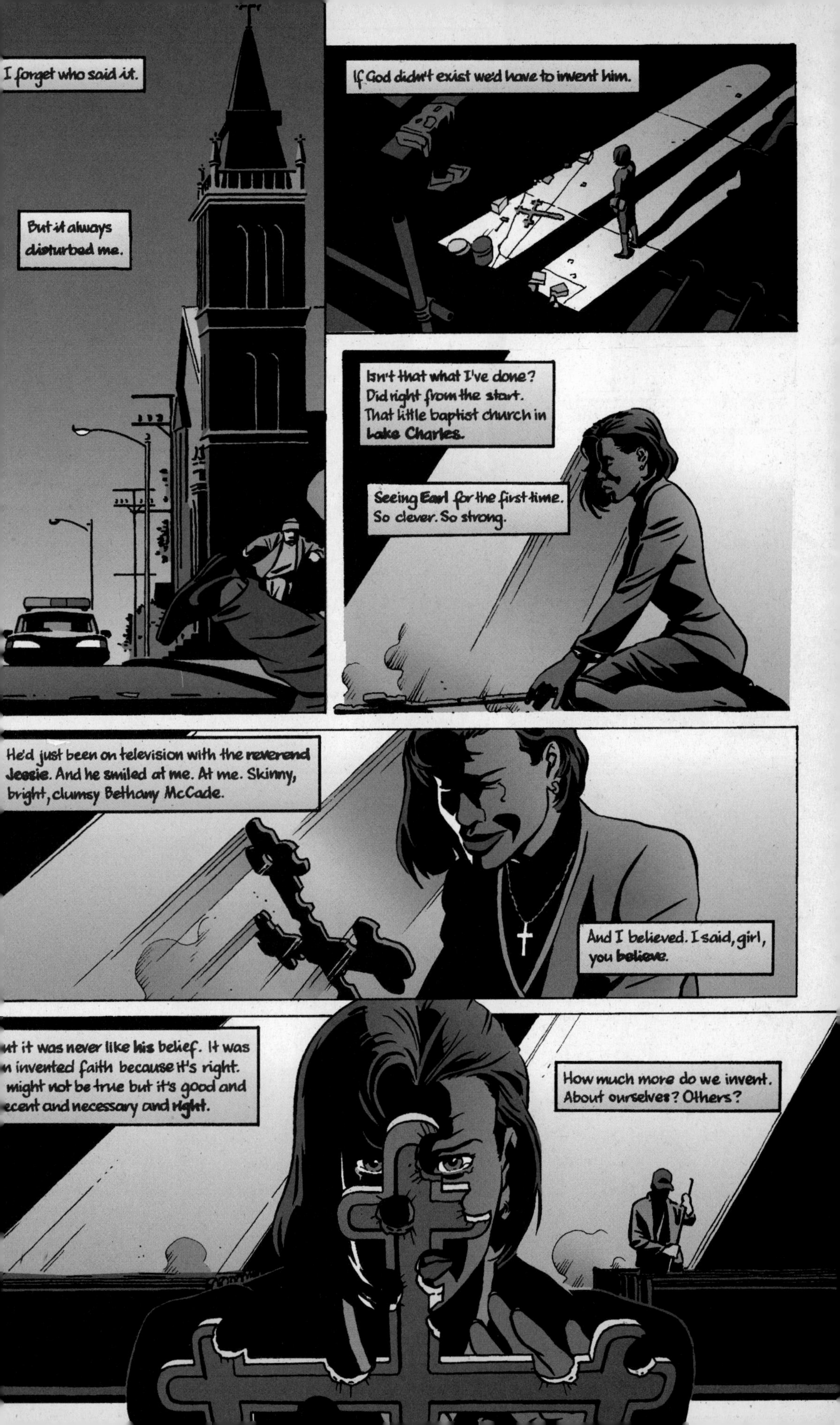
I forget who said it.
But it always disturbed me.
If God didn't exist we'd have to invent him.
Isn't that what I've done? Did right from the start. That little baptist church in Lake Charles.
Seeing Earl for the first time. So clever. So strong.
He'd just been on television with the reverend Jessie. And he smiled at me. At me. Skinny, bright, clumsy Bethany McCade.
And I believed. I said, girl, you believe.
ut it was never like his belief. It was n invented faith because it's right. might not be true but it's good and ecent and necessary and right.
How much more do we invent. About ourselves? Others?

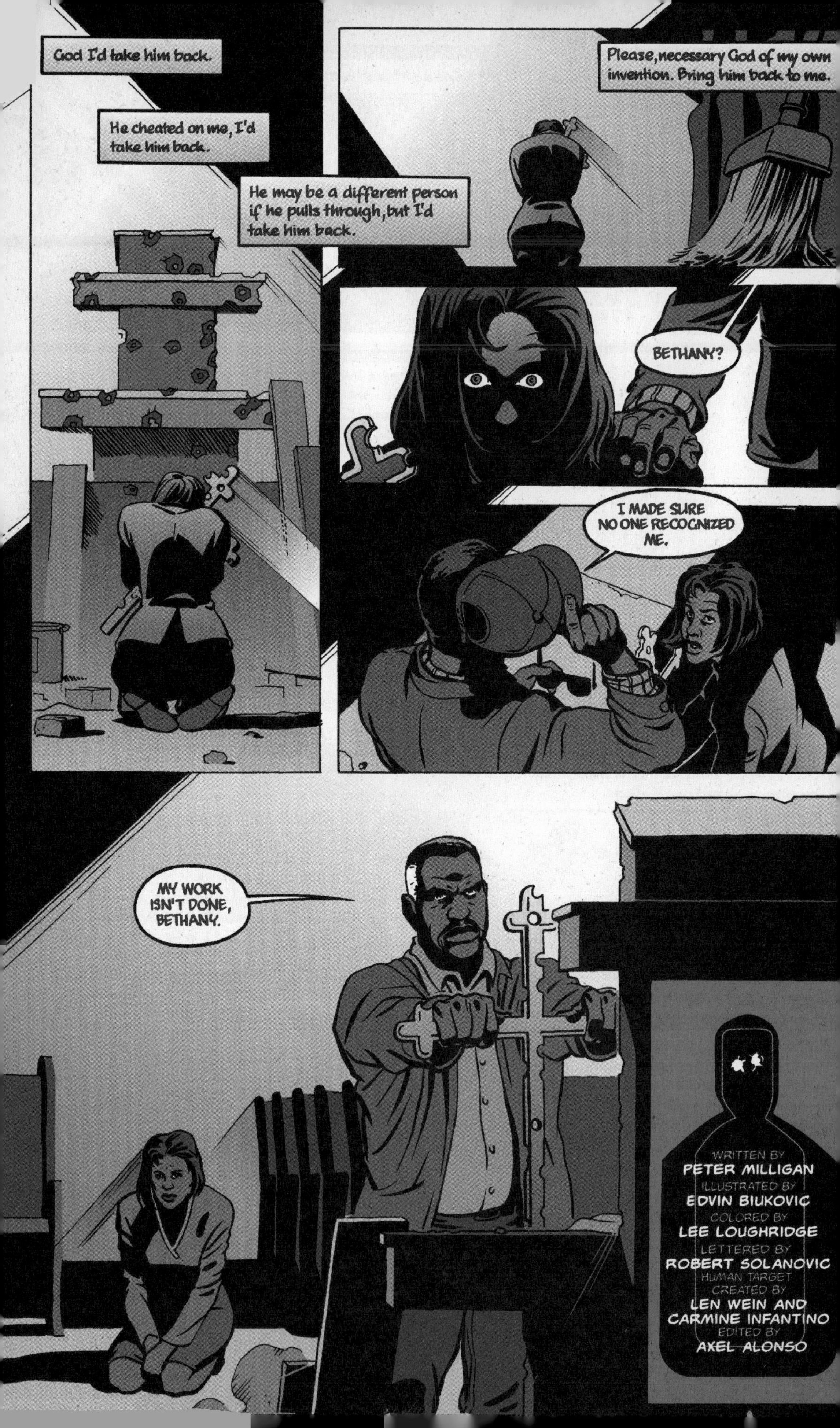
God I'd take him back.
He cheated on me, I'd take him back.
He may be a different person if he pulls through, but I'd take him back.
Please, necessary God of my own invention. Bring him back to me.
BETHANY?
I MADE SURE NO ONE RECOGNIZED ME.
MY WORK ISN'T DONE, BETHANY.
WRITTEN BY PETER MILLIGAN
ILLUSTRATED BY EDVIN BIUKOVIC
COLORED BY LEE LOUGHRIDGE
LETTERED BY ROBERT SOLANOVIC
HUMAN TARGET CREATED BY LEN WEIN AND CARMINE INFANTINO
EDITED BY AXEL ALONSO

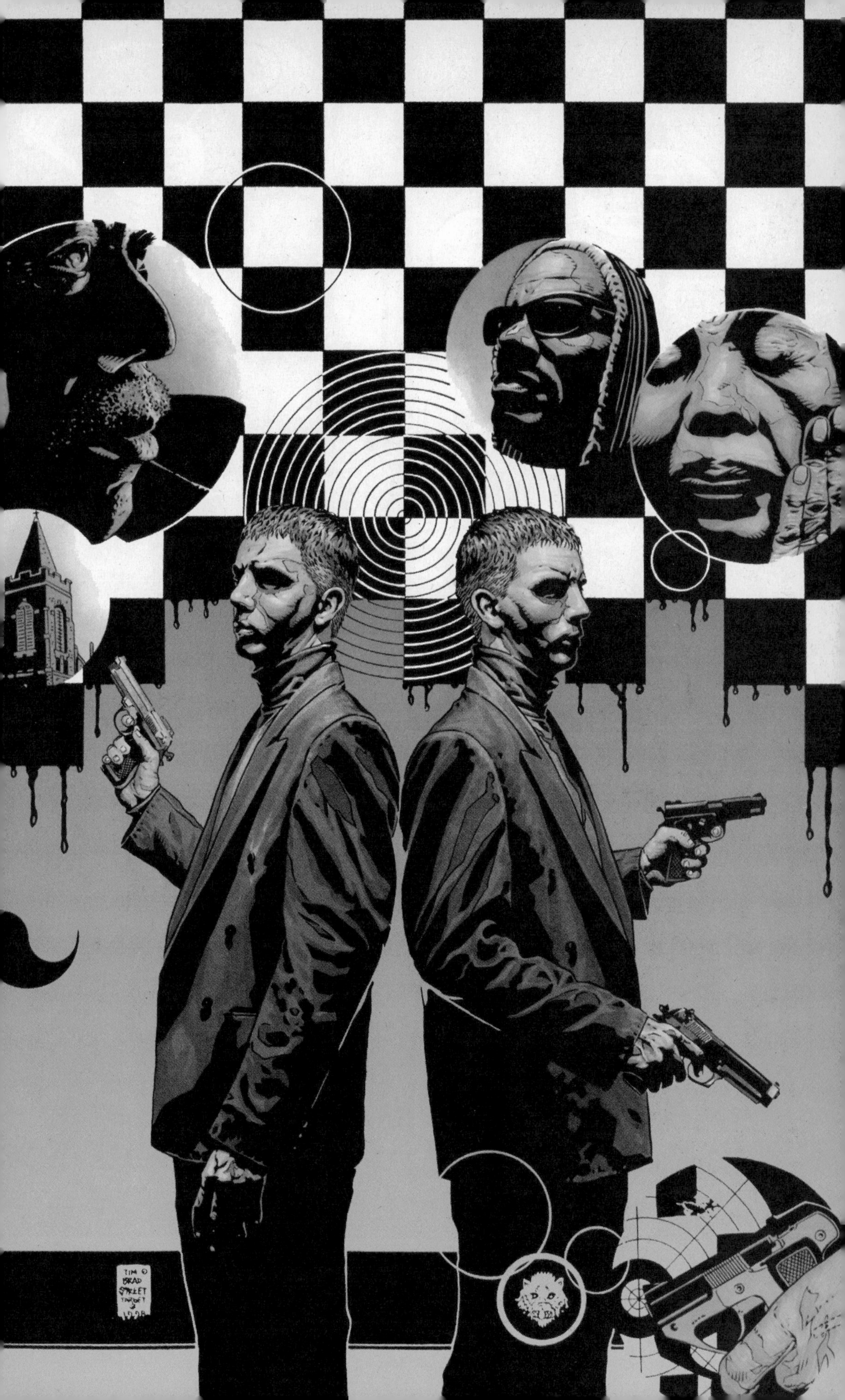
TIM ©
BRAD
STREET
1998

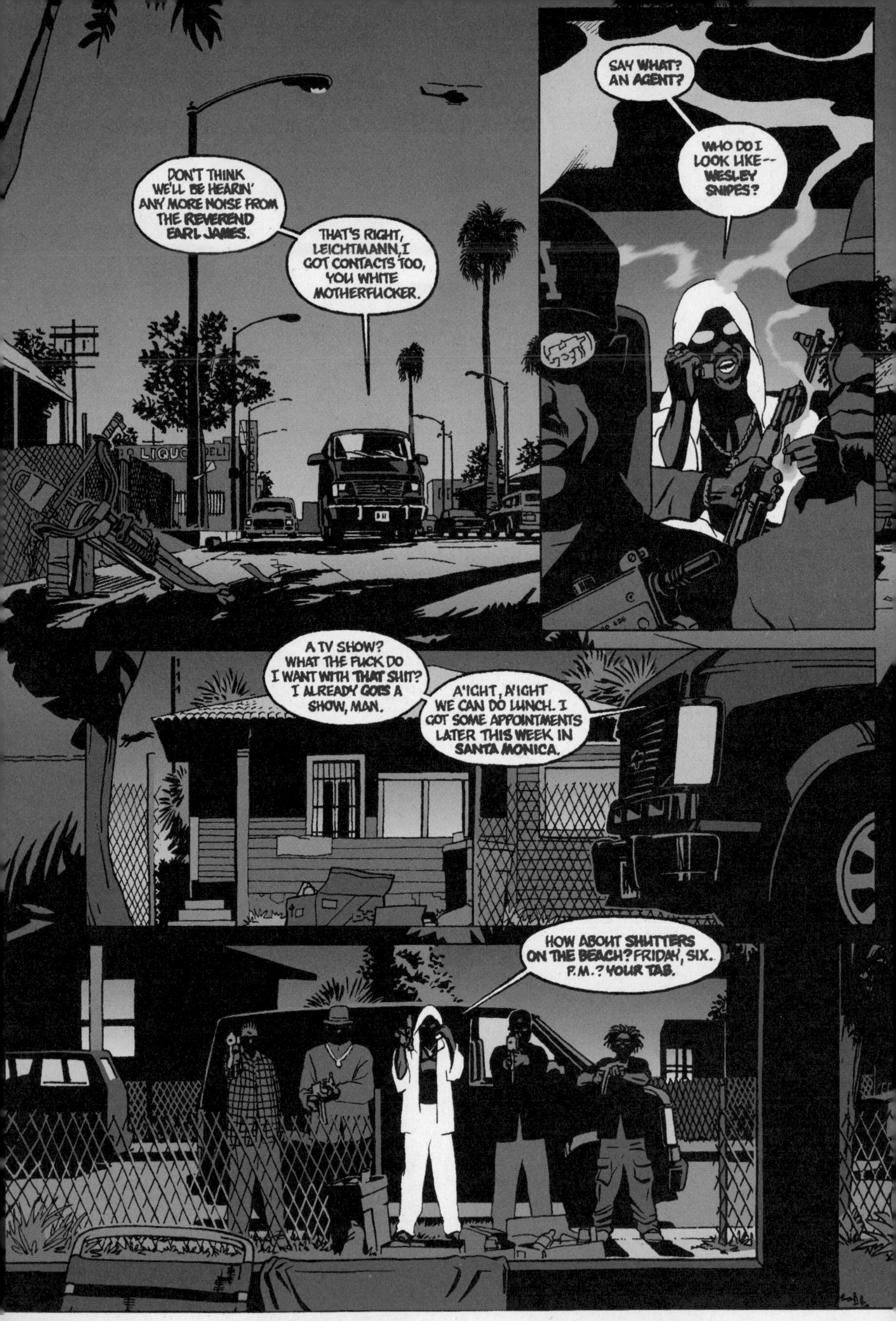
DON'T THINK WE'LL BE HEARIN' ANY MORE NOISE FROM THE REVEREND EARL JAMES.
THAT'S RIGHT, LEICHTMANN, I GOT CONTACTS TOO, YOU WHITE MOTHERFUCKER.
SAY WHAT? AN AGENT?
WHO DO I LOOK LIKE-- WESLEY SNIPES?
A TV SHOW? WHAT THE FUCK DO I WANT WITH THAT SHIT? I ALREADY GOTS A SHOW, MAN.
A'IGHT, A'IGHT WE CAN DO LUNCH. I GOT SOME APPOINTMENTS LATER THIS WEEK IN SANTA MONICA.
HOW ABOUT SHUTTERS ON THE BEACH? FRIDAY, SIX. P.M.? YOUR TAB.

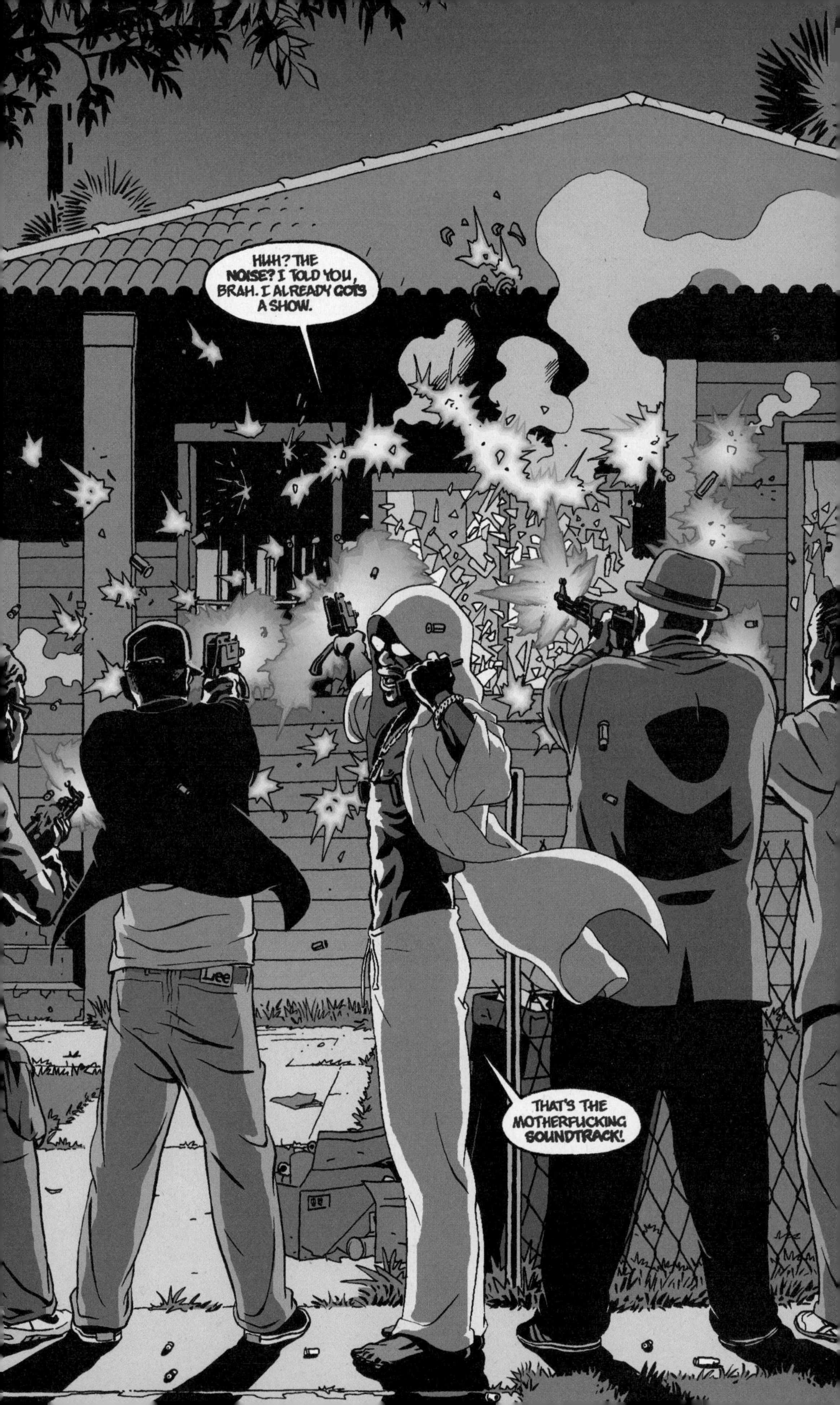
HUH? THE NOISE? I TOLD YOU, BRAH. I ALREADY GOTS A SHOW.
THAT'S THE MOTHERFUCKING SOUNDTRACK!
Lee

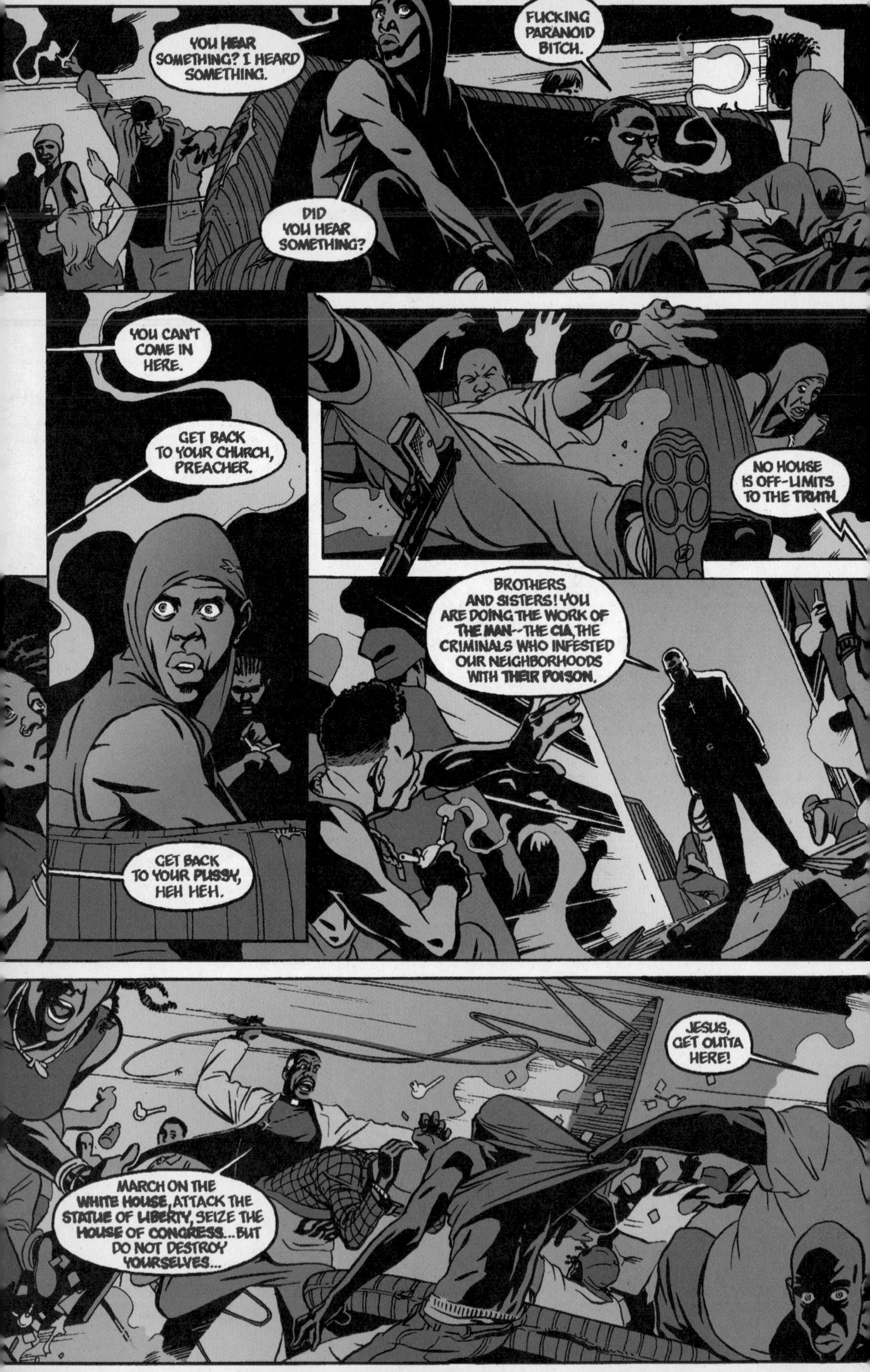

YOU HEAR SOMETHING? I HEARD SOMETHING.
FUCKING PARANOID BITCH.
DID YOU HEAR SOMETHING?
YOU CAN'T COME IN HERE.
GET BACK TO YOUR CHURCH, PREACHER.
GET BACK TO YOUR PUSSY, HEH HEH.
NO HOUSE IS OFF-LIMITS TO THE TRUTH.
BROTHERS AND SISTERS! YOU ARE DOING THE WORK OF THE MAN--THE CIA, THE CRIMINALS WHO INFESTED OUR NEIGHBORHOODS WITH THEIR POISON.
JESUS, GET OUTTA HERE!
MARCH ON THE WHITE HOUSE, ATTACK THE STATUE OF LIBERTY, SEIZE THE HOUSE OF CONGRESS...BUT DO NOT DESTROY YOURSELVES...

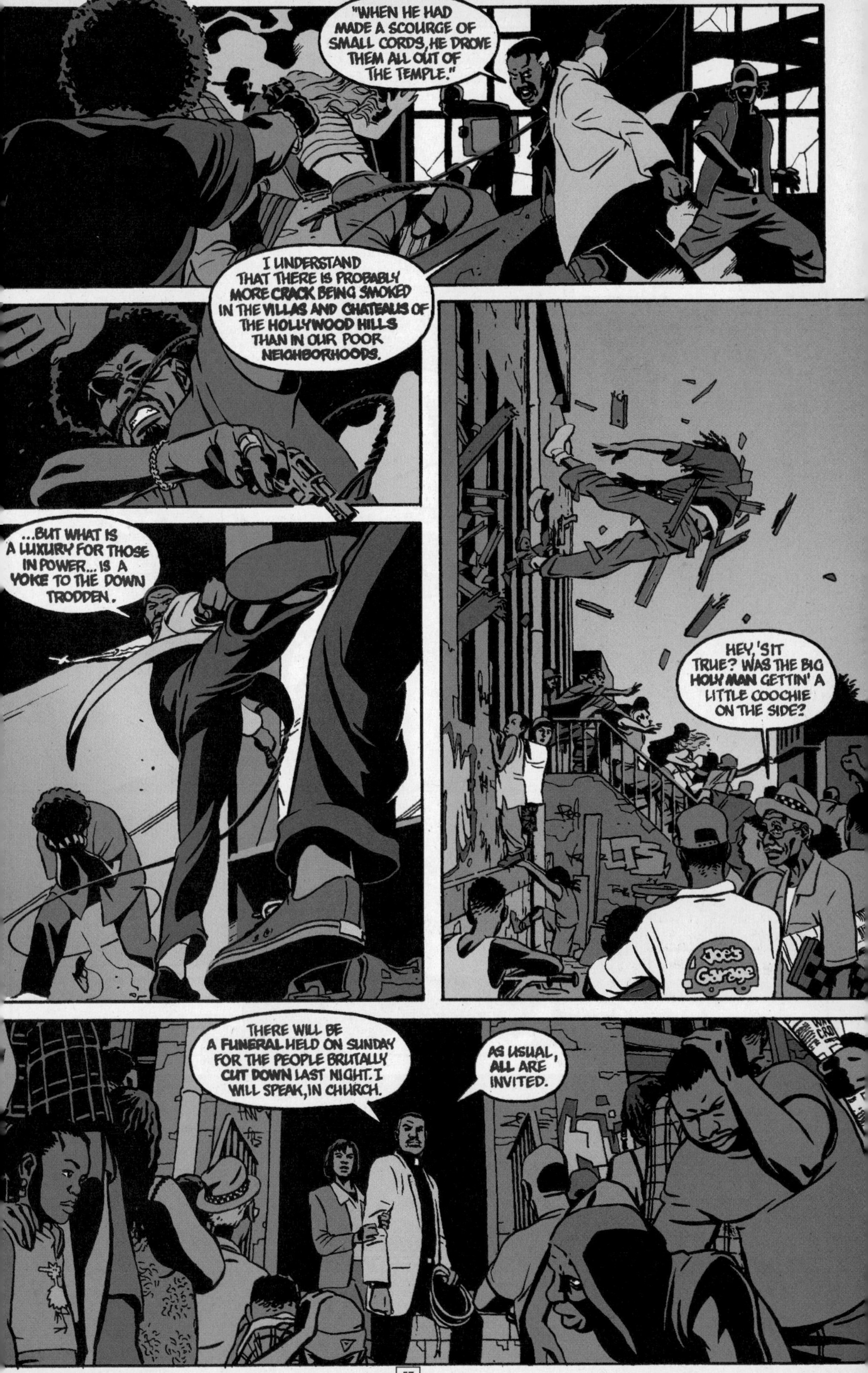
"WHEN HE HAD MADE A SCOURGE OF SMALL CORDS, HE DROVE THEM ALL OUT OF THE TEMPLE."
I UNDERSTAND THAT THERE IS PROBABLY MORE CRACK BEING SMOKED IN THE VILLAS AND CHATEAUS OF THE HOLLYWOOD HILLS THAN IN OUR POOR NEIGHBORHOODS.
...BUT WHAT IS A LUXURY FOR THOSE IN POWER... IS A YOKE TO THE DOWN TRODDEN.
HEY, 'SIT TRUE? WAS THE BIG HOLY MAN GETTIN' A LITTLE COOCHIE ON THE SIDE?
Joe's Garage
THERE WILL BE A FUNERAL HELD ON SUNDAY FOR THE PEOPLE BRUTALLY CUT DOWN LAST NIGHT. I WILL SPEAK, IN CHURCH.
AS USUAL, ALL ARE INVITED.

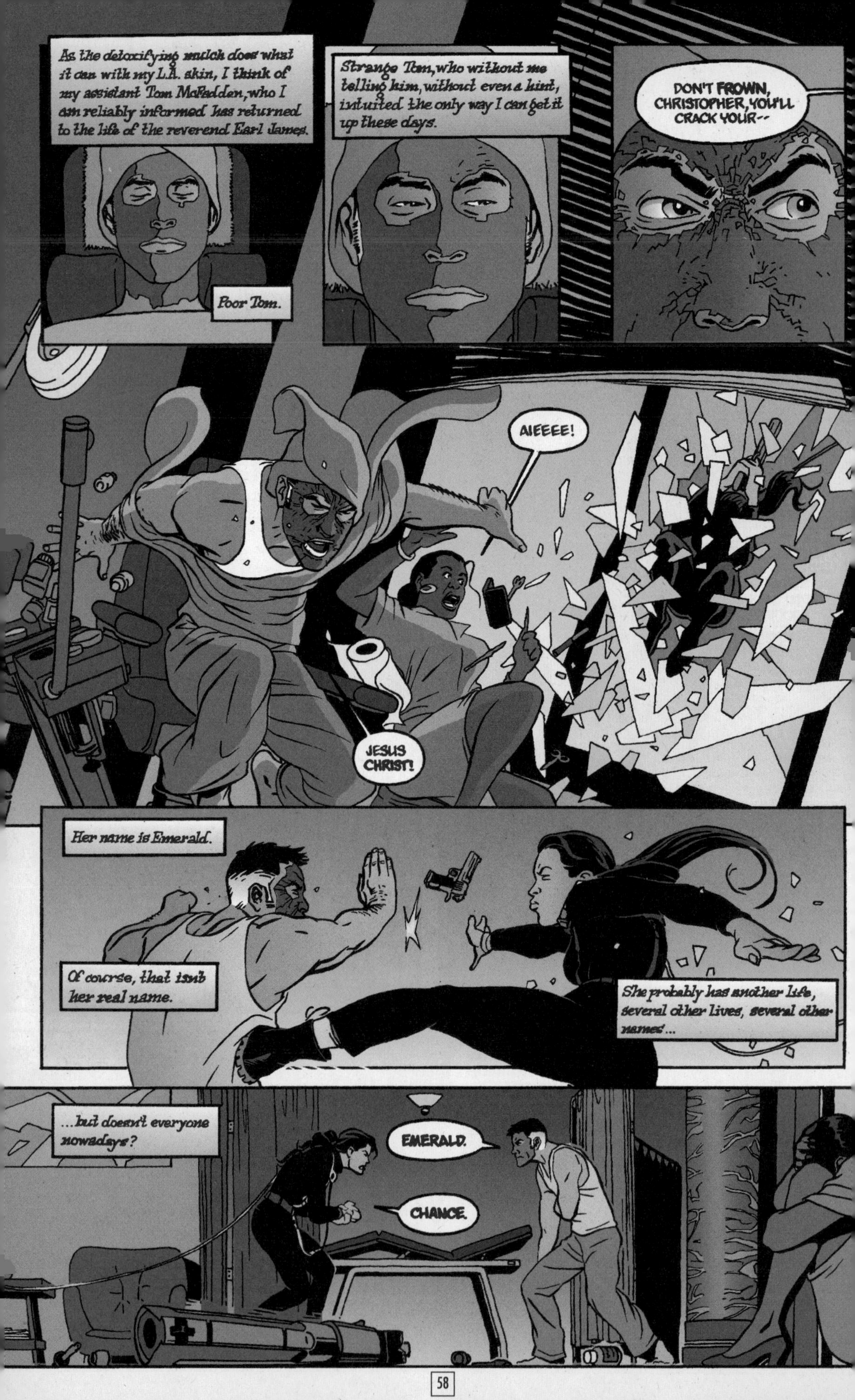
As the detoxifying mulch does what it can with my L.A. skin, I think of my assistant Tom McFadden, who I am reliably informed has returned to the life of the reverend Earl James.
Poor Tom.
Strange Tom, who without me telling him, without even a hint, intuited the only way I can get it up these days.
DON'T FROWN, CHRISTOPHER, YOU'LL CRACK YOUR--
AIEEEE!
JESUS CHRIST!
Her name is Emerald.
Of course, that isn't her real name.
She probably has another life, several other lives, several other names...
...but doesn't everyone nowadays?
EMERALD.
CHANCE.

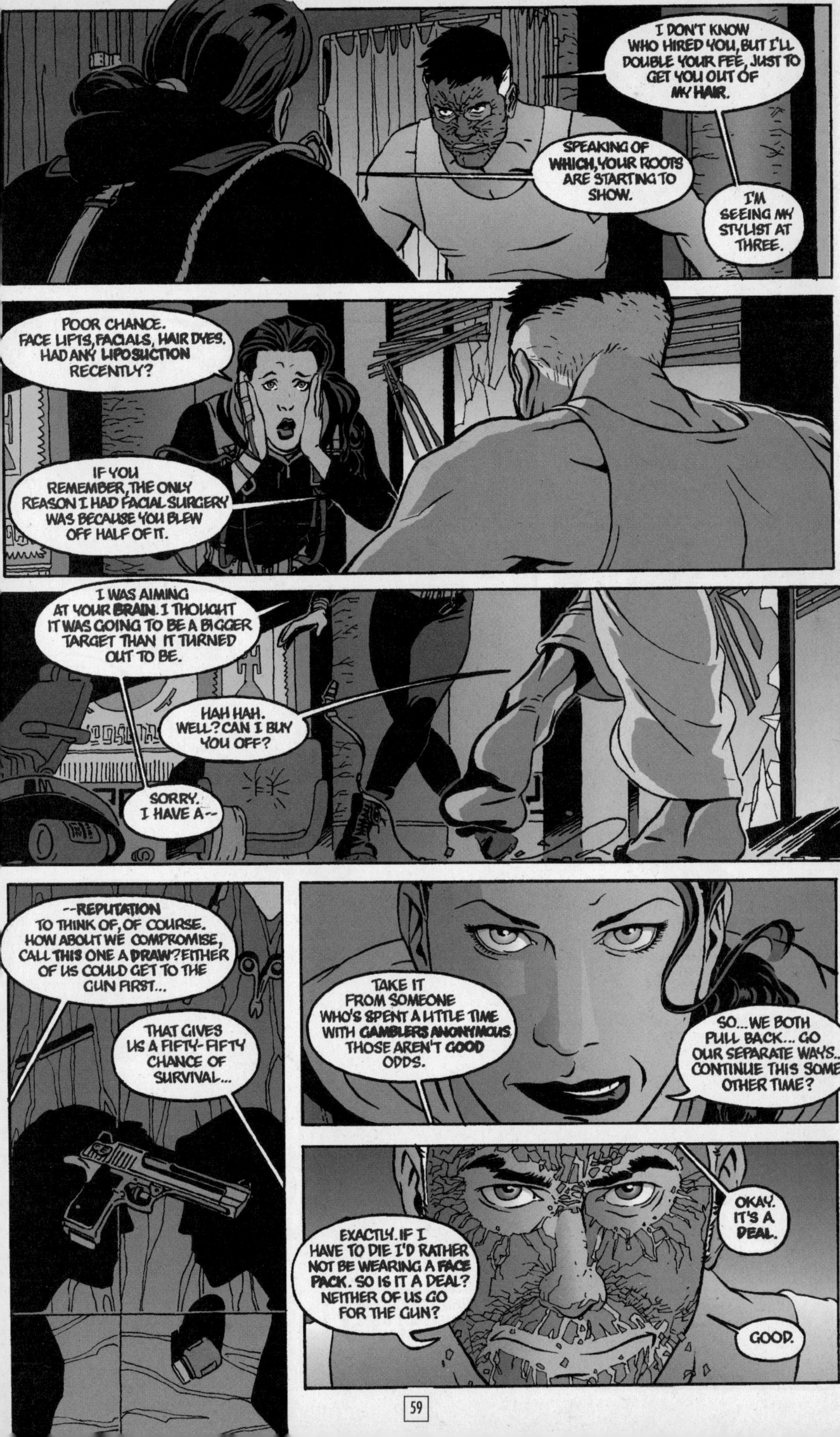

I DON'T KNOW WHO HIRED YOU, BUT I'LL DOUBLE YOUR FEE, JUST TO GET YOU OUT OF MY HAIR.
SPEAKING OF WHICH, YOUR ROOTS ARE STARTING TO SHOW.
I'M SEEING MY STYLIST AT THREE.
POOR CHANCE. FACE LIFTS, FACIALS, HAIR DYES. HAD ANY LIPOSUCTION RECENTLY?
IF YOU REMEMBER, THE ONLY REASON I HAD FACIAL SURGERY WAS BECAUSE YOU BLEW OFF HALF OF IT.
I WAS AIMING AT YOUR BRAIN. I THOUGHT IT WAS GOING TO BE A BIGGER TARGET THAN IT TURNED OUT TO BE.
HAH HAH. WELL? CAN I BUY YOU OFF?
SORRY. I HAVE A--
--REPUTATION TO THINK OF, OF COURSE. HOW ABOUT WE COMPROMISE, CALL THIS ONE A DRAW? EITHER OF US COULD GET TO THE GUN FIRST...
THAT GIVES US A FIFTY-FIFTY CHANCE OF SURVIVAL...
TAKE IT FROM SOMEONE WHO'S SPENT A LITTLE TIME WITH GAMBLERS ANONYMOUS. THOSE AREN'T GOOD ODDS.
SO... WE BOTH PULL BACK... GO OUR SEPARATE WAYS... CONTINUE THIS SOME OTHER TIME?
EXACTLY. IF I HAVE TO DIE I'D RATHER NOT BE WEARING A FACE PACK. SO IS IT A DEAL? NEITHER OF US GO FOR THE GUN?
OKAY. IT'S A DEAL.
GOOD.

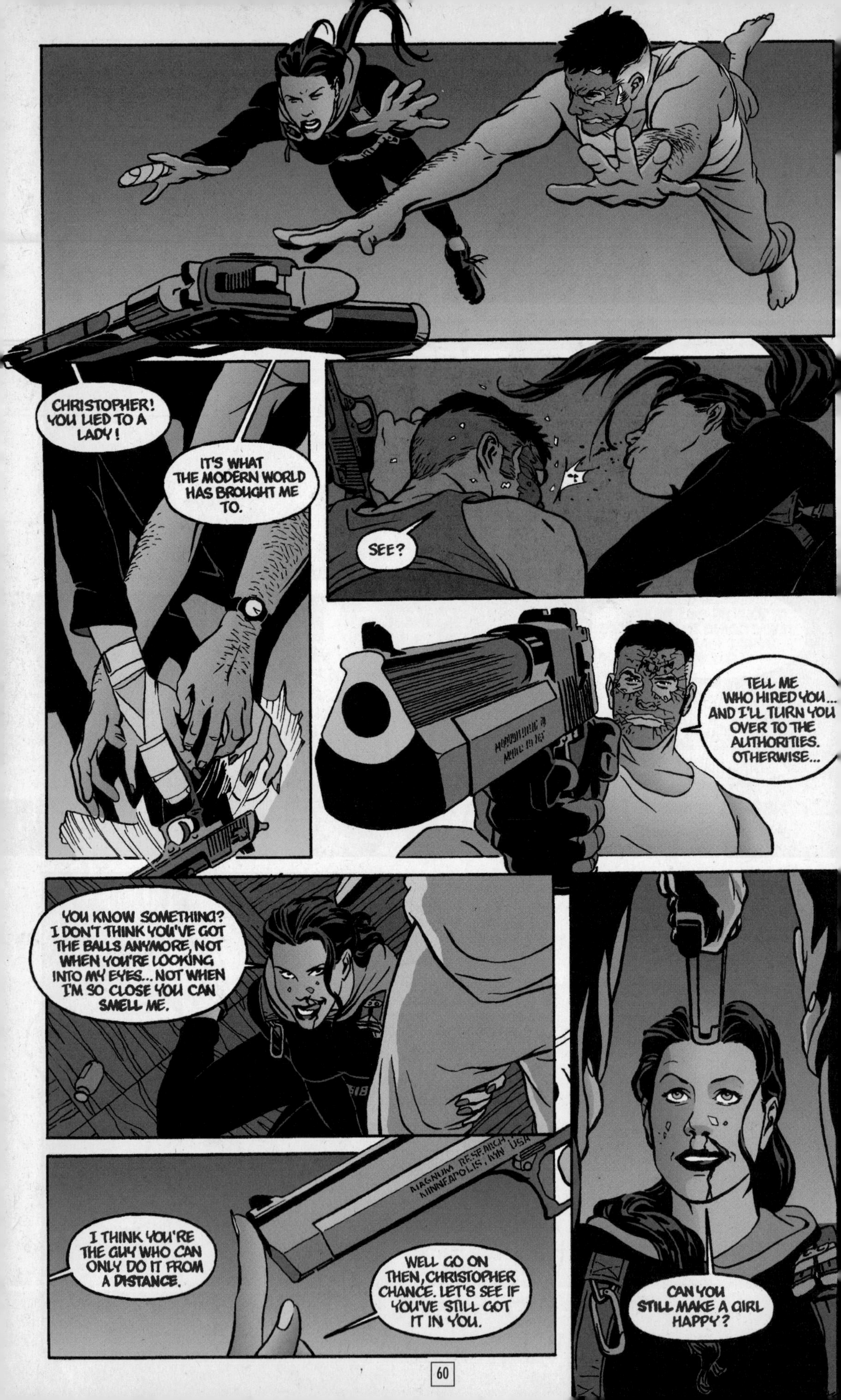
CHRISTOPHER! YOU LIED TO A LADY!
IT'S WHAT THE MODERN WORLD HAS BROUGHT ME TO.
SEE?
TELL ME WHO HIRED YOU... AND I'LL TURN YOU OVER TO THE AUTHORITIES. OTHERWISE...
YOU KNOW SOMETHING? I DON'T THINK YOU'VE GOT THE BALLS ANYMORE, NOT WHEN YOU'RE LOOKING INTO MY EYES... NOT WHEN I'M SO CLOSE YOU CAN SMELL ME.
MAGNUM RESEARCH MINNEAPOLIS, MN USA
I THINK YOU'RE THE GUY WHO CAN ONLY DO IT FROM A DISTANCE.
WELL GO ON THEN, CHRISTOPHER CHANCE. LET'S SEE IF YOU'VE STILL GOT IT IN YOU.
CAN YOU STILL MAKE A GIRL HAPPY?

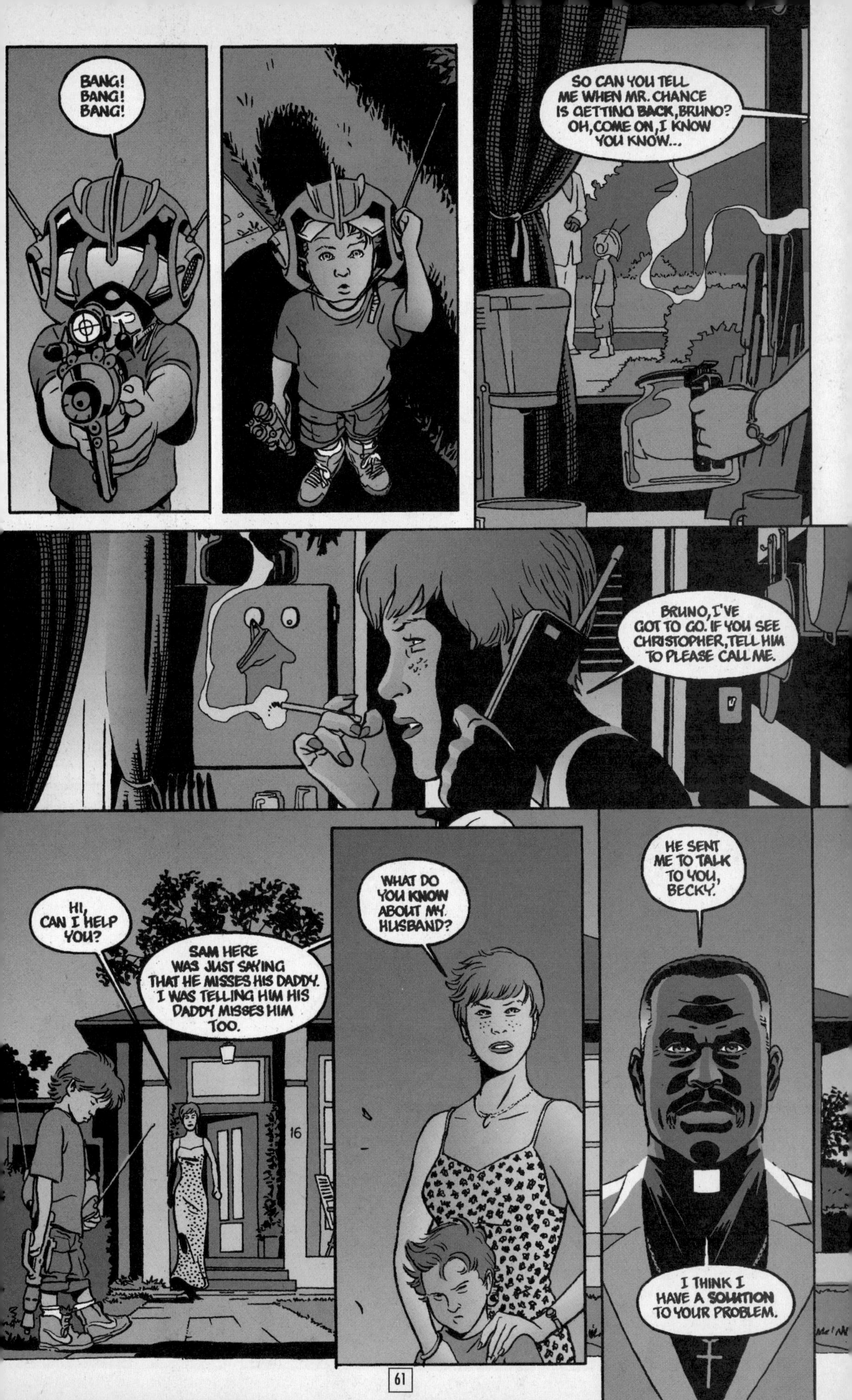
BANG! BANG! BANG!
SO CAN YOU TELL ME WHEN MR. CHANCE IS GETTING BACK, BRUNO? OH, COME ON, I KNOW YOU KNOW...
BRUNO, I'VE GOT TO GO. IF YOU SEE CHRISTOPHER, TELL HIM TO PLEASE CALL ME.
HI, CAN I HELP YOU?
SAM HERE WAS JUST SAYING THAT HE MISSES HIS DADDY. I WAS TELLING HIM HIS DADDY MISSES HIM TOO.
16
WHAT DO YOU KNOW ABOUT MY HUSBAND?
HE SENT ME TO TALK TO YOU, BECKY.
I THINK I HAVE A SOLUTION TO YOUR PROBLEM.

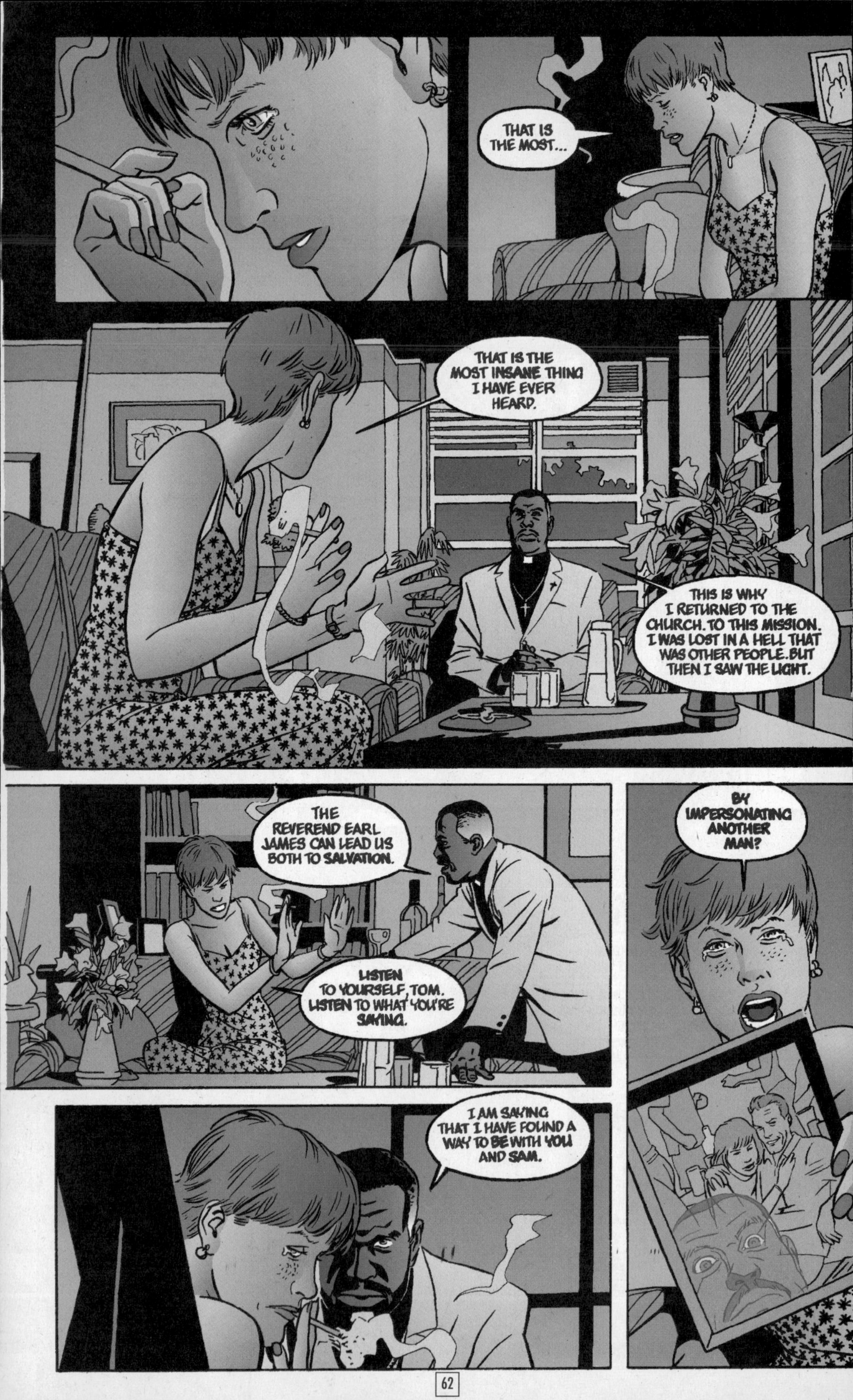

THAT IS THE MOST...
THAT IS THE MOST INSANE THING I HAVE EVER HEARD.
THIS IS WHY I RETURNED TO THE CHURCH. TO THIS MISSION. I WAS LOST IN A HELL THAT WAS OTHER PEOPLE. BUT THEN I SAW THE LIGHT.
THE REVEREND EARL JAMES CAN LEAD US BOTH TO SALVATION.
LISTEN TO YOURSELF, TOM. LISTEN TO WHAT YOU'RE SAYING.
BY IMPERSONATING ANOTHER MAN?
I AM SAYING THAT I HAVE FOUND A WAY TO BE WITH YOU AND SAM.

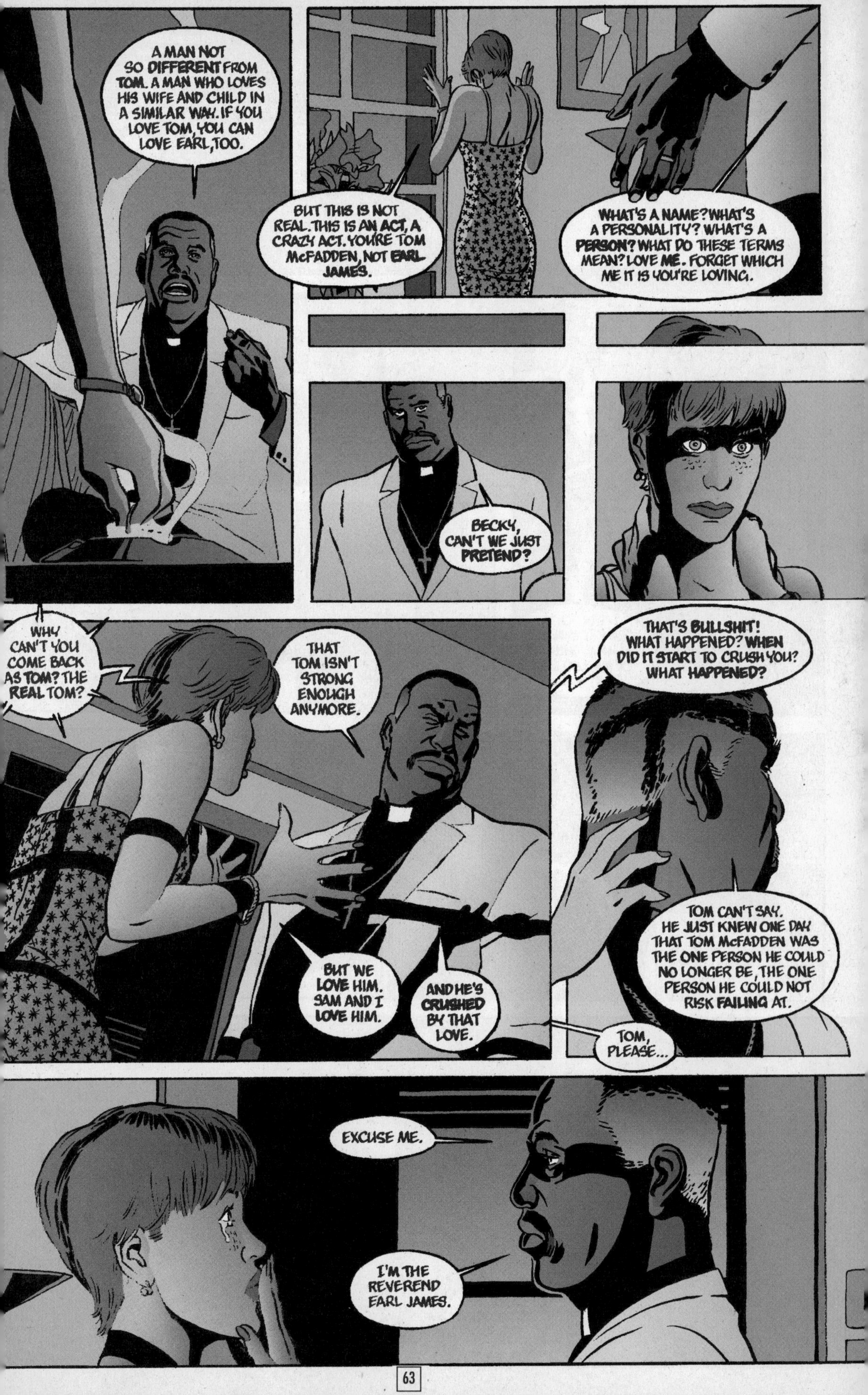
A MAN NOT SO DIFFERENT FROM TOM. A MAN WHO LOVES HIS WIFE AND CHILD IN A SIMILAR WAY. IF YOU LOVE TOM, YOU CAN LOVE EARL, TOO.
BUT THIS IS NOT REAL. THIS IS AN ACT, A CRAZY ACT. YOU'RE TOM McFADDEN, NOT EARL JAMES.
WHAT'S A NAME? WHAT'S A PERSONALITY? WHAT'S A PERSON? WHAT DO THESE TERMS MEAN? LOVE ME. FORGET WHICH ME IT IS YOU'RE LOVING.
BECKY, CAN'T WE JUST PRETEND?
WHY CAN'T YOU COME BACK AS TOM? THE REAL TOM?
THAT TOM ISN'T STRONG ENOUGH ANYMORE.
BUT WE LOVE HIM. SAM AND I LOVE HIM.
AND HE'S CRUSHED BY THAT LOVE.
THAT'S BULLSHIT! WHAT HAPPENED? WHEN DID IT START TO CRUSH YOU? WHAT HAPPENED?
TOM CAN'T SAY. HE JUST KNEW ONE DAY THAT TOM McFADDEN WAS THE ONE PERSON HE COULD NO LONGER BE, THE ONE PERSON HE COULD NOT RISK FAILING AT.
TOM, PLEASE...
EXCUSE ME.
I'M THE REVEREND EARL JAMES.

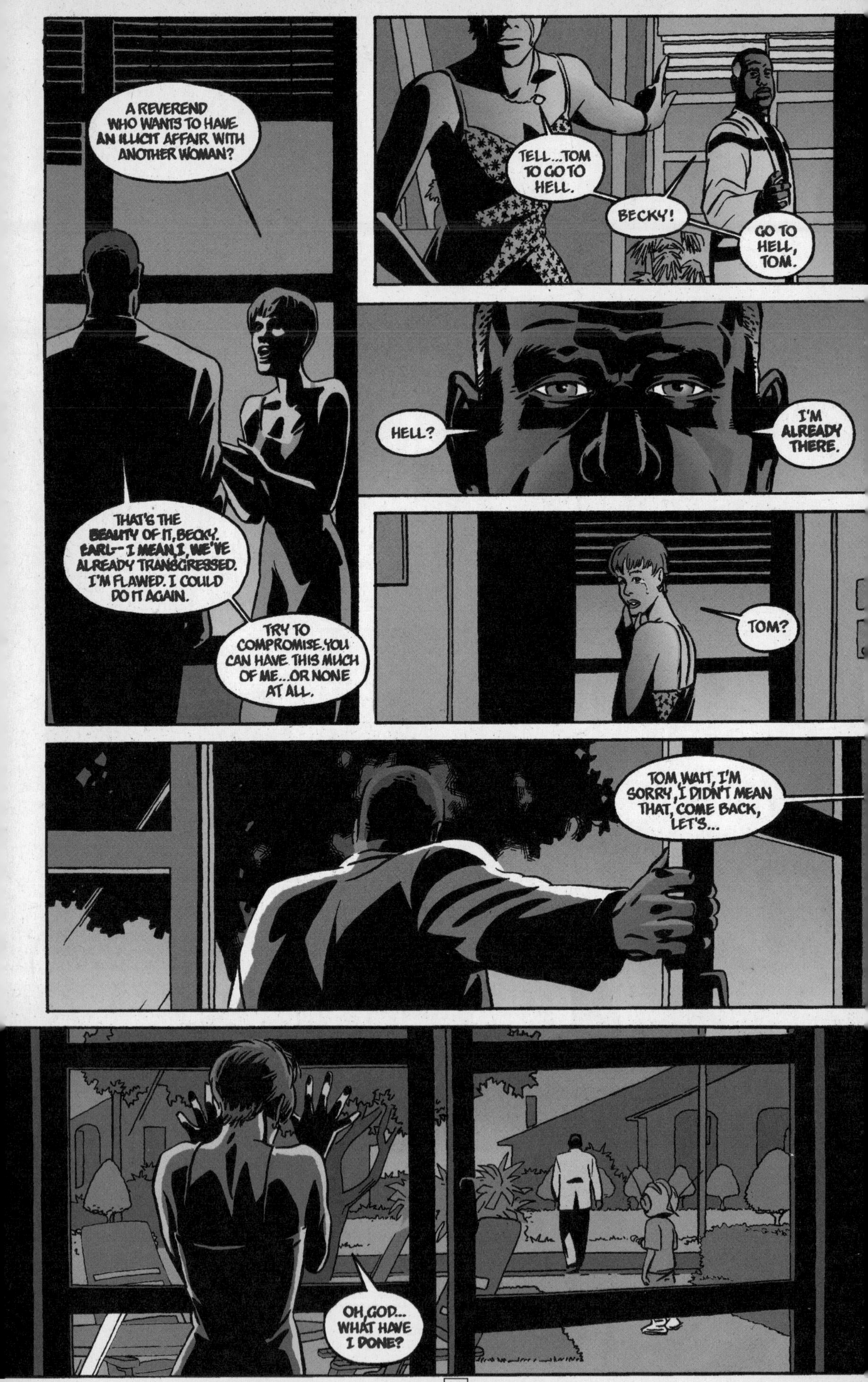
A REVEREND WHO WANTS TO HAVE AN ILLICIT AFFAIR WITH ANOTHER WOMAN?
THAT'S THE BEAUTY OF IT, BECKY. EARL-- I MEAN, I, WE'VE ALREADY TRANSGRESSED. I'M FLAWED. I COULD DO IT AGAIN.
TRY TO COMPROMISE. YOU CAN HAVE THIS MUCH OF ME...OR NONE AT ALL.
TELL...TOM TO GO TO HELL.
BECKY!
GO TO HELL, TOM.
HELL?
I'M ALREADY THERE.
TOM?
TOM WAIT, I'M SORRY, I DIDN'T MEAN THAT, COME BACK, LET'S...
OH, GOD... WHAT HAVE I DONE?

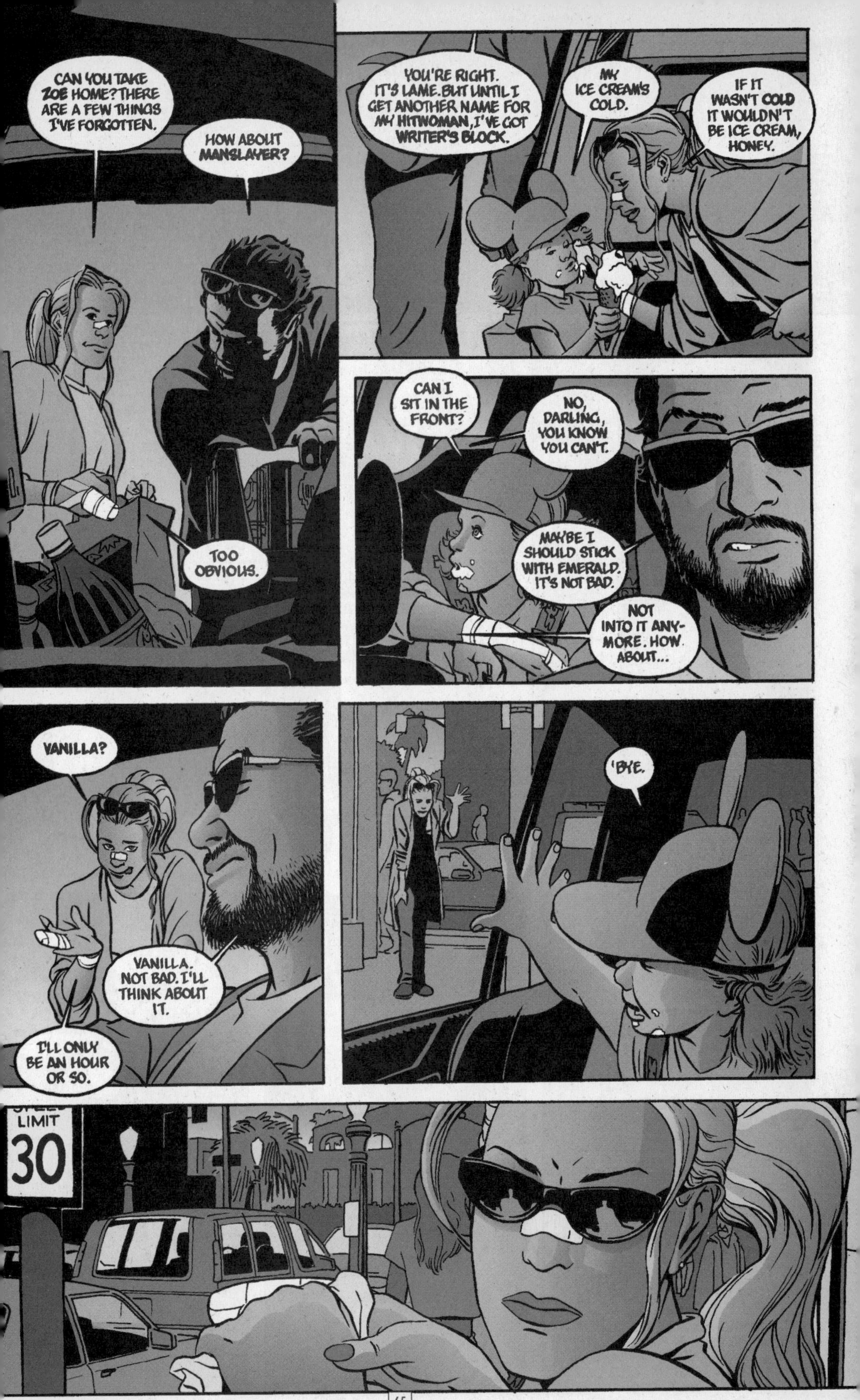

CAN YOU TAKE ZOE HOME? THERE ARE A FEW THINGS I'VE FORGOTTEN.
HOW ABOUT MANSLAYER?
TOO OBVIOUS.
YOU'RE RIGHT. IT'S LAME. BUT UNTIL I GET ANOTHER NAME FOR MY HITWOMAN, I'VE GOT WRITER'S BLOCK.
MY ICE CREAM'S COLD.
IF IT WASN'T COLD IT WOULDN'T BE ICE CREAM, HONEY.
CAN I SIT IN THE FRONT?
NO, DARLING, YOU KNOW YOU CAN'T.
MAYBE I SHOULD STICK WITH EMERALD. IT'S NOT BAD.
NOT INTO IT ANY-MORE. HOW ABOUT...
VANILLA?
VANILLA. NOT BAD. I'LL THINK ABOUT IT.
I'LL ONLY BE AN HOUR OR SO.
'BYE.
LIMIT
30

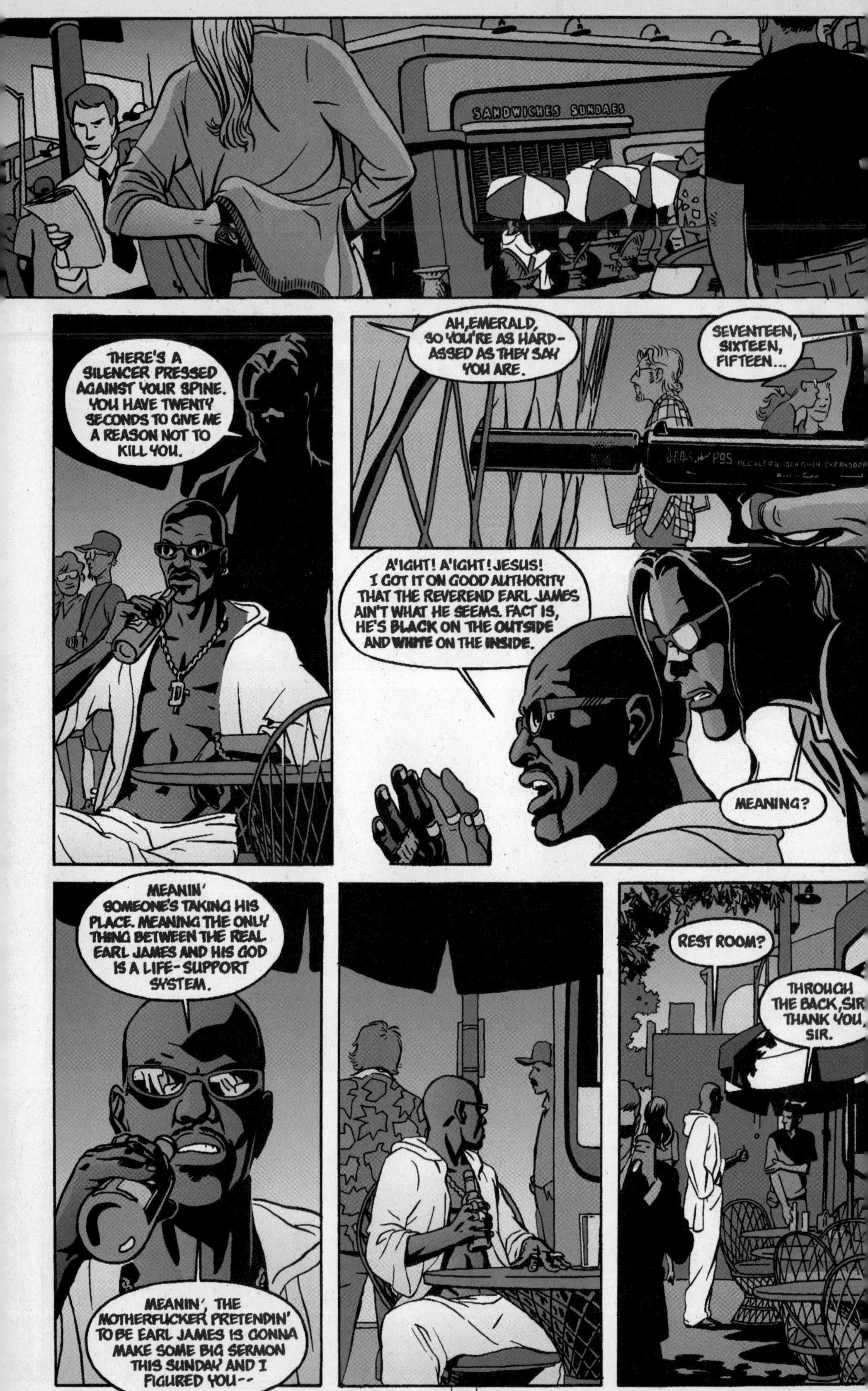
SANDWICHES SUNDAES
THERE'S A SILENCER PRESSED AGAINST YOUR SPINE. YOU HAVE TWENTY SECONDS TO GIVE ME A REASON NOT TO KILL YOU.
AH,EMERALD, SO YOU'RE AS HARD-ASSED AS THEY SAY YOU ARE.
SEVENTEEN, SIXTEEN, FIFTEEN...
A'IGHT! A'IGHT! JESUS! I GOT IT ON GOOD AUTHORITY THAT THE REVEREND EARL JAMES AIN'T WHAT HE SEEMS. FACT IS, HE'S BLACK ON THE OUTSIDE AND WHITE ON THE INSIDE.
MEANING?
MEANIN' SOMEONE'S TAKING HIS PLACE. MEANING THE ONLY THING BETWEEN THE REAL EARL JAMES AND HIS GOD IS A LIFE-SUPPORT SYSTEM.
MEANIN', THE MOTHERFUCKER PRETENDIN' TO BE EARL JAMES IS GONNA MAKE SOME BIG SERMON THIS SUNDAY AND I FIGURED YOU--
REST ROOM?
THROUGH THE BACK,SIR.
THANK YOU, SIR.

THAT WENT WELL...A PERFECT SOLUTION.

ALL OUR PROBLEMS WILL SOON BE OVER.

EARL JAMES BECOMES A MARTYR. MOWN DOWN IN HIS CHURCH AS HE REPENTS HIS SINS.

EMERALD THINKS SHE HAS KILLED CHRISTOPHER CHANCE, AND SO LEAVES HIM ALONE.

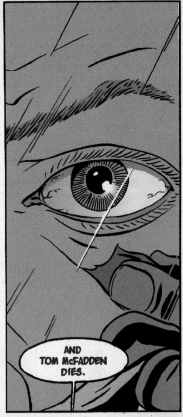

AND TOM McFADDEN DIES.

Becky and Sam will be able to build their lives again, knowing I won't be back, knowing...

Why's everyone looking at me?

OH NO...

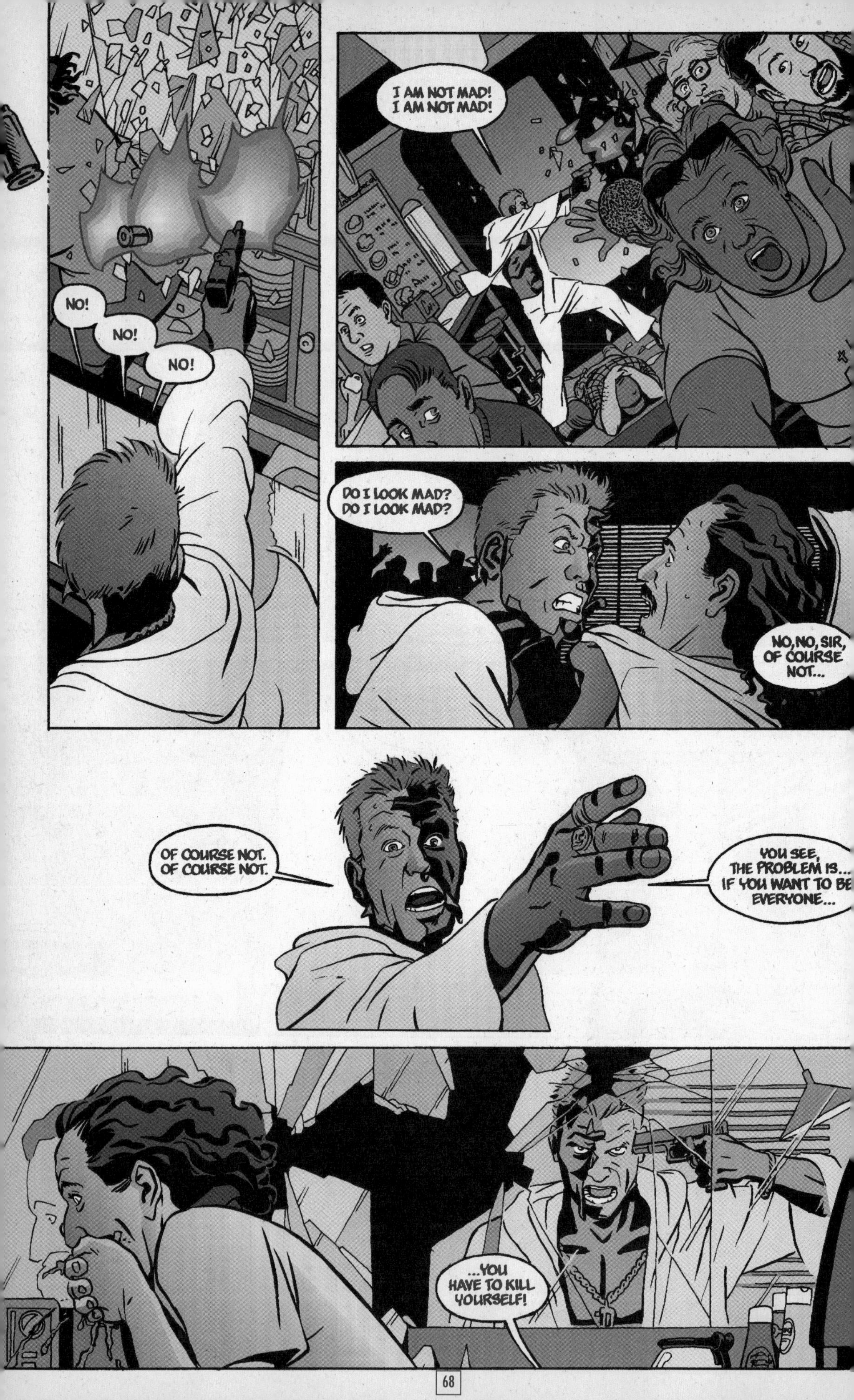
NO!
NO!
NO!
I AM NOT MAD! I AM NOT MAD!
DO I LOOK MAD? DO I LOOK MAD?
NO, NO, SIR, OF COURSE NOT...
OF COURSE NOT. OF COURSE NOT.
YOU SEE, THE PROBLEM IS... IF YOU WANT TO BE EVERYONE...
...YOU HAVE TO KILL YOURSELF!

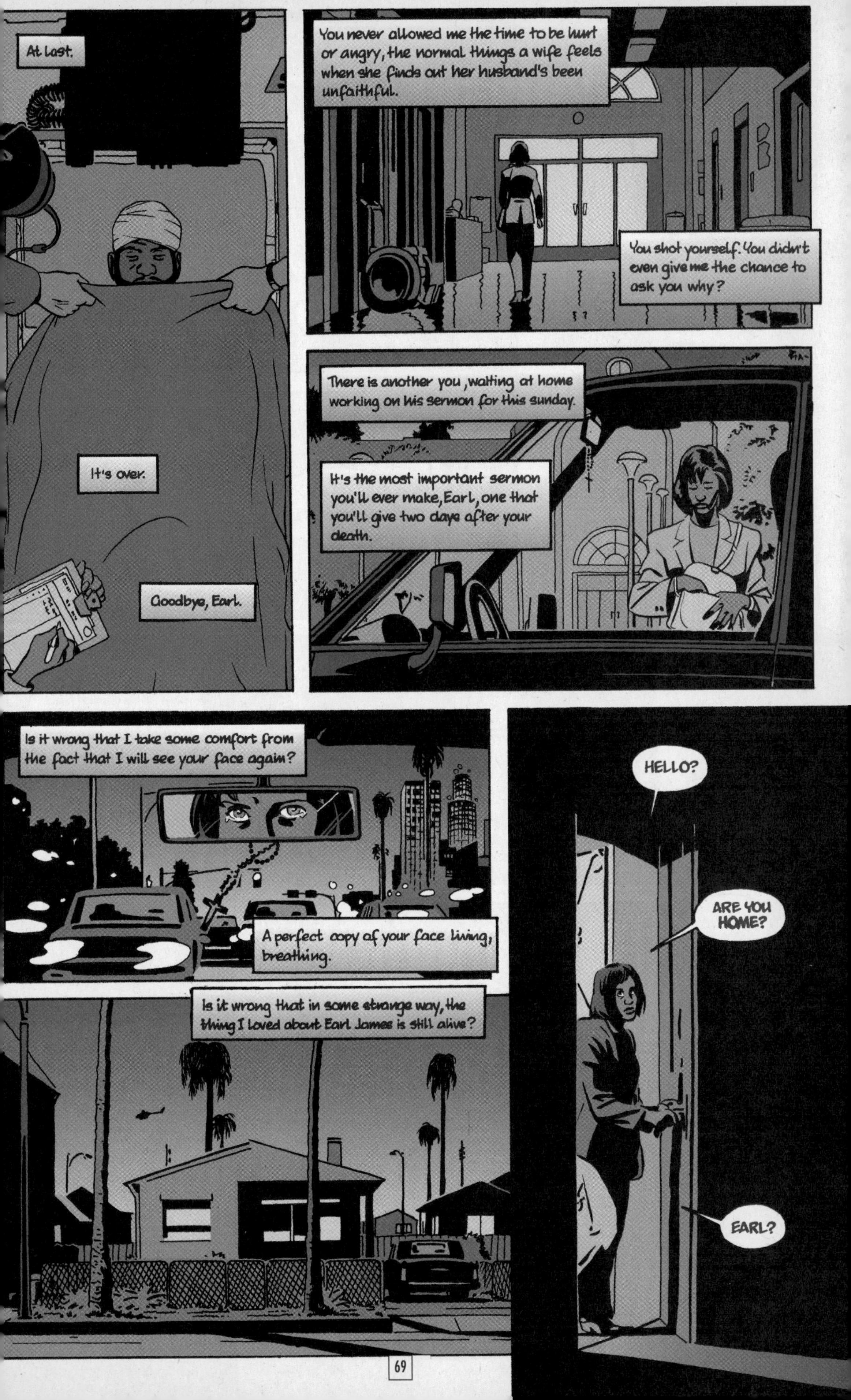
At Last.
It's over.
Goodbye, Earl.
You never allowed me the time to be hurt or angry, the normal things a wife feels when she finds out her husband's been unfaithful.
You shot yourself. You didn't even give me the chance to ask you why?
There is another you, waiting at home working on his sermon for this sunday.
It's the most important sermon you'll ever make, Earl, one that you'll give two days after your death.
Is it wrong that I take some comfort from the fact that I will see your face again?
A perfect copy of your face living, breathing.
Is it wrong that in some strange way, the thing I loved about Earl James is still alive?
HELLO?
ARE YOU HOME?
EARL?

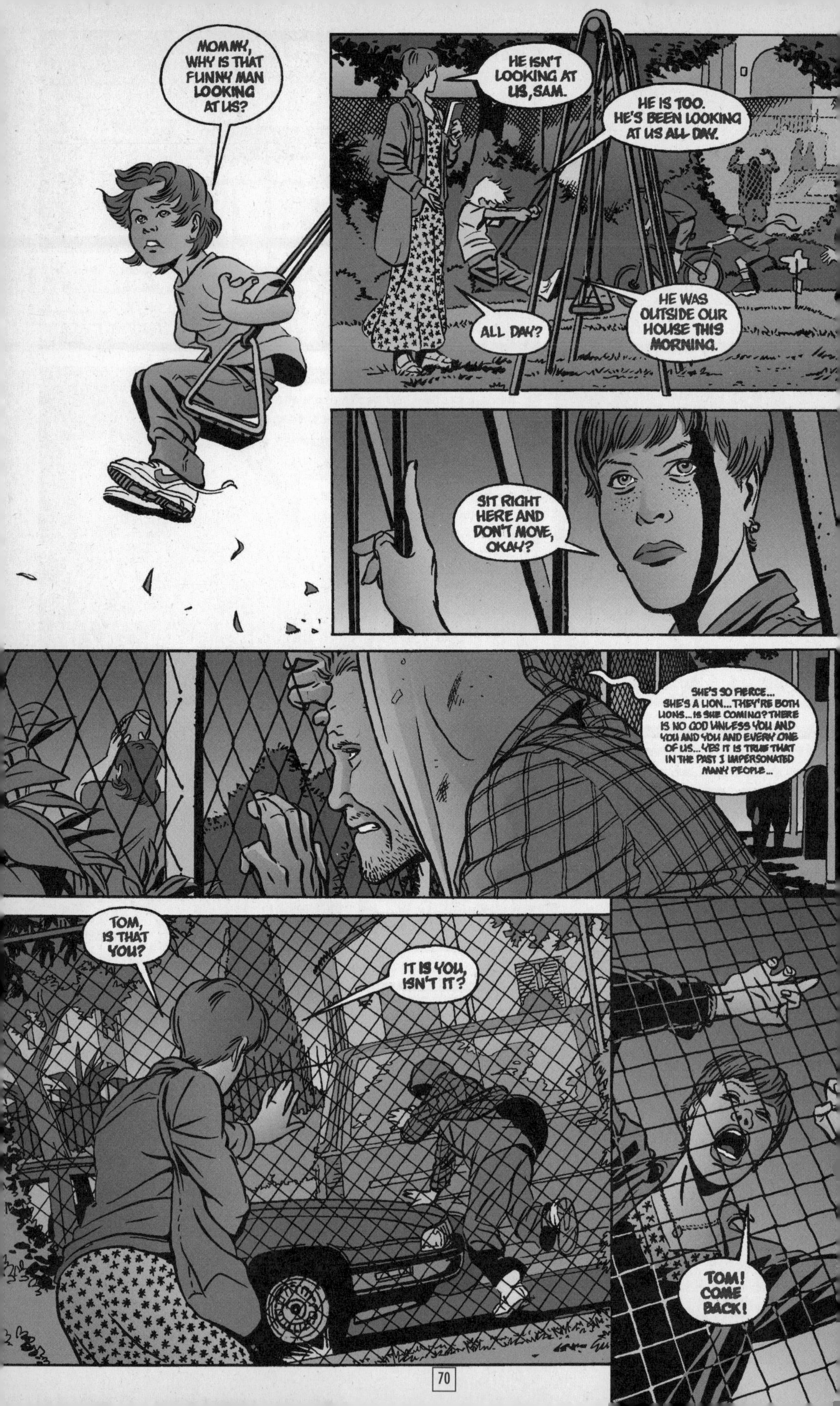
MOMMY, WHY IS THAT FUNNY MAN LOOKING AT US?
HE ISN'T LOOKING AT US, SAM.
HE IS TOO. HE'S BEEN LOOKING AT US ALL DAY.
ALL DAY?
HE WAS OUTSIDE OUR HOUSE THIS MORNING.
SIT RIGHT HERE AND DON'T MOVE, OKAY?
SHE'S SO FIERCE... SHE'S A LION... THEY'RE BOTH LIONS... IS SHE COMING? THERE IS NO GOD UNLESS YOU AND YOU AND YOU AND EVERY ONE OF US... YES IT IS TRUE THAT IN THE PAST I IMPERSONATED MANY PEOPLE...
TOM, IS THAT YOU?
IT IS YOU, ISN'T IT?
TOM! COME BACK!

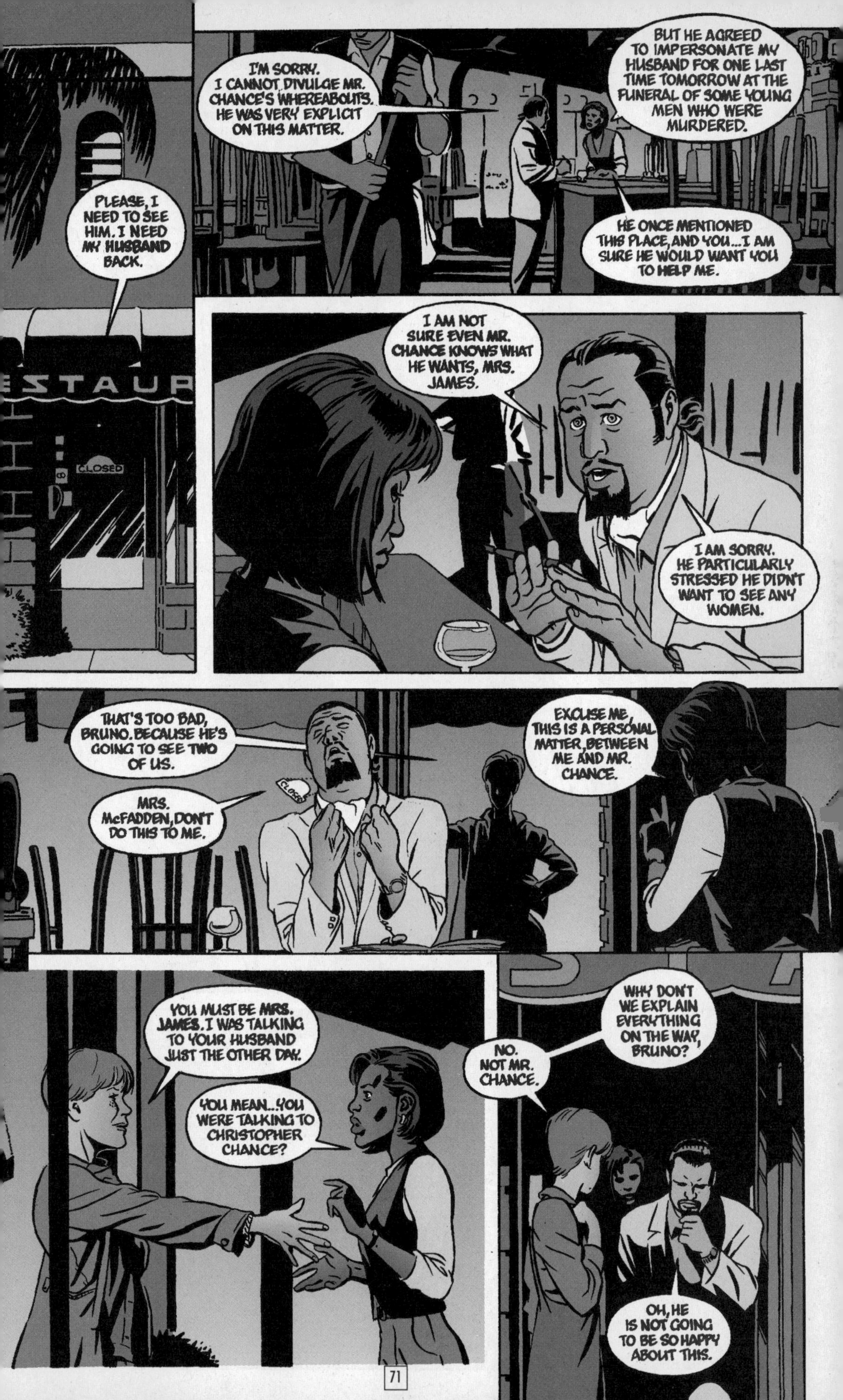
PLEASE, I NEED TO SEE HIM. I NEED MY HUSBAND BACK.
ESTAUR
CLOSED
I'M SORRY. I CANNOT DIVULGE MR. CHANCE'S WHEREABOUTS. HE WAS VERY EXPLICIT ON THIS MATTER.
BUT HE AGREED TO IMPERSONATE MY HUSBAND FOR ONE LAST TIME TOMORROW AT THE FUNERAL OF SOME YOUNG MEN WHO WERE MURDERED.
HE ONCE MENTIONED THIS PLACE, AND YOU...I AM SURE HE WOULD WANT YOU TO HELP ME.
I AM NOT SURE EVEN MR. CHANCE KNOWS WHAT HE WANTS, MRS. JAMES.
I AM SORRY. HE PARTICULARLY STRESSED HE DIDN'T WANT TO SEE ANY WOMEN.
THAT'S TOO BAD, BRUNO. BECAUSE HE'S GOING TO SEE TWO OF US.
MRS. McFADDEN, DON'T DO THIS TO ME.
EXCUSE ME, THIS IS A PERSONAL MATTER, BETWEEN ME AND MR. CHANCE.
YOU MUST BE MRS. JAMES. I WAS TALKING TO YOUR HUSBAND JUST THE OTHER DAY.
YOU MEAN...YOU WERE TALKING TO CHRISTOPHER CHANCE?
NO. NOT MR. CHANCE.
WHY DON'T WE EXPLAIN EVERYTHING ON THE WAY, BRUNO?
OH, HE IS NOT GOING TO BE SO HAPPY ABOUT THIS.

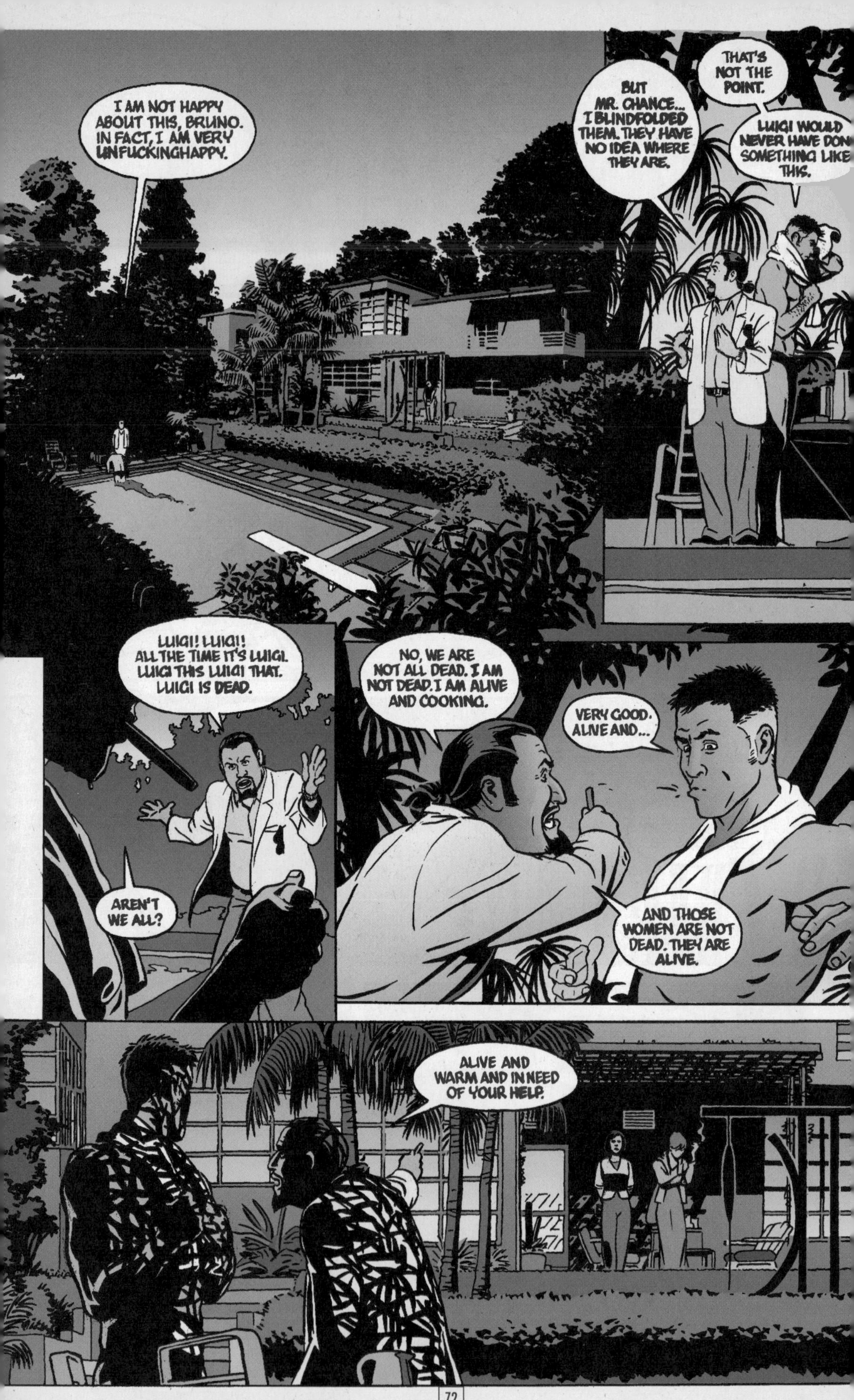
I AM NOT HAPPY ABOUT THIS, BRUNO. IN FACT, I AM VERY UNFUCKINGHAPPY.
BUT MR. CHANCE... I BLINDFOLDED THEM. THEY HAVE NO IDEA WHERE THEY ARE.
THAT'S NOT THE POINT.
LUIGI WOULD NEVER HAVE DONE SOMETHING LIKE THIS.
LUIGI! LUIGI! ALL THE TIME IT'S LUIGI. LUIGI THIS LUIGI THAT. LUIGI IS DEAD.
AREN'T WE ALL?
NO, WE ARE NOT ALL DEAD. I AM NOT DEAD. I AM ALIVE AND COOKING.
VERY GOOD. ALIVE AND...
AND THOSE WOMEN ARE NOT DEAD. THEY ARE ALIVE.
ALIVE AND WARM AND IN NEED OF YOUR HELP.

LADIES, I GIVE YOU CHRISTOPHER CHANCE, MASTER OF DISGUISE, THE PRINCE OF DECEPTION, THE KING OF--

YEAH, OKAY, BRUNO, WE GET THE MESSAGE.

CHRIS, YOU HAVE TO HELP US!

I CAN'T HELP ANYONE, BECKY.

FOR GOD'S SAKE YOU HAVE TO TRY. WE BOTH NEED YOU. WE'VE BOTH LOST OUR HUSBANDS.

DO YOU KNOW WHOM YOU'RE ASKING FOR HELP?

SOMEONE WHO THE OTHER DAY HAD THE CHANCE TO SHOOT AN ASSASSIN WITH A CONTRACT ON HIS HEAD... BUT WAS TOO INEFFECTUAL, TOO PATHETIC TO DO IT.

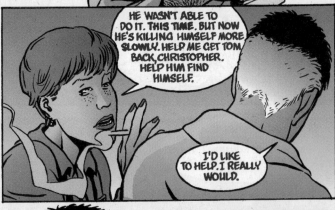

HE WASN'T ABLE TO DO IT, THIS TIME, BUT NOW HE'S KILLING HIMSELF MORE SLOWLY. HELP ME GET TOM BACK, CHRISTOPHER. HELP HIM FIND HIMSELF.

I'D LIKE TO HELP. I REALLY WOULD.

TOM ALSO TRIED TO SHOOT SOMEONE YESTERDAY.

WHO?

HIMSELF.

MY GOD, HOW IS HE?

MY HUSBAND IS DEAD, MR. CHANCE. BUT HE MUST NOT BE DEAD-- NOT YET, NOT UNTIL HE HAS MADE ONE LAST SERMON. UNLESS THAT HAPPENS, ALL HIS WORK WILL HAVE BEEN IN VAIN.

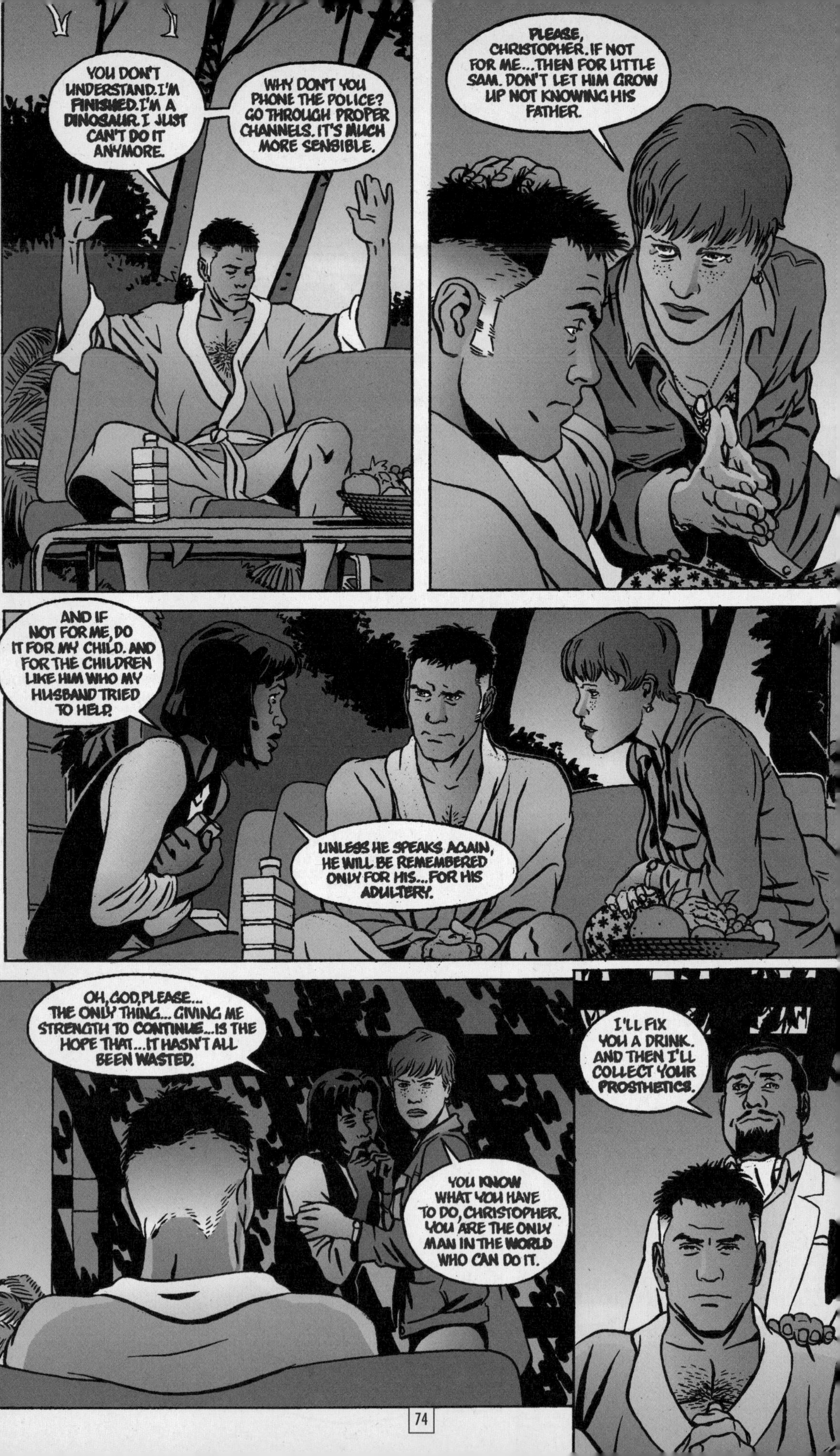

YOU DON'T UNDERSTAND. I'M FINISHED. I'M A DINOSAUR. I JUST CAN'T DO IT ANYMORE.
WHY DON'T YOU PHONE THE POLICE? GO THROUGH PROPER CHANNELS. IT'S MUCH MORE SENSIBLE.
PLEASE, CHRISTOPHER. IF NOT FOR ME...THEN FOR LITTLE SAM. DON'T LET HIM GROW UP NOT KNOWING HIS FATHER.
AND IF NOT FOR ME, DO IT FOR MY CHILD. AND FOR THE CHILDREN LIKE HIM WHO MY HUSBAND TRIED TO HELP.
UNLESS HE SPEAKS AGAIN, HE WILL BE REMEMBERED ONLY FOR HIS...FOR HIS ADULTERY.
OH, GOD, PLEASE... THE ONLY THING... GIVING ME STRENGTH TO CONTINUE...IS THE HOPE THAT...IT HASN'T ALL BEEN WASTED.
YOU KNOW WHAT YOU HAVE TO DO, CHRISTOPHER. YOU ARE THE ONLY MAN IN THE WORLD WHO CAN DO IT.
I'LL FIX YOU A DRINK. AND THEN I'LL COLLECT YOUR PROSTHETICS.

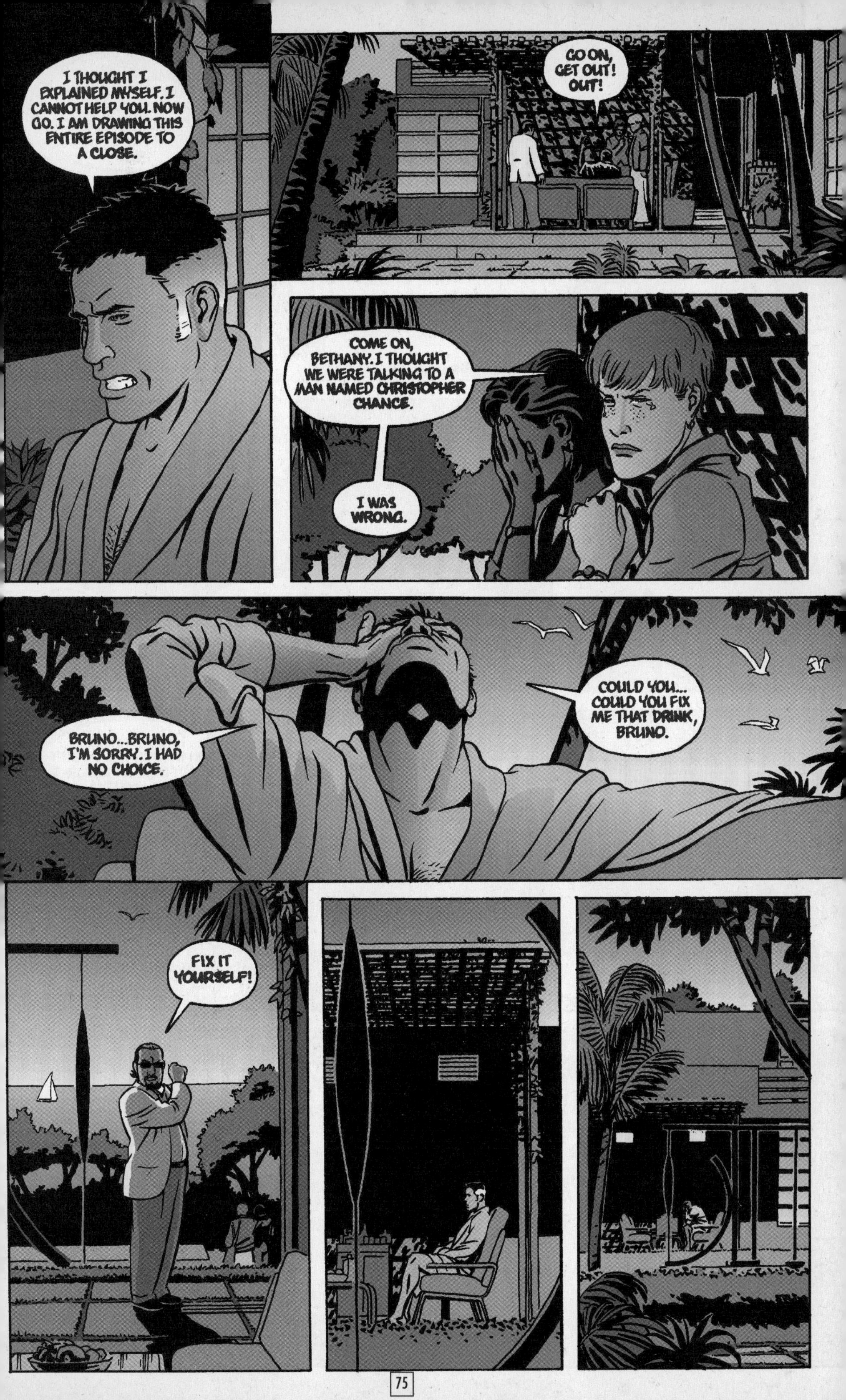
I THOUGHT I EXPLAINED MYSELF. I CANNOT HELP YOU. NOW GO. I AM DRAWING THIS ENTIRE EPISODE TO A CLOSE.
GO ON, GET OUT! OUT!
COME ON, BETHANY. I THOUGHT WE WERE TALKING TO A MAN NAMED CHRISTOPHER CHANCE.
I WAS WRONG.
BRUNO...BRUNO, I'M SORRY. I HAD NO CHOICE.
COULD YOU... COULD YOU FIX ME THAT DRINK, BRUNO.
FIX IT YOURSELF!

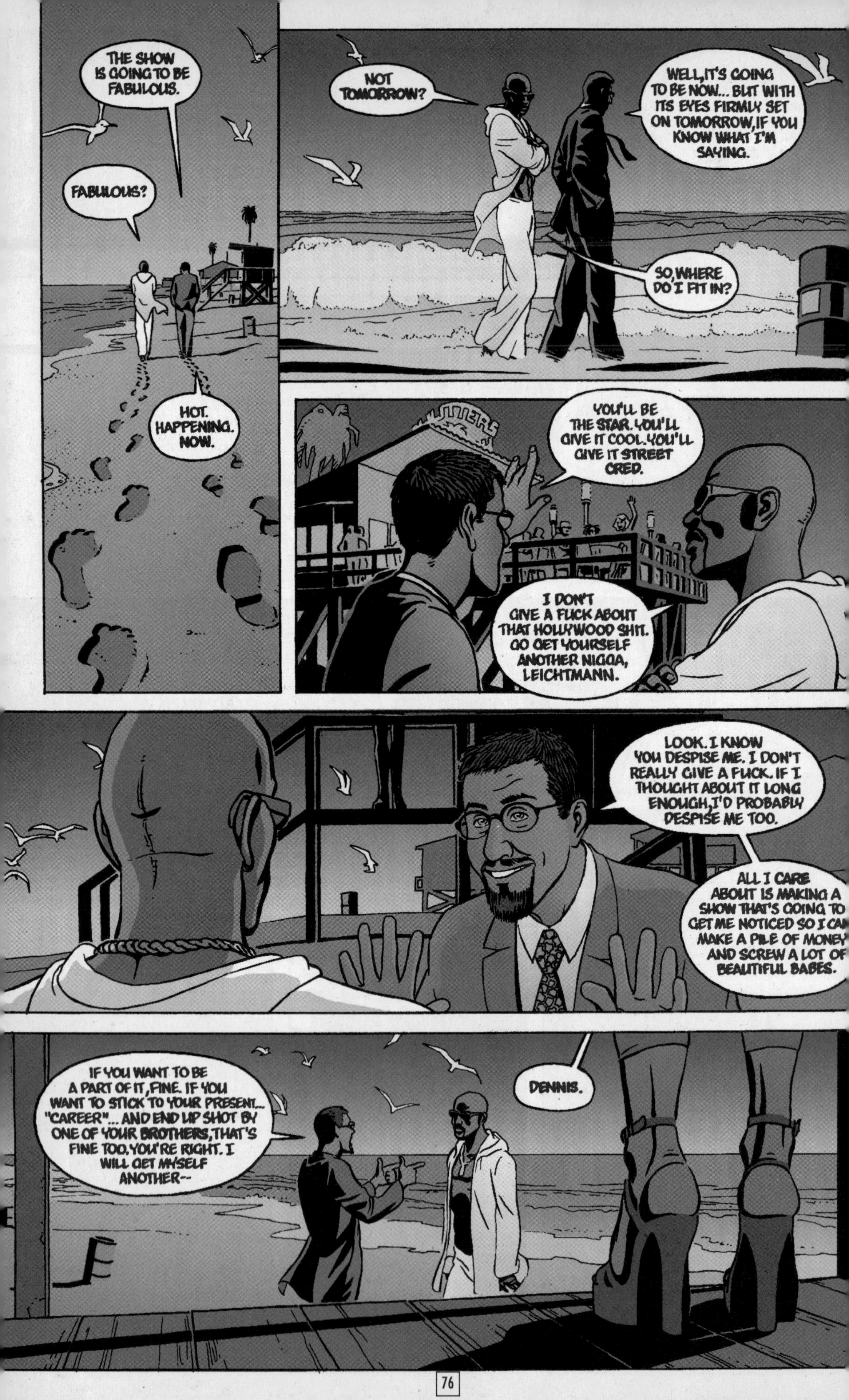
THE SHOW IS GOING TO BE FABULOUS.
FABULOUS?
HOT. HAPPENING. NOW.
NOT TOMORROW?
WELL, IT'S GOING TO BE NOW... BUT WITH ITS EYES FIRMLY SET ON TOMORROW, IF YOU KNOW WHAT I'M SAYING.
SO, WHERE DO I FIT IN?
YOU'LL BE THE STAR. YOU'LL GIVE IT COOL. YOU'LL GIVE IT STREET CRED.
I DON'T GIVE A FUCK ABOUT THAT HOLLYWOOD SHIT. GO GET YOURSELF ANOTHER NIGGA, LEICHTMANN.
LOOK. I KNOW YOU DESPISE ME. I DON'T REALLY GIVE A FUCK. IF I THOUGHT ABOUT IT LONG ENOUGH, I'D PROBABLY DESPISE ME TOO.
ALL I CARE ABOUT IS MAKING A SHOW THAT'S GOING TO GET ME NOTICED SO I CAN MAKE A PILE OF MONEY AND SCREW A LOT OF BEAUTIFUL BABES.
IF YOU WANT TO BE A PART OF IT, FINE. IF YOU WANT TO STICK TO YOUR PRESENT... "CAREER"... AND END UP SHOT BY ONE OF YOUR BROTHERS, THAT'S FINE TOO. YOU'RE RIGHT. I WILL GET MYSELF ANOTHER--
DENNIS.

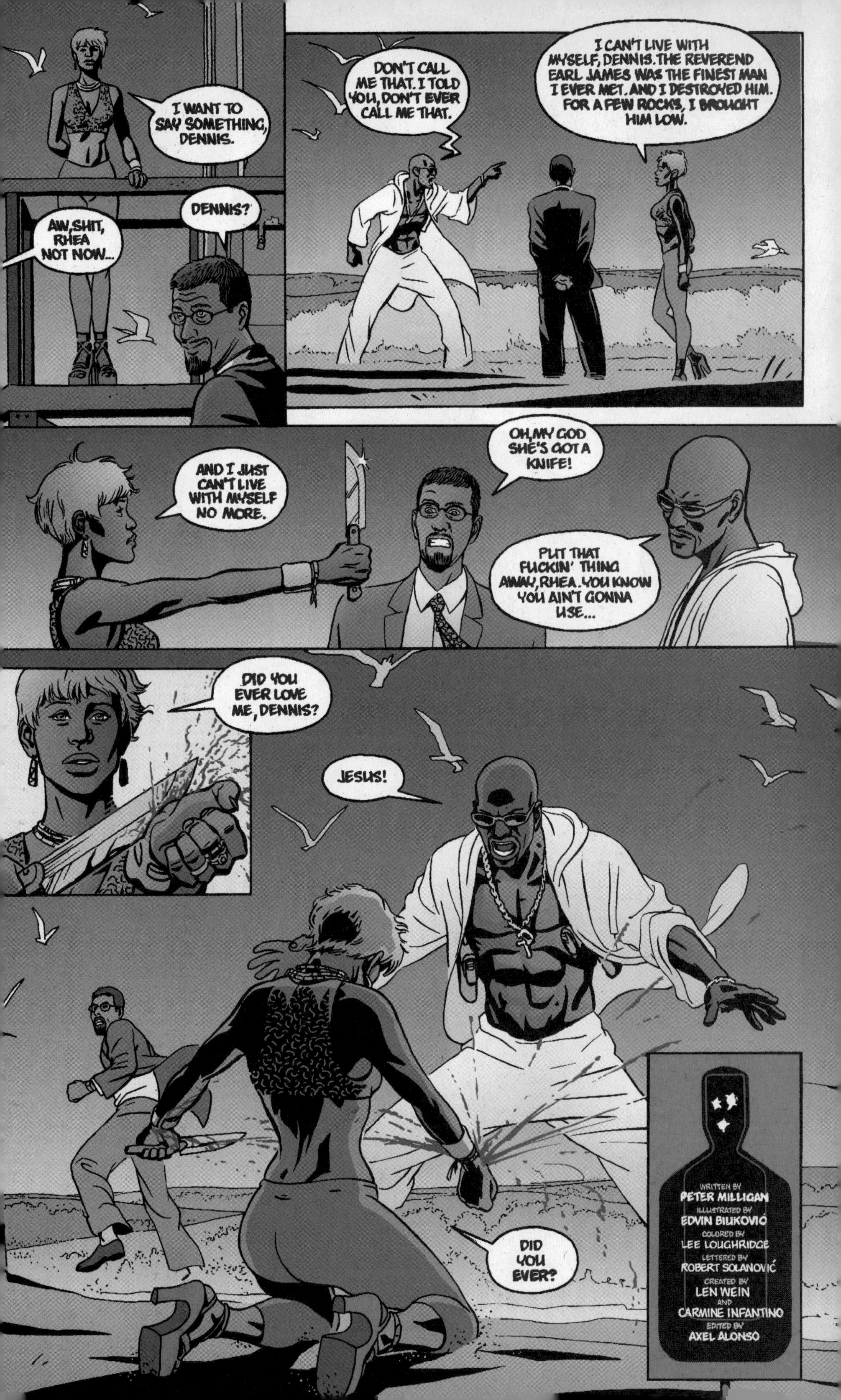
I WANT TO SAY SOMETHING, DENNIS.
DENNIS?
AW, SHIT, RHEA NOT NOW...
DON'T CALL ME THAT. I TOLD YOU, DON'T EVER CALL ME THAT.
I CAN'T LIVE WITH MYSELF, DENNIS. THE REVEREND EARL JAMES WAS THE FINEST MAN I EVER MET. AND I DESTROYED HIM. FOR A FEW ROCKS, I BROUGHT HIM LOW.
AND I JUST CAN'T LIVE WITH MYSELF NO MORE.
OH, MY GOD SHE'S GOT A KNIFE!
PUT THAT FUCKIN' THING AWAY, RHEA. YOU KNOW YOU AIN'T GONNA USE...
DID YOU EVER LOVE ME, DENNIS?
JESUS!
DID YOU EVER?
WRITTEN BY
PETER MILLIGAN
ILLUSTRATED BY
EDVIN BIUKOVIĆ
COLORED BY
LEE LOUGHRIDGE
LETTERED BY
ROBERT SOLANOVIĆ
CREATED BY
LEN WEIN
AND
CARMINE INFANTINO
EDITED BY
AXEL ALONSO

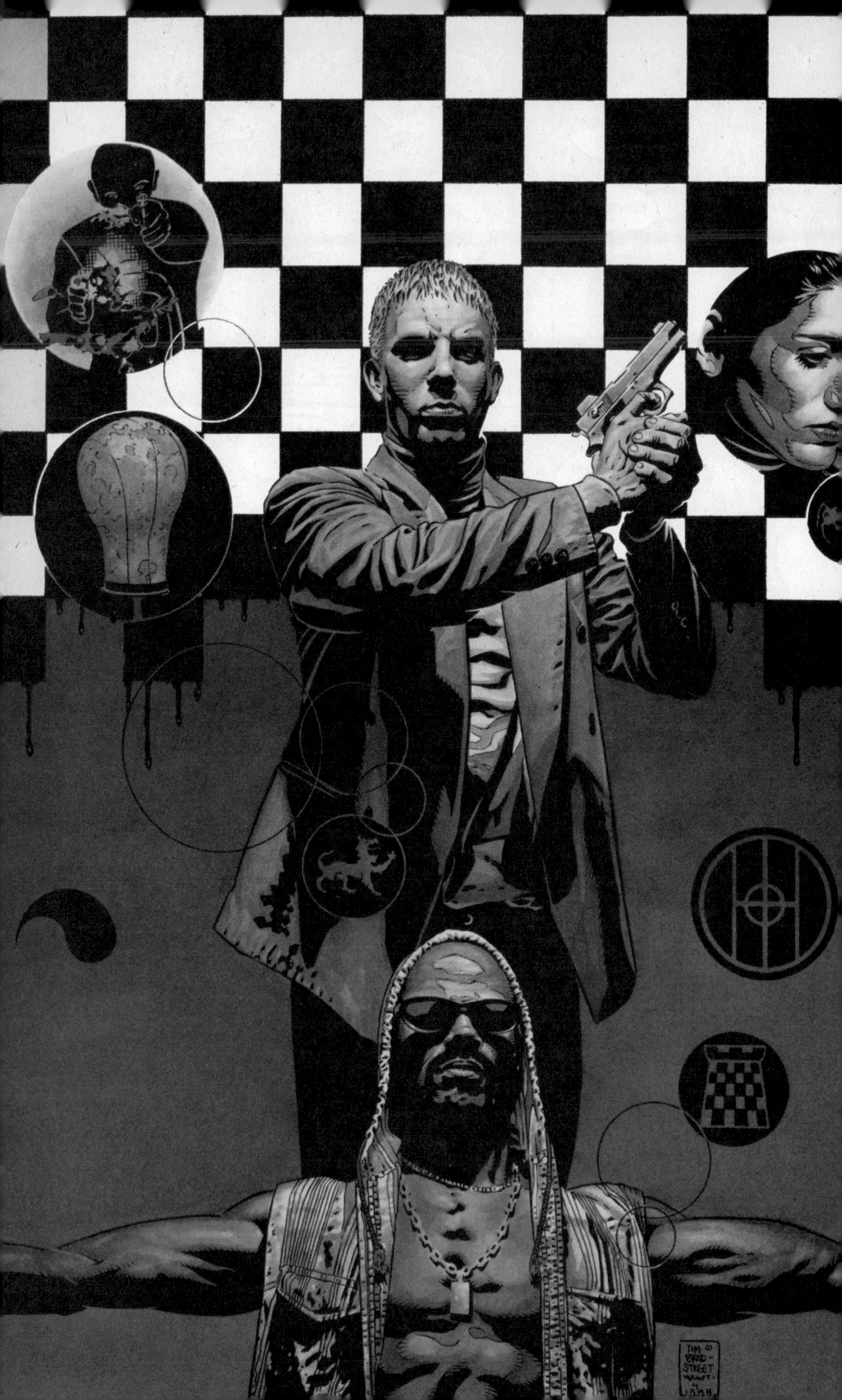

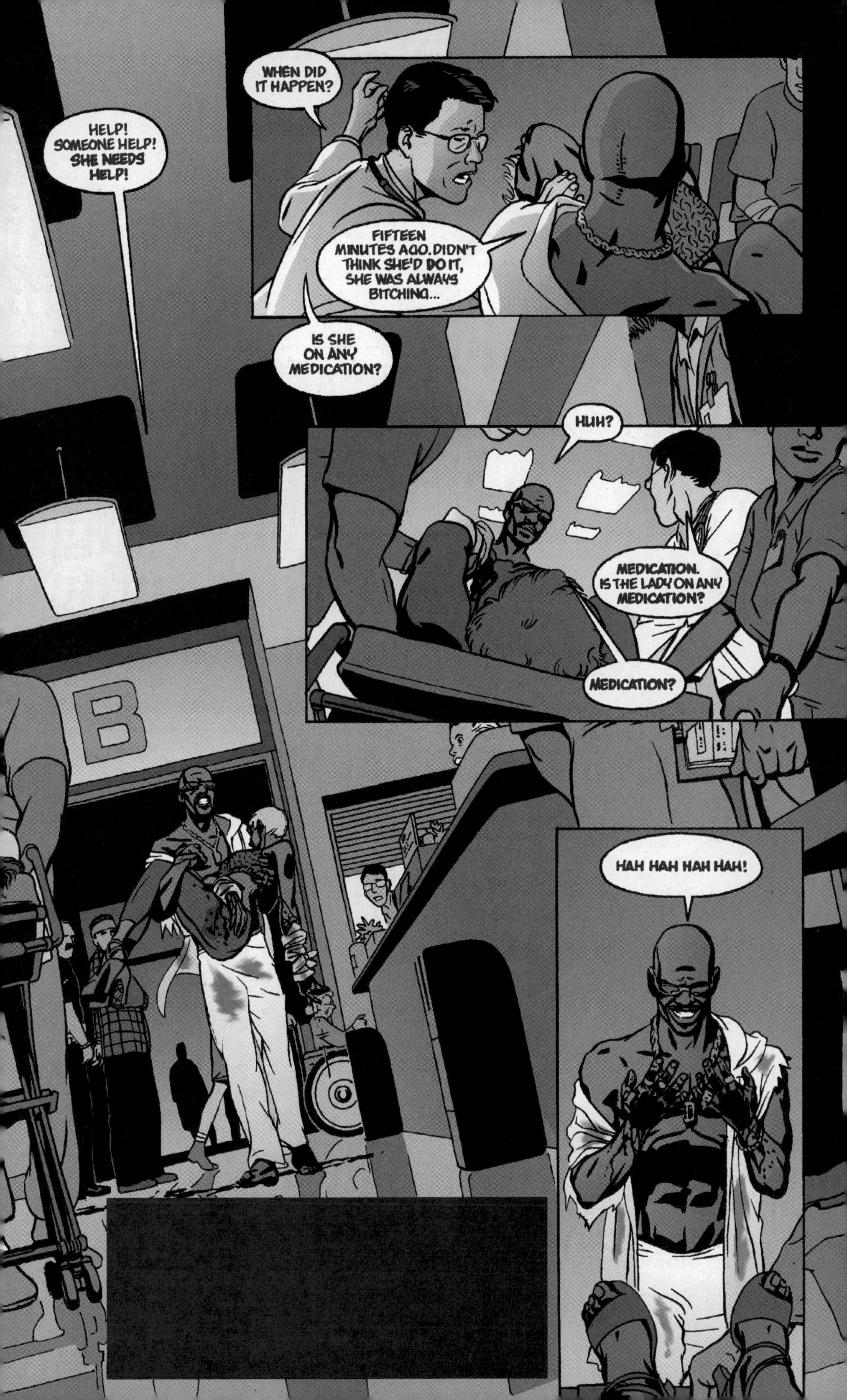
HELP! SOMEONE HELP! SHE NEEDS HELP!
WHEN DID IT HAPPEN?
FIFTEEN MINUTES AGO. DIDN'T THINK SHE'D DO IT, SHE WAS ALWAYS BITCHING...
IS SHE ON ANY MEDICATION?
HUH?
MEDICATION. IS THE LADY ON ANY MEDICATION?
MEDICATION?
HAH HAH HAH HAH!

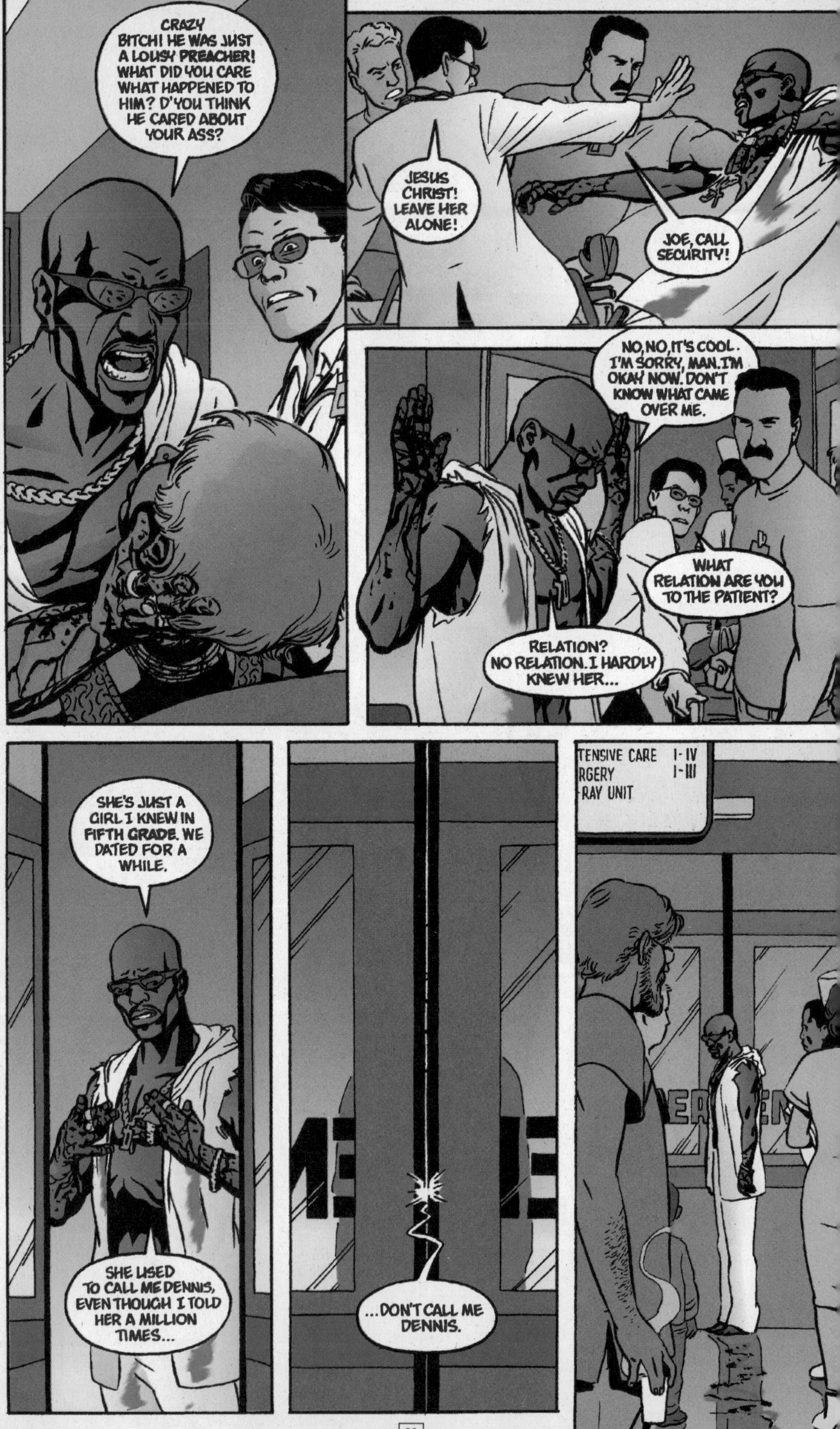
CRAZY BITCH! HE WAS JUST A LOUSY PREACHER! WHAT DID YOU CARE WHAT HAPPENED TO HIM? D'YOU THINK HE CARED ABOUT YOUR ASS?
JESUS CHRIST! LEAVE HER ALONE!
JOE, CALL SECURITY!
NO, NO, IT'S COOL. I'M SORRY, MAN. I'M OKAY NOW. DON'T KNOW WHAT CAME OVER ME.
WHAT RELATION ARE YOU TO THE PATIENT?
RELATION? NO RELATION. I HARDLY KNEW HER...
SHE'S JUST A GIRL I KNEW IN FIFTH GRADE. WE DATED FOR A WHILE.
SHE USED TO CALL ME DENNIS, EVEN THOUGH I TOLD HER A MILLION TIMES...
...DON'T CALL ME DENNIS.
TENSIVE CARE I-IV
RGERY I-III
-RAY UNIT

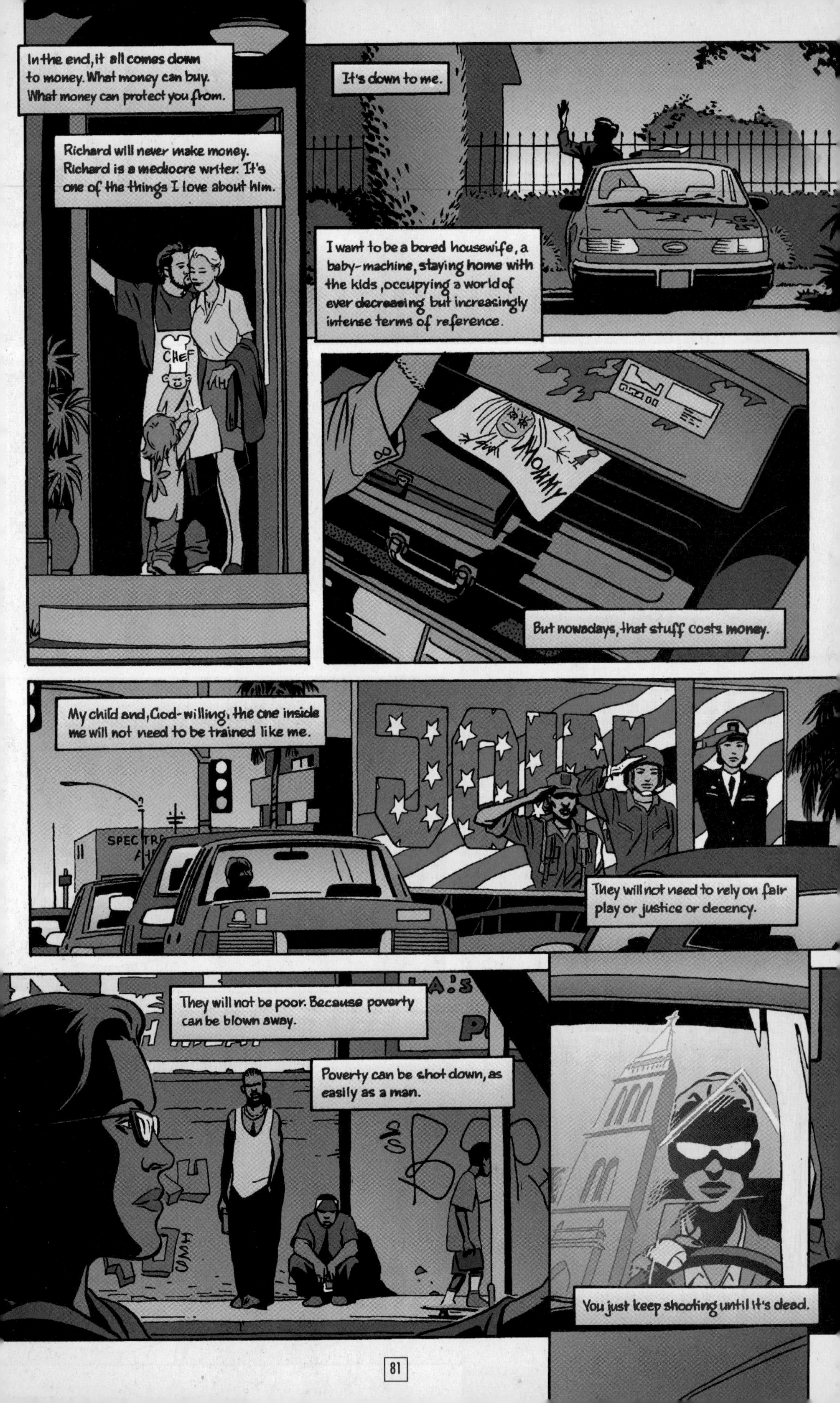
In the end, it all comes down to money. What money can buy. What money can protect you from.
Richard will never make money. Richard is a mediocre writer. It's one of the things I love about him.
CHEF
It's down to me.
I want to be a bored housewife, a baby-machine, staying home with the kids, occupying a world of ever decreasing but increasingly intense terms of reference.
MOMMY
But nowadays, that stuff costs money.
My child and, God-willing, the one inside me will not need to be trained like me.
They will not need to rely on fair play or justice or decency.
They will not be poor. Because poverty can be blown away.
Poverty can be shot down, as easily as a man.
You just keep shooting until it's dead.

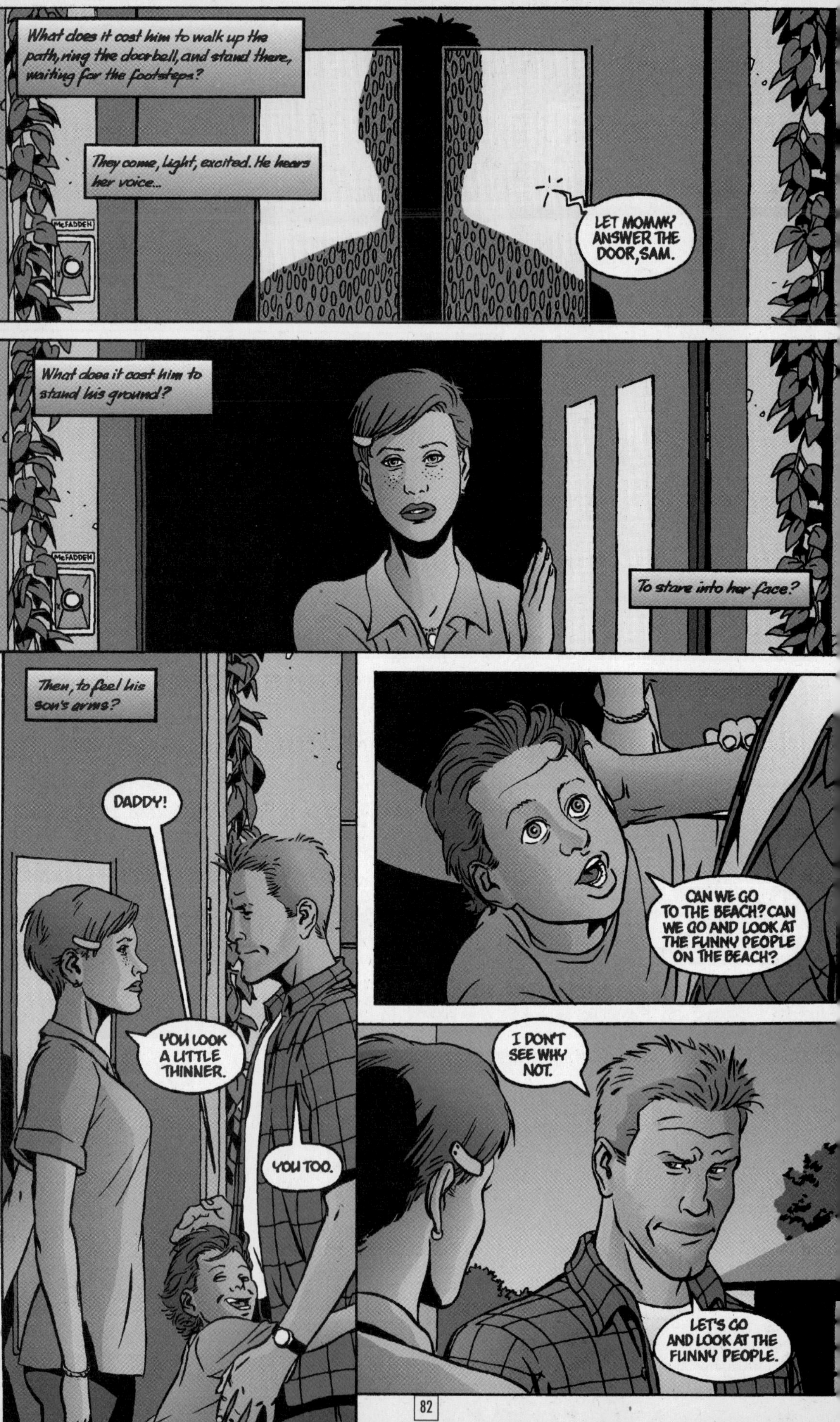

What does it cost him to walk up the path, ring the doorbell, and stand there, waiting for the footsteps?
They come, light, excited. He hears her voice...
McFADDEN
LET MOMMY ANSWER THE DOOR, SAM.
What does it cost him to stand his ground?
McFADDEN
To stare into her face?
Then, to feel his son's arms?
DADDY!
YOU LOOK A LITTLE THINNER.
YOU TOO.
CAN WE GO TO THE BEACH? CAN WE GO AND LOOK AT THE FUNNY PEOPLE ON THE BEACH?
I DON'T SEE WHY NOT.
LET'S GO AND LOOK AT THE FUNNY PEOPLE.

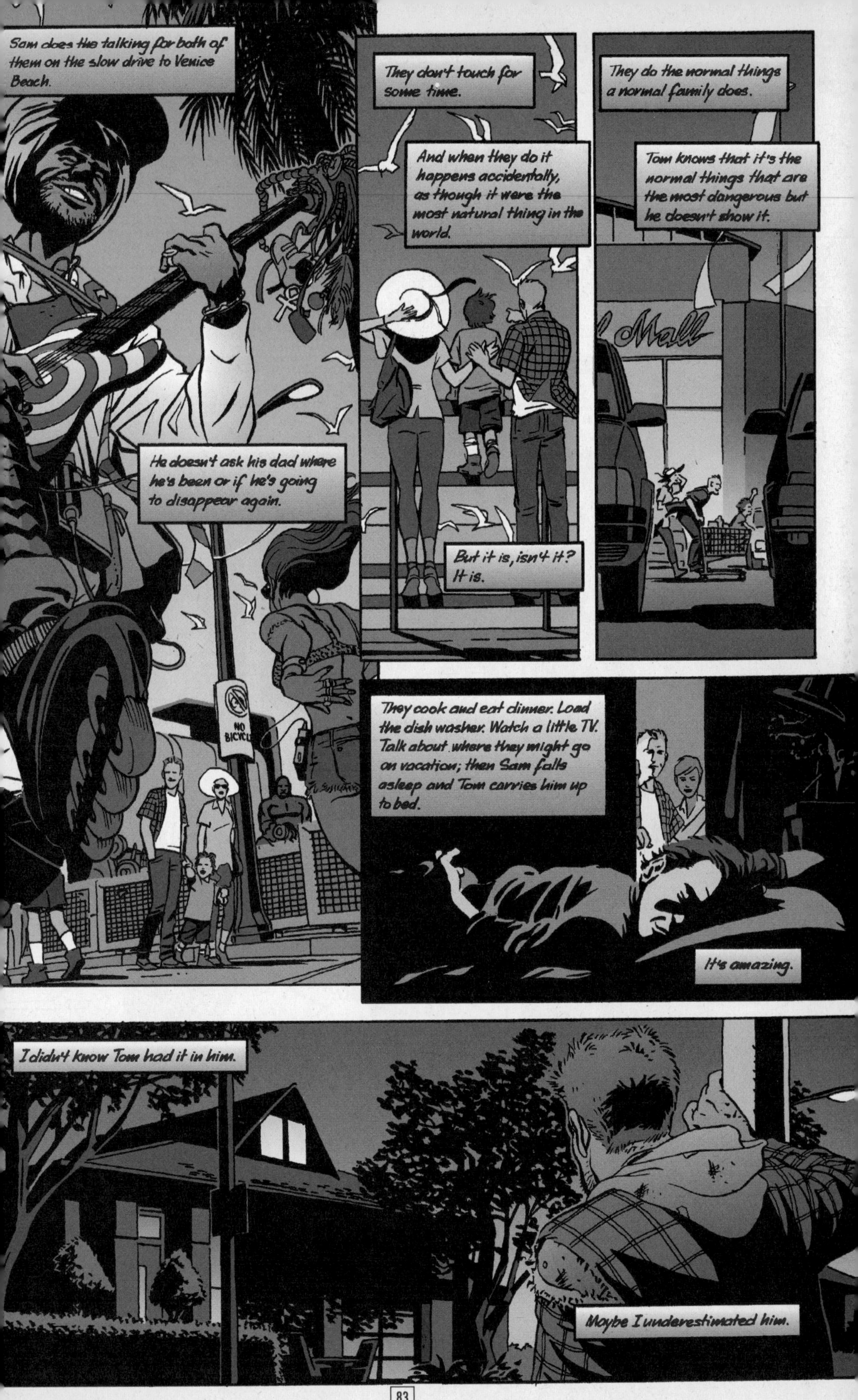

Sam does the talking for both of them on the slow drive to Venice Beach.
He doesn't ask his dad where he's been or if he's going to disappear again.
NO BICYCL
They don't touch for some time.
And when they do it happens accidentally, as though it were the most natural thing in the world.
But it is, isn't it? It is.
They do the normal things a normal family does.
Tom knows that it's the normal things that are the most dangerous but he doesn't show it.
Mall
They cook and eat dinner. Load the dish washer. Watch a little TV. Talk about where they might go on vacation; then Sam falls asleep and Tom carries him up to bed.
It's amazing.
I didn't know Tom had it in him.
Maybe I underestimated him.

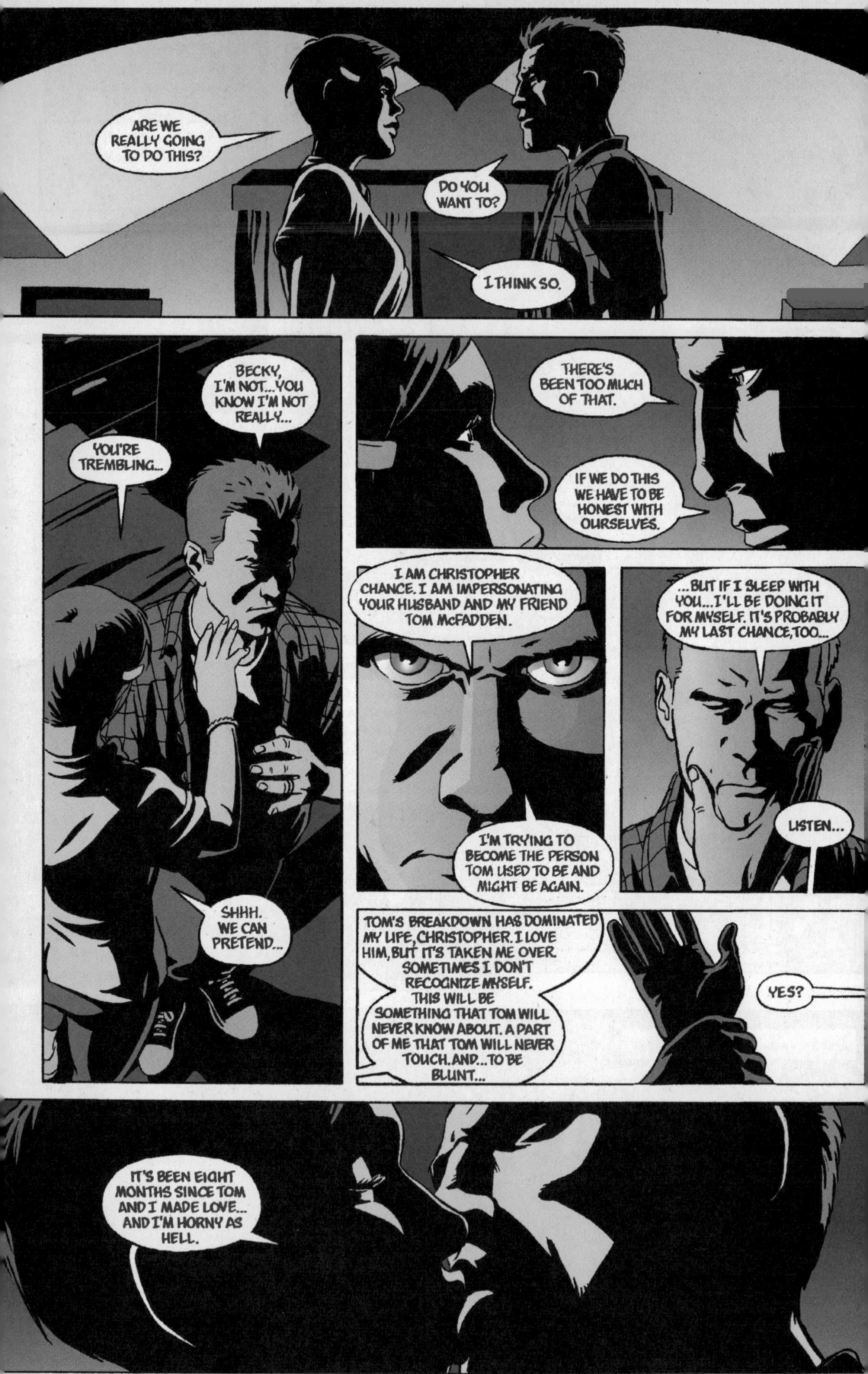

ARE WE REALLY GOING TO DO THIS?
DO YOU WANT TO?
I THINK SO.
BECKY, I'M NOT...YOU KNOW I'M NOT REALLY...
YOU'RE TREMBLING...
SHHH. WE CAN PRETEND...
THERE'S BEEN TOO MUCH OF THAT.
IF WE DO THIS WE HAVE TO BE HONEST WITH OURSELVES.
I AM CHRISTOPHER CHANCE. I AM IMPERSONATING YOUR HUSBAND AND MY FRIEND TOM McFADDEN.
I'M TRYING TO BECOME THE PERSON TOM USED TO BE AND MIGHT BE AGAIN.
...BUT IF I SLEEP WITH YOU...I'LL BE DOING IT FOR MYSELF. IT'S PROBABLY MY LAST CHANCE, TOO...
LISTEN...
YES?
TOM'S BREAKDOWN HAS DOMINATED MY LIFE, CHRISTOPHER. I LOVE HIM, BUT IT'S TAKEN ME OVER. SOMETIMES I DON'T RECOGNIZE MYSELF. THIS WILL BE SOMETHING THAT TOM WILL NEVER KNOW ABOUT. A PART OF ME THAT TOM WILL NEVER TOUCH. AND...TO BE BLUNT...
IT'S BEEN EIGHT MONTHS SINCE TOM AND I MADE LOVE... AND I'M HORNY AS HELL.

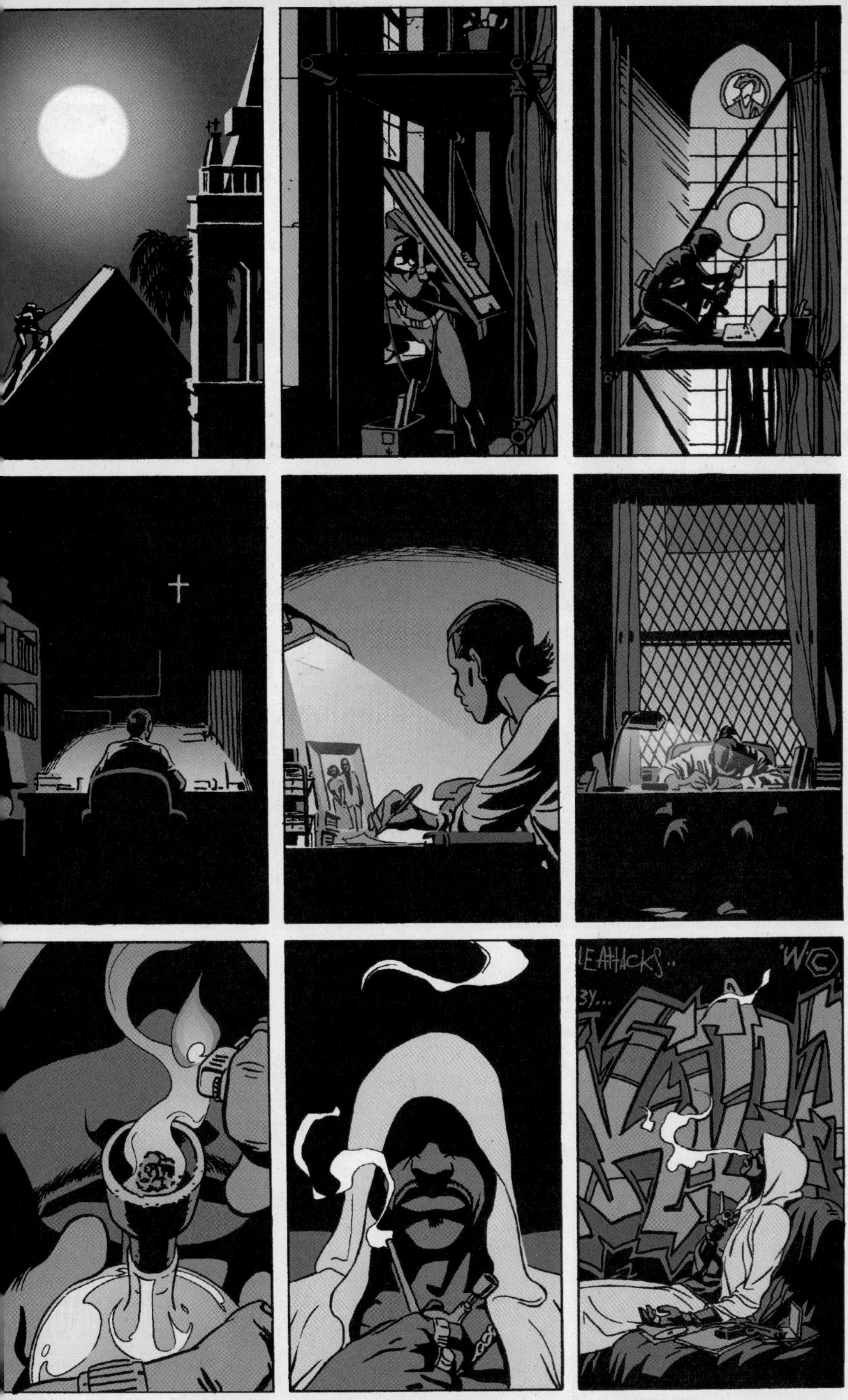
LEATTACKS..
W·C
3Y...

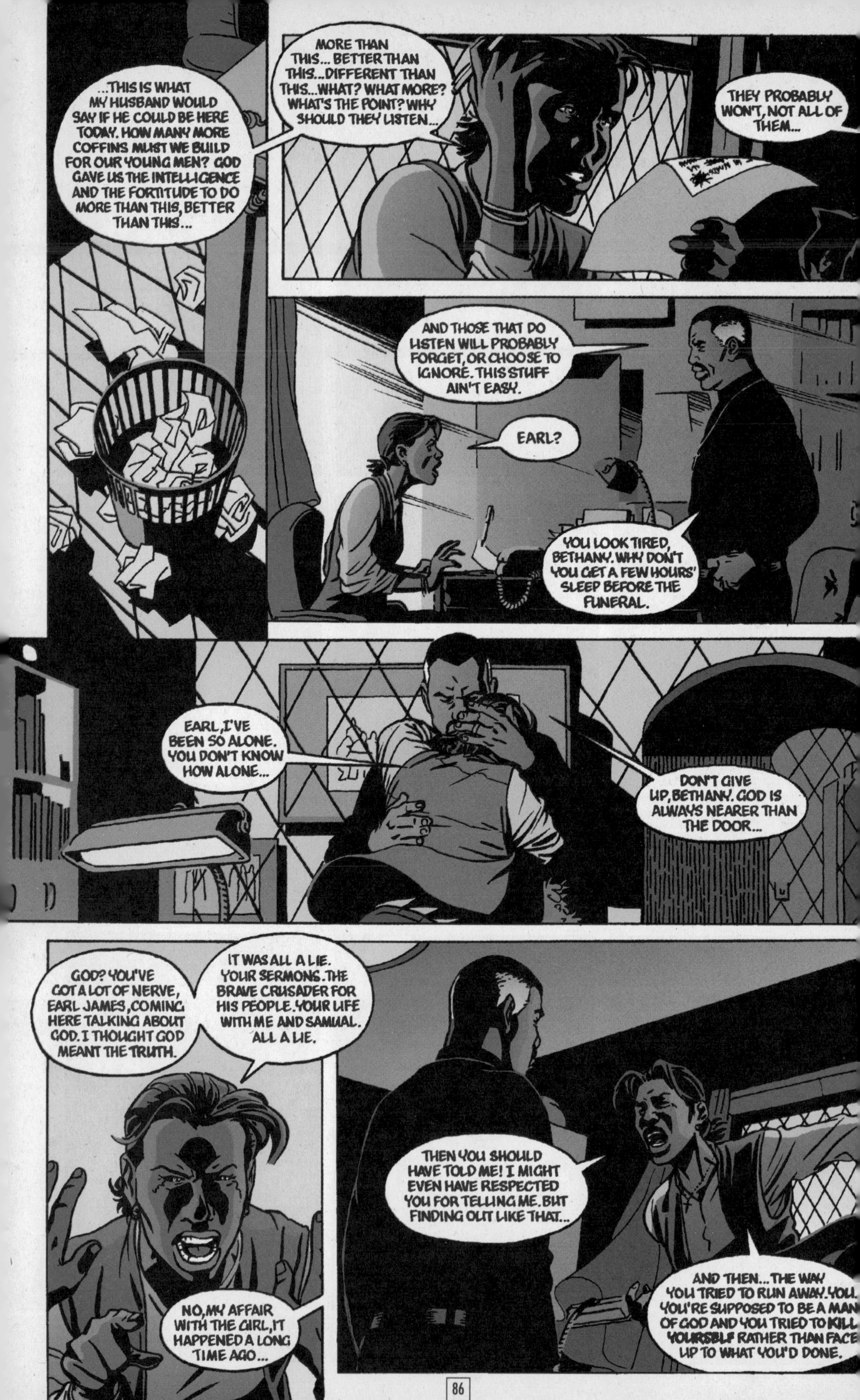
...THIS IS WHAT MY HUSBAND WOULD SAY IF HE COULD BE HERE TODAY. HOW MANY MORE COFFINS MUST WE BUILD FOR OUR YOUNG MEN? GOD GAVE US THE INTELLIGENCE AND THE FORTITUDE TO DO MORE THAN THIS, BETTER THAN THIS...
MORE THAN THIS... BETTER THAN THIS...DIFFERENT THAN THIS...WHAT? WHAT MORE? WHAT'S THE POINT? WHY SHOULD THEY LISTEN...
THEY PROBABLY WON'T, NOT ALL OF THEM...
AND THOSE THAT DO LISTEN WILL PROBABLY FORGET, OR CHOOSE TO IGNORE. THIS STUFF AIN'T EASY.
EARL?
YOU LOOK TIRED, BETHANY. WHY DON'T YOU GET A FEW HOURS' SLEEP BEFORE THE FUNERAL.
EARL, I'VE BEEN SO ALONE. YOU DON'T KNOW HOW ALONE...
DON'T GIVE UP, BETHANY. GOD IS ALWAYS NEARER THAN THE DOOR...
GOD? YOU'VE GOT A LOT OF NERVE, EARL JAMES, COMING HERE TALKING ABOUT GOD. I THOUGHT GOD MEANT THE TRUTH.
IT WAS ALL A LIE. YOUR SERMONS. THE BRAVE CRUSADER FOR HIS PEOPLE. YOUR LIFE WITH ME AND SAMUAL. ALL A LIE.
NO, MY AFFAIR WITH THE GIRL, IT HAPPENED A LONG TIME AGO...
THEN YOU SHOULD HAVE TOLD ME! I MIGHT EVEN HAVE RESPECTED YOU FOR TELLING ME. BUT FINDING OUT LIKE THAT...
AND THEN... THE WAY YOU TRIED TO RUN AWAY. YOU. YOU'RE SUPPOSED TO BE A MAN OF GOD AND YOU TRIED TO KILL YOURSELF RATHER THAN FACE UP TO WHAT YOU'D DONE.

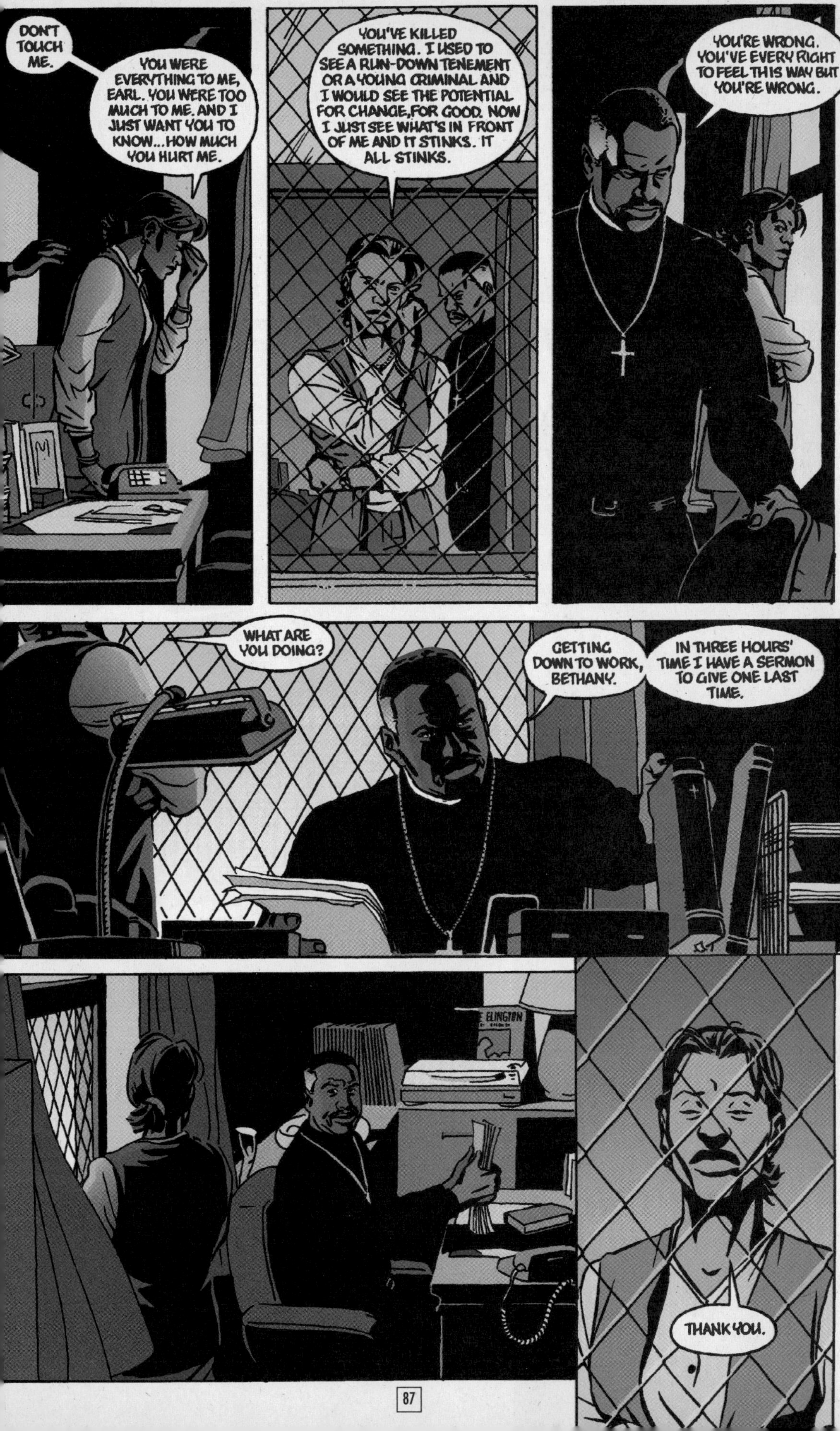

DON'T TOUCH ME.
YOU WERE EVERYTHING TO ME, EARL. YOU WERE TOO MUCH TO ME. AND I JUST WANT YOU TO KNOW...HOW MUCH YOU HURT ME.
YOU'VE KILLED SOMETHING. I USED TO SEE A RUN-DOWN TENEMENT OR A YOUNG CRIMINAL AND I WOULD SEE THE POTENTIAL FOR CHANGE, FOR GOOD. NOW I JUST SEE WHAT'S IN FRONT OF ME AND IT STINKS. IT ALL STINKS.
YOU'RE WRONG. YOU'VE EVERY RIGHT TO FEEL THIS WAY BUT YOU'RE WRONG.
WHAT ARE YOU DOING?
GETTING DOWN TO WORK, BETHANY.
IN THREE HOURS' TIME I HAVE A SERMON TO GIVE ONE LAST TIME.
THANK YOU.

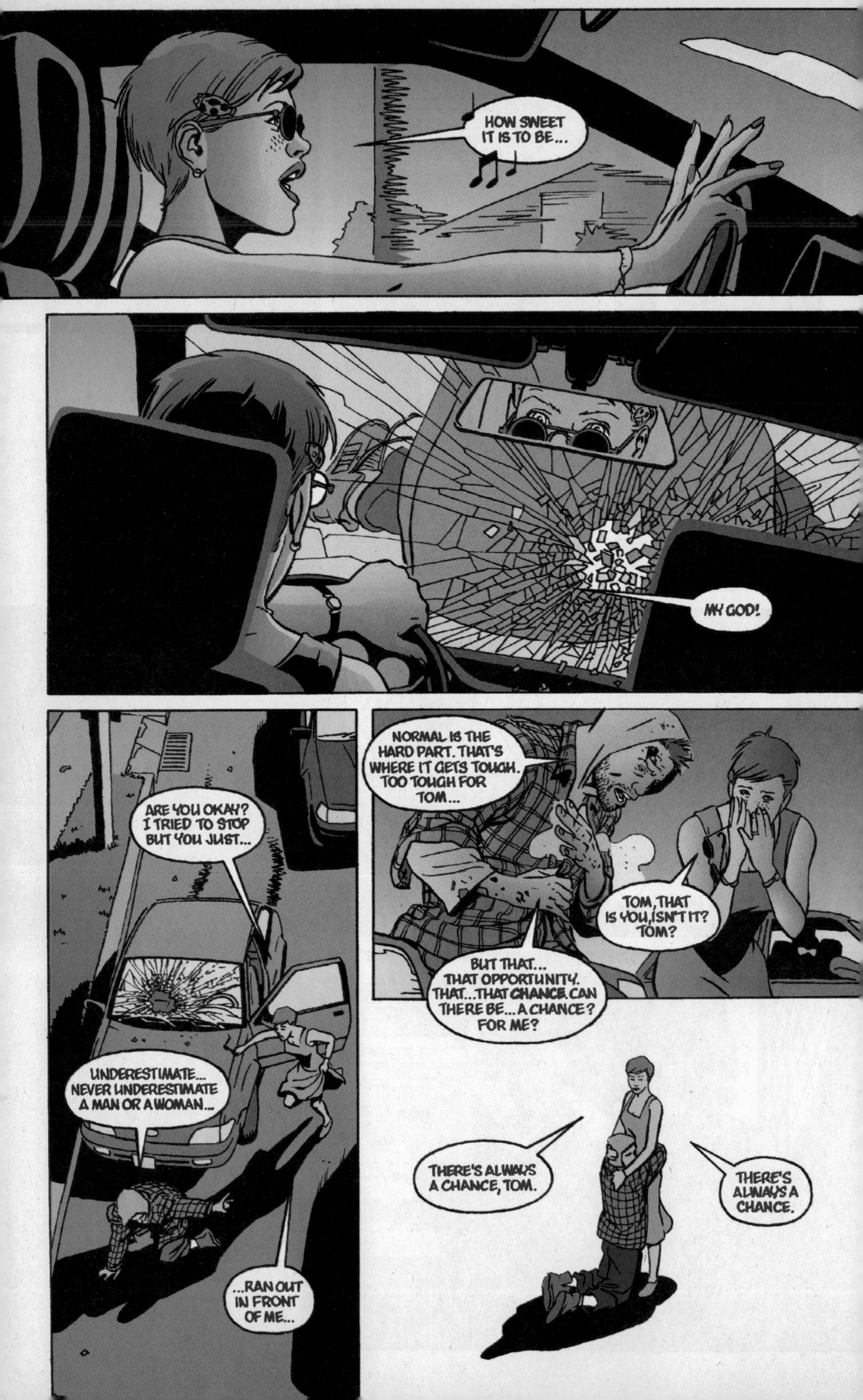
HOW SWEET IT IS TO BE...
MY GOD!
ARE YOU OKAY? I TRIED TO STOP BUT YOU JUST...
...RAN OUT IN FRONT OF ME...
UNDERESTIMATE... NEVER UNDERESTIMATE A MAN OR A WOMAN...
NORMAL IS THE HARD PART. THAT'S WHERE IT GETS TOUGH. TOO TOUGH FOR TOM...
TOM, THAT IS YOU, ISN'T IT? TOM?
BUT THAT... THAT OPPORTUNITY. THAT...THAT CHANCE. CAN THERE BE...A CHANCE? FOR ME?
THERE'S ALWAYS A CHANCE, TOM.
THERE'S ALWAYS A CHANCE.

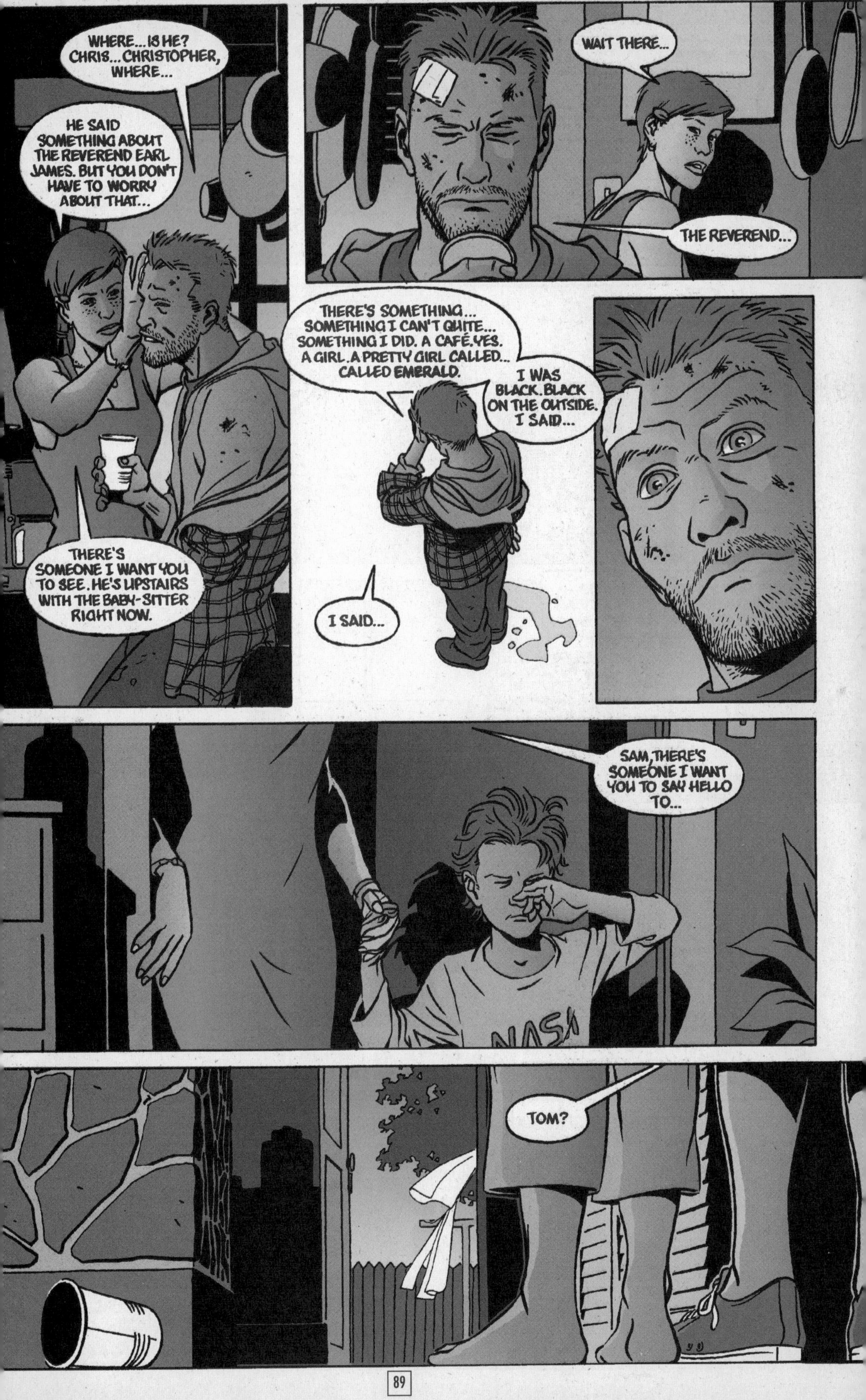
WHERE... IS HE? CHRIS... CHRISTOPHER, WHERE...
HE SAID SOMETHING ABOUT THE REVEREND EARL JAMES. BUT YOU DON'T HAVE TO WORRY ABOUT THAT...
THERE'S SOMEONE I WANT YOU TO SEE. HE'S UPSTAIRS WITH THE BABY-SITTER RIGHT NOW.
WAIT THERE...
THE REVEREND...
THERE'S SOMETHING... SOMETHING I CAN'T QUITE... SOMETHING I DID. A CAFÉ. YES. A GIRL. A PRETTY GIRL CALLED... CALLED EMERALD.
I WAS BLACK. BLACK ON THE OUTSIDE. I SAID...
I SAID...
SAM, THERE'S SOMEONE I WANT YOU TO SAY HELLO TO...
NASA
TOM?

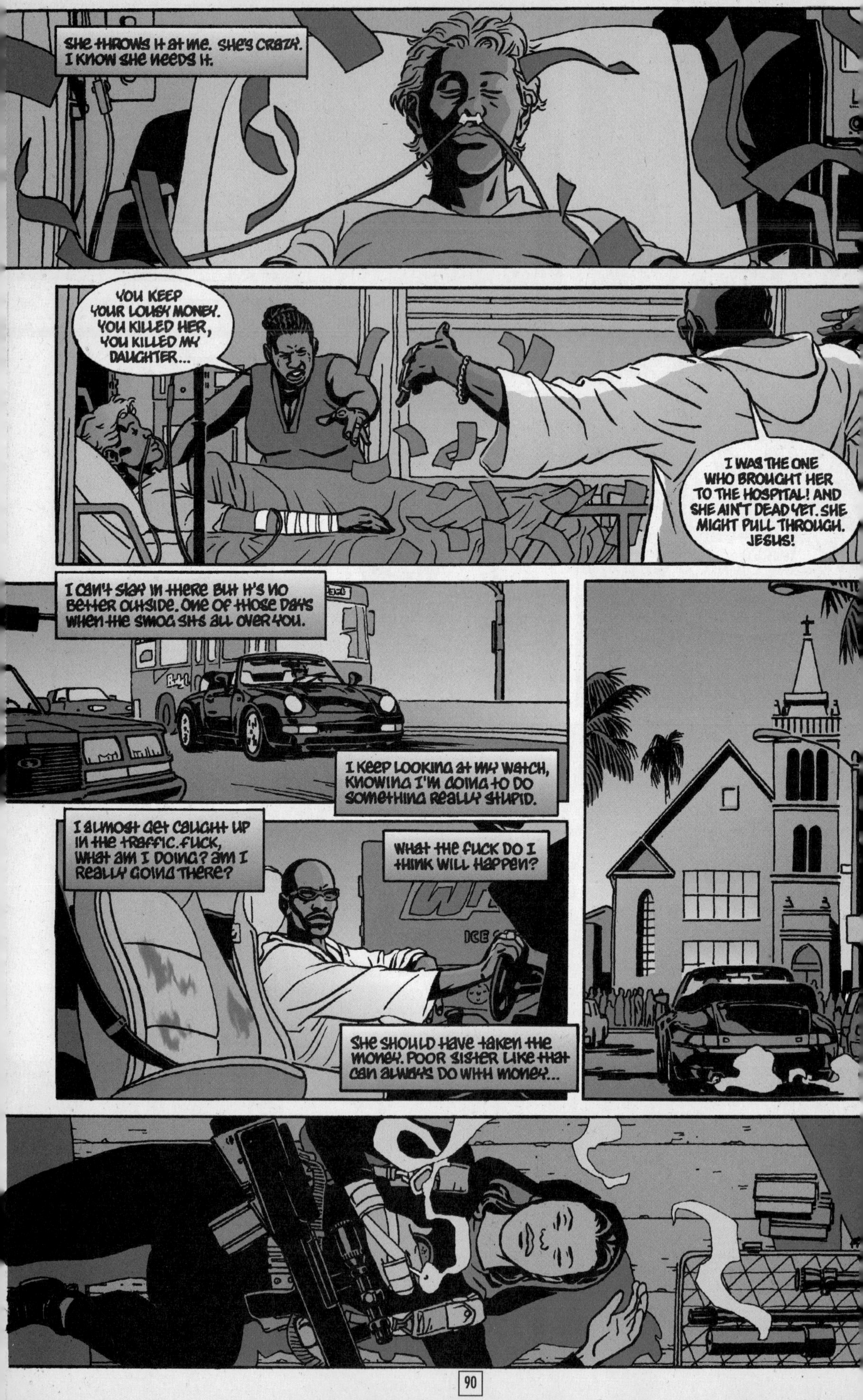
SHE THROWS IT AT ME. SHE'S CRAZY. I KNOW SHE NEEDS IT.
YOU KEEP YOUR LOUSY MONEY. YOU KILLED HER, YOU KILLED MY DAUGHTER...
I WAS THE ONE WHO BROUGHT HER TO THE HOSPITAL! AND SHE AIN'T DEAD YET. SHE MIGHT PULL THROUGH. JESUS!
I CAN'T STAY IN THERE BUT IT'S NO BETTER OUTSIDE. ONE OF THOSE DAYS WHEN THE SMOG SITS ALL OVER YOU.
I KEEP LOOKING AT MY WATCH, KNOWING I'M GOING TO DO SOMETHING REALLY STUPID.
I ALMOST GET CAUGHT UP IN THE TRAFFIC. FUCK, WHAT AM I DOING? AM I REALLY GOING THERE?
WHAT THE FUCK DO I THINK WILL HAPPEN?
SHE SHOULD HAVE TAKEN THE MONEY. POOR SISTER LIKE THAT CAN ALWAYS DO WITH MONEY...

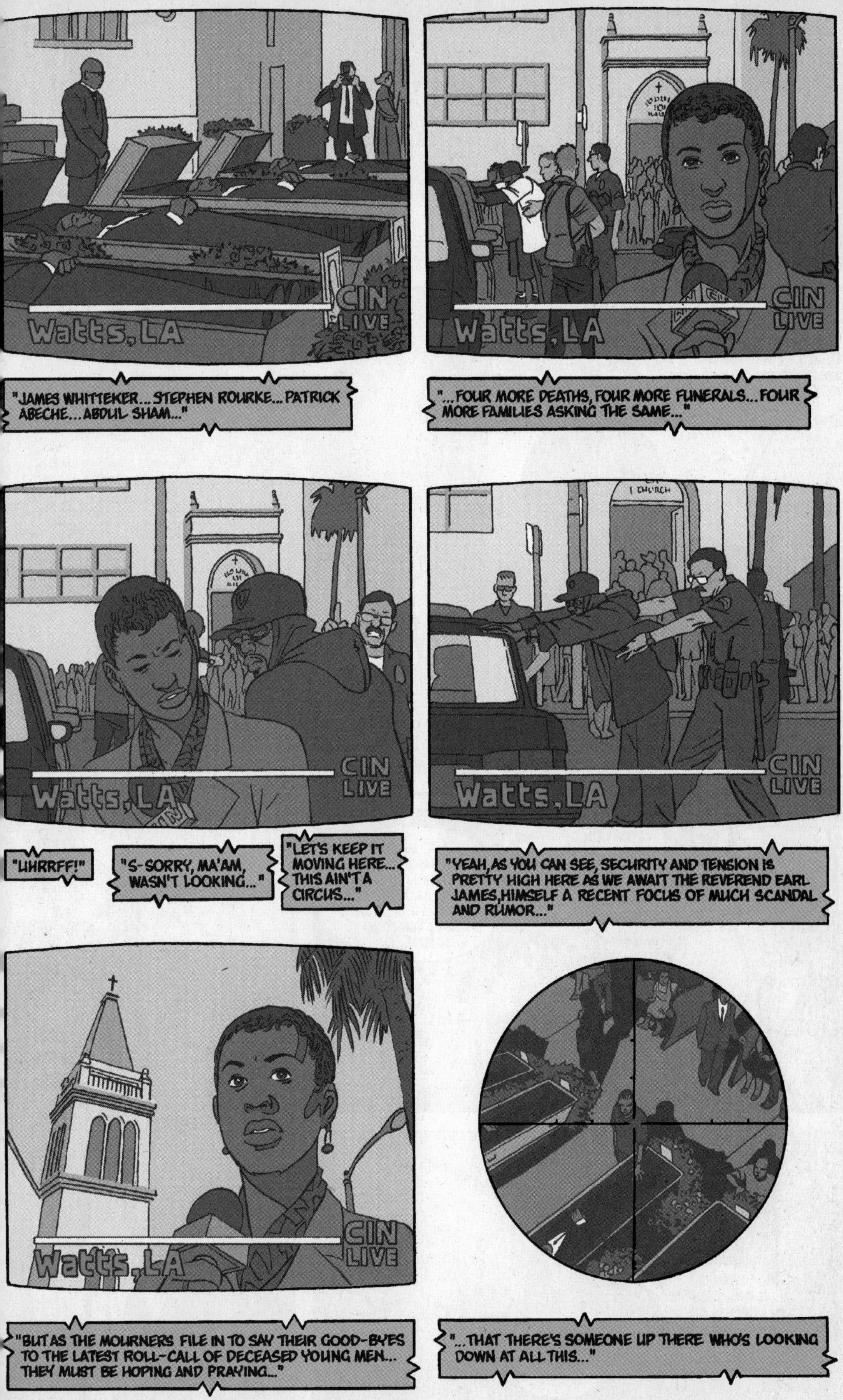
CIN
LIVE
Watts, LA
"JAMES WHITTEKER... STEPHEN ROURKE... PATRICK ABECHE... ABDUL SHAM..."
CIN
LIVE
Watts, LA
"...FOUR MORE DEATHS, FOUR MORE FUNERALS... FOUR MORE FAMILIES ASKING THE SAME..."
CIN
LIVE
Watts, LA
"UHRRFF!"
"S-SORRY, MA'AM, WASN'T LOOKING..."
"LET'S KEEP IT MOVING HERE... THIS AIN'T A CIRCUS..."
CIN
LIVE
Watts, LA
"YEAH, AS YOU CAN SEE, SECURITY AND TENSION IS PRETTY HIGH HERE AS WE AWAIT THE REVEREND EARL JAMES, HIMSELF A RECENT FOCUS OF MUCH SCANDAL AND RUMOR..."
CIN
LIVE
Watts, LA
"BUT AS THE MOURNERS FILE IN TO SAY THEIR GOOD-BYES TO THE LATEST ROLL-CALL OF DECEASED YOUNG MEN... THEY MUST BE HOPING AND PRAYING..."
"...THAT THERE'S SOMEONE UP THERE WHO'S LOOKING DOWN AT ALL THIS..."

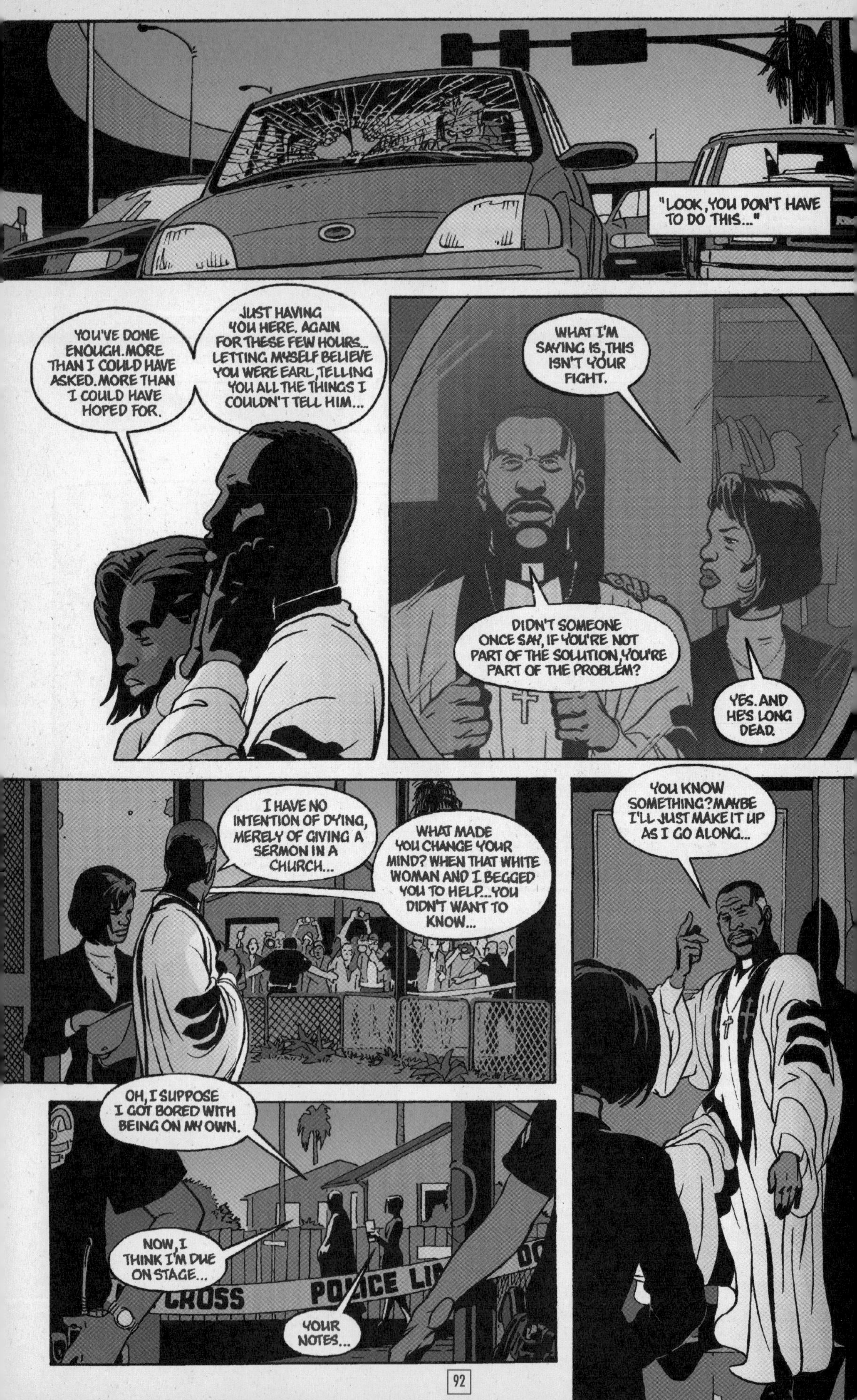
"LOOK, YOU DON'T HAVE TO DO THIS..."
YOU'VE DONE ENOUGH. MORE THAN I COULD HAVE ASKED. MORE THAN I COULD HAVE HOPED FOR.
JUST HAVING YOU HERE. AGAIN FOR THESE FEW HOURS... LETTING MYSELF BELIEVE YOU WERE EARL, TELLING YOU ALL THE THINGS I COULDN'T TELL HIM...
WHAT I'M SAYING IS, THIS ISN'T YOUR FIGHT.
DIDN'T SOMEONE ONCE SAY, IF YOU'RE NOT PART OF THE SOLUTION, YOU'RE PART OF THE PROBLEM?
YES. AND HE'S LONG DEAD.
I HAVE NO INTENTION OF DYING, MERELY OF GIVING A SERMON IN A CHURCH...
WHAT MADE YOU CHANGE YOUR MIND? WHEN THAT WHITE WOMAN AND I BEGGED YOU TO HELP... YOU DIDN'T WANT TO KNOW...
OH, I SUPPOSE I GOT BORED WITH BEING ON MY OWN.
NOW, I THINK I'M DUE ON STAGE...
YOUR NOTES...
CROSS
POLICE LI
YOU KNOW SOMETHING? MAYBE I'LL JUST MAKE IT UP AS I GO ALONG...

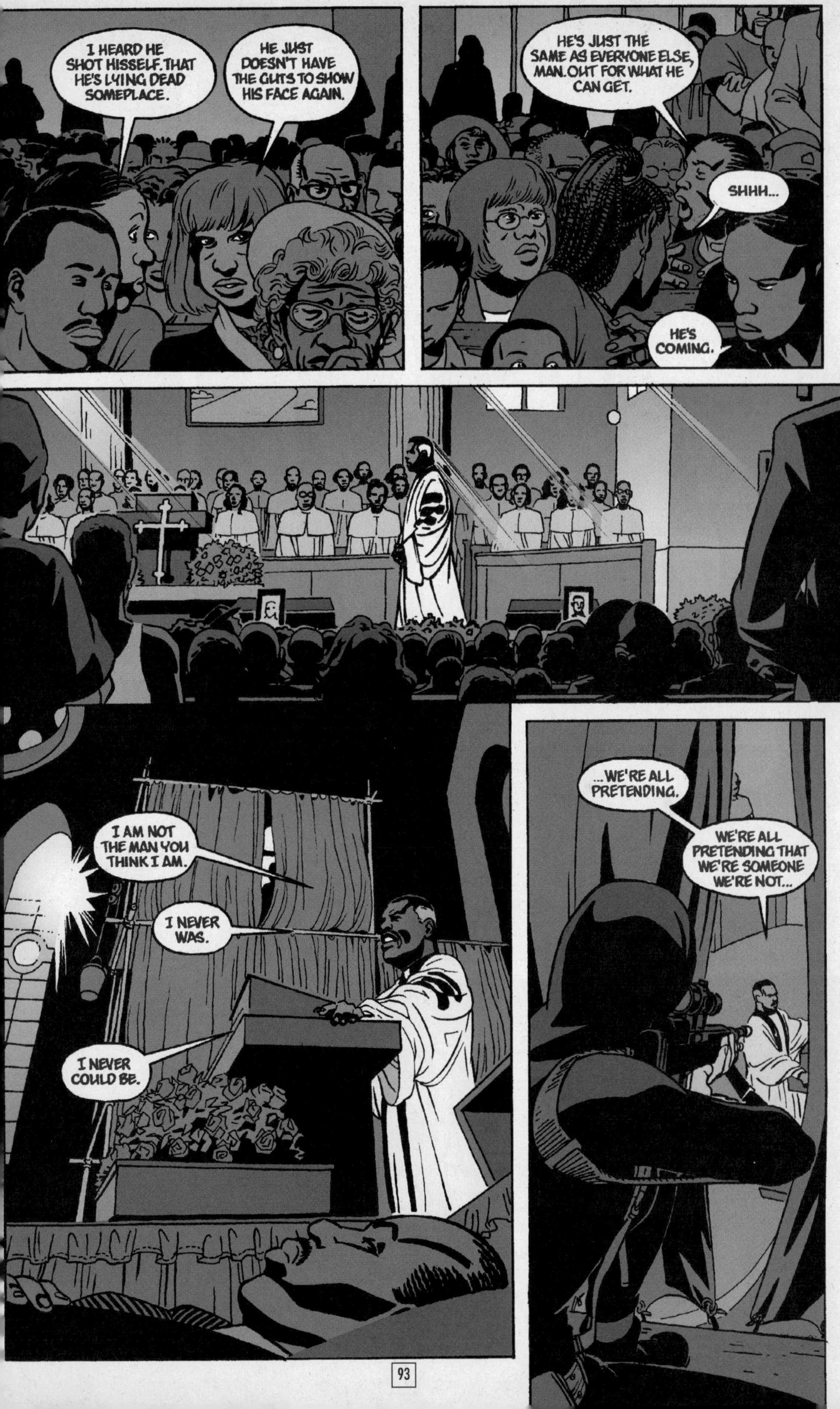
I HEARD HE SHOT HISSELF. THAT HE'S LYING DEAD SOMEPLACE.
HE JUST DOESN'T HAVE THE GUTS TO SHOW HIS FACE AGAIN.
HE'S JUST THE SAME AS EVERYONE ELSE, MAN. OUT FOR WHAT HE CAN GET.
SHHH...
HE'S COMING.
I AM NOT THE MAN YOU THINK I AM.
I NEVER WAS.
I NEVER COULD BE.
...WE'RE ALL PRETENDING.
WE'RE ALL PRETENDING THAT WE'RE SOMEONE WE'RE NOT...

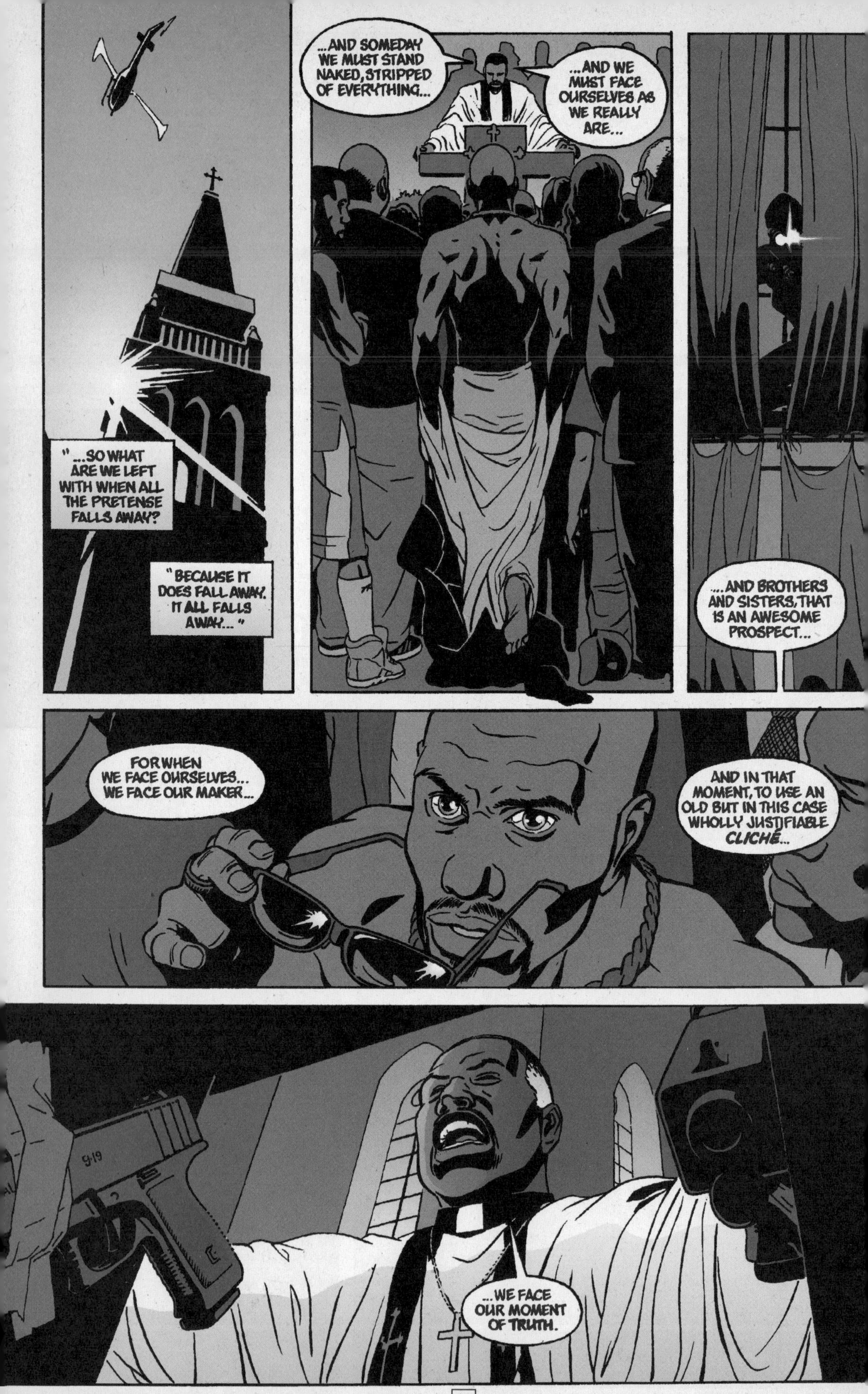
"...SO WHAT ARE WE LEFT WITH WHEN ALL THE PRETENSE FALLS AWAY?
"BECAUSE IT DOES FALL AWAY. IT ALL FALLS AWAY..."
...AND SOMEDAY WE MUST STAND NAKED, STRIPPED OF EVERYTHING...
...AND WE MUST FACE OURSELVES AS WE REALLY ARE...
....AND BROTHERS AND SISTERS, THAT IS AN AWESOME PROSPECT...
FOR WHEN WE FACE OURSELVES... WE FACE OUR MAKER...
AND IN THAT MOMENT, TO USE AN OLD BUT IN THIS CASE WHOLLY JUSTIFIABLE *CLICHÉ*...
...WE FACE OUR MOMENT OF TRUTH.

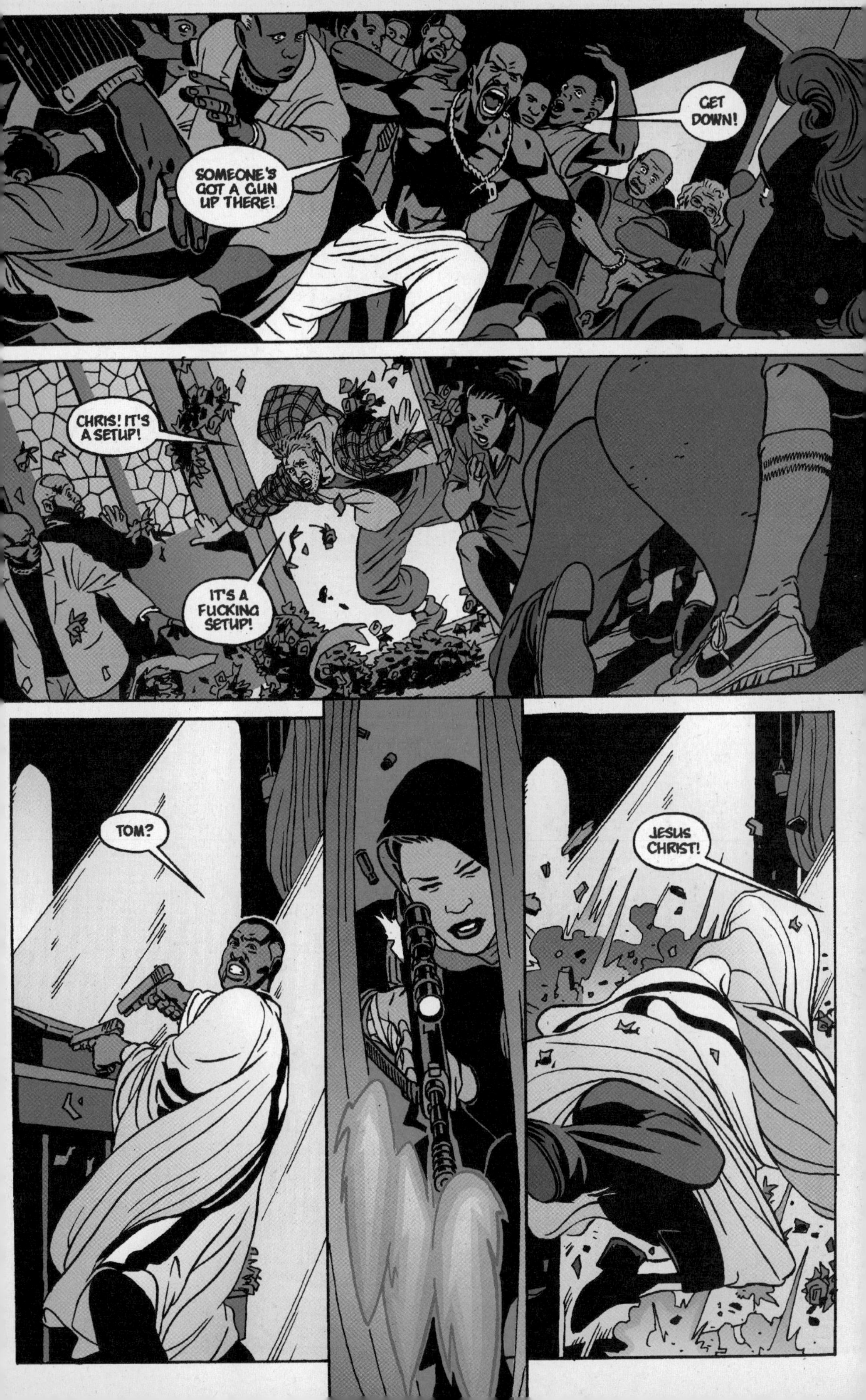
SOMEONE'S GOT A GUN UP THERE!
GET DOWN!
CHRIS! IT'S A SETUP!
IT'S A FUCKING SETUP!
TOM?
JESUS CHRIST!

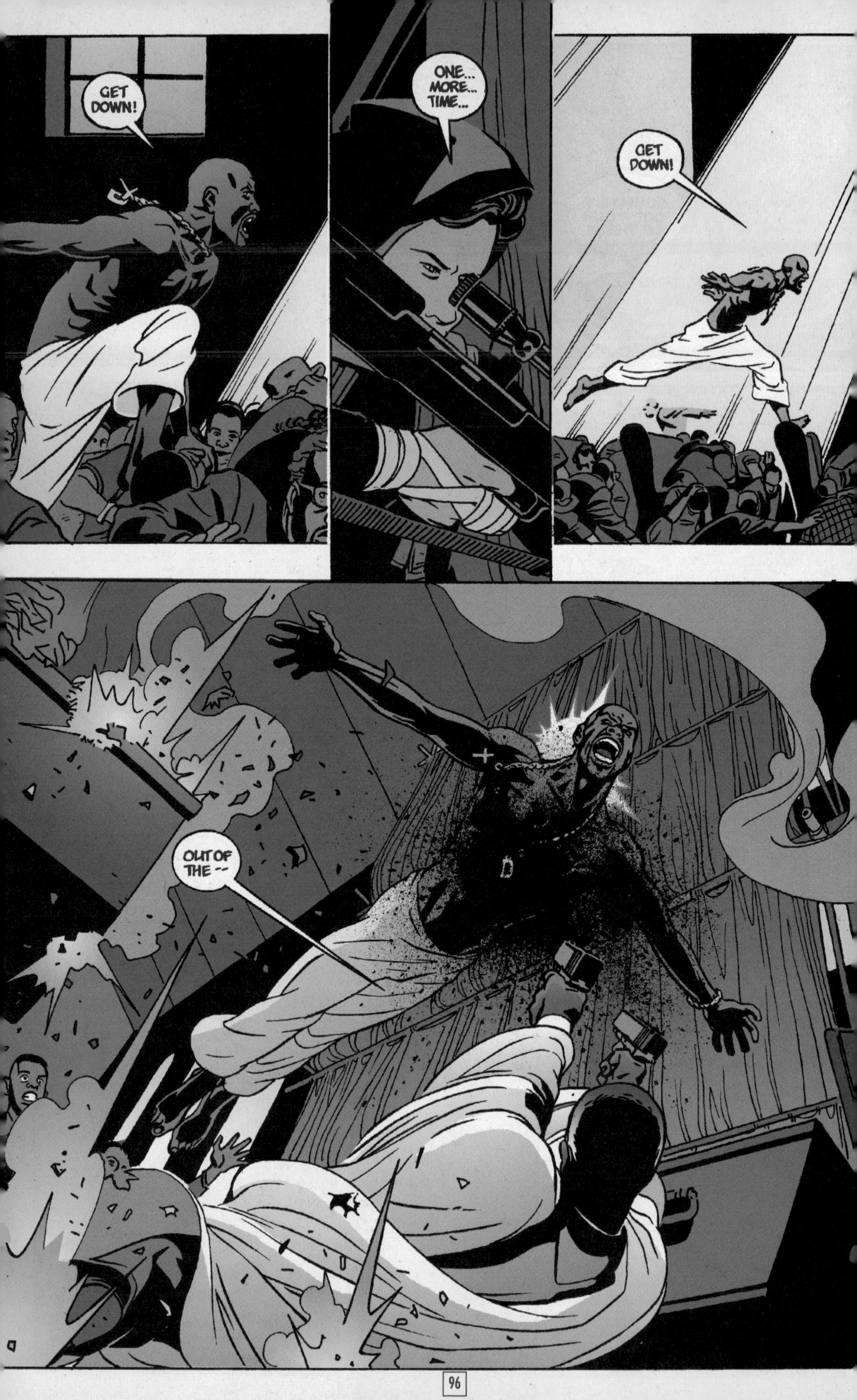
GET DOWN!
ONE... MORE... TIME...
GET DOWN!
OUT OF THE --

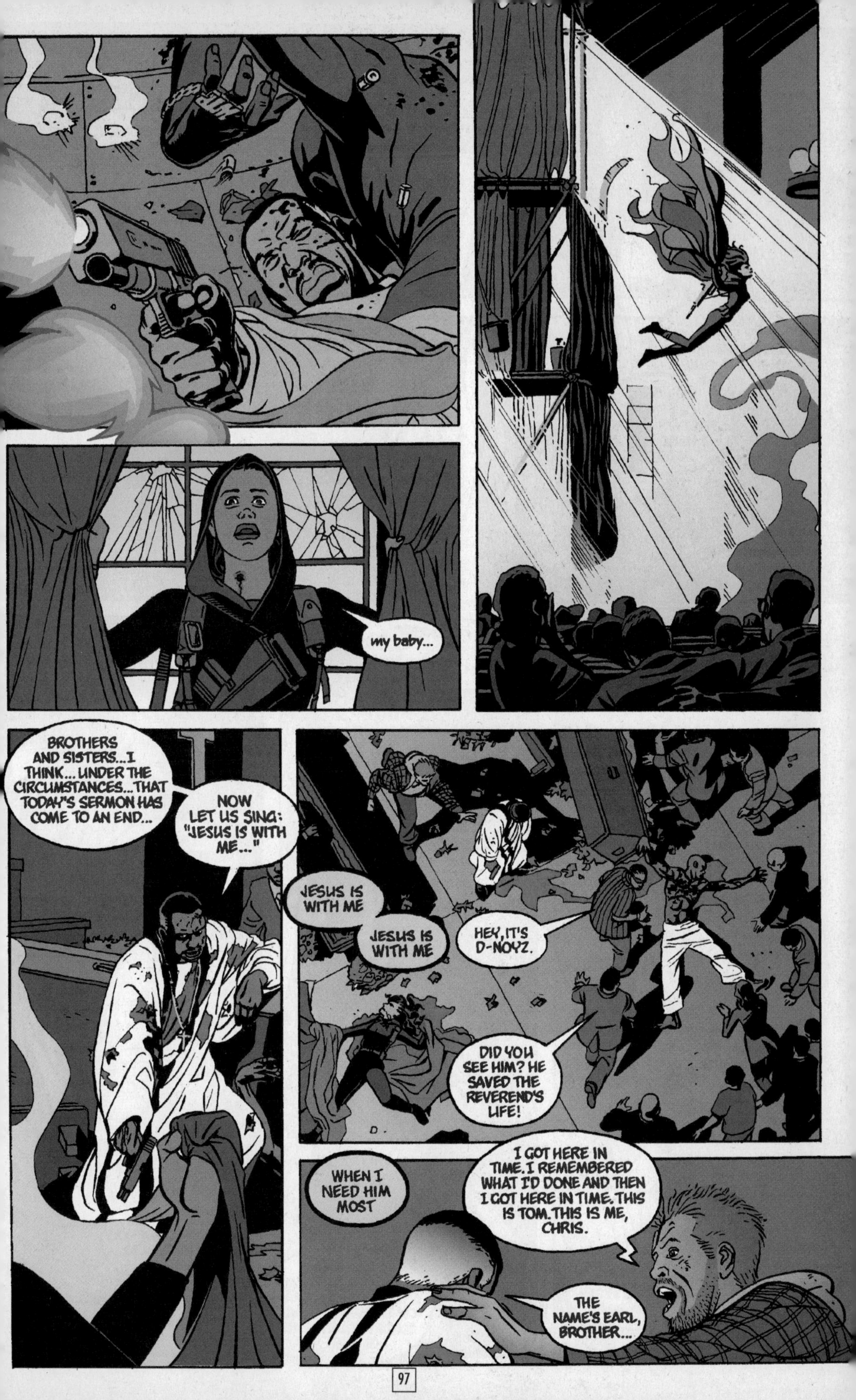
my baby...
BROTHERS AND SISTERS...I THINK... UNDER THE CIRCUMSTANCES...THAT TODAY'S SERMON HAS COME TO AN END...
NOW LET US SING: "JESUS IS WITH ME..."
JESUS IS WITH ME
JESUS IS WITH ME
HEY, IT'S D-NOYZ.
DID YOU SEE HIM? HE SAVED THE REVEREND'S LIFE!
WHEN I NEED HIM MOST
I GOT HERE IN TIME. I REMEMBERED WHAT I'D DONE AND THEN I GOT HERE IN TIME. THIS IS TOM. THIS IS ME, CHRIS.
THE NAME'S EARL, BROTHER...

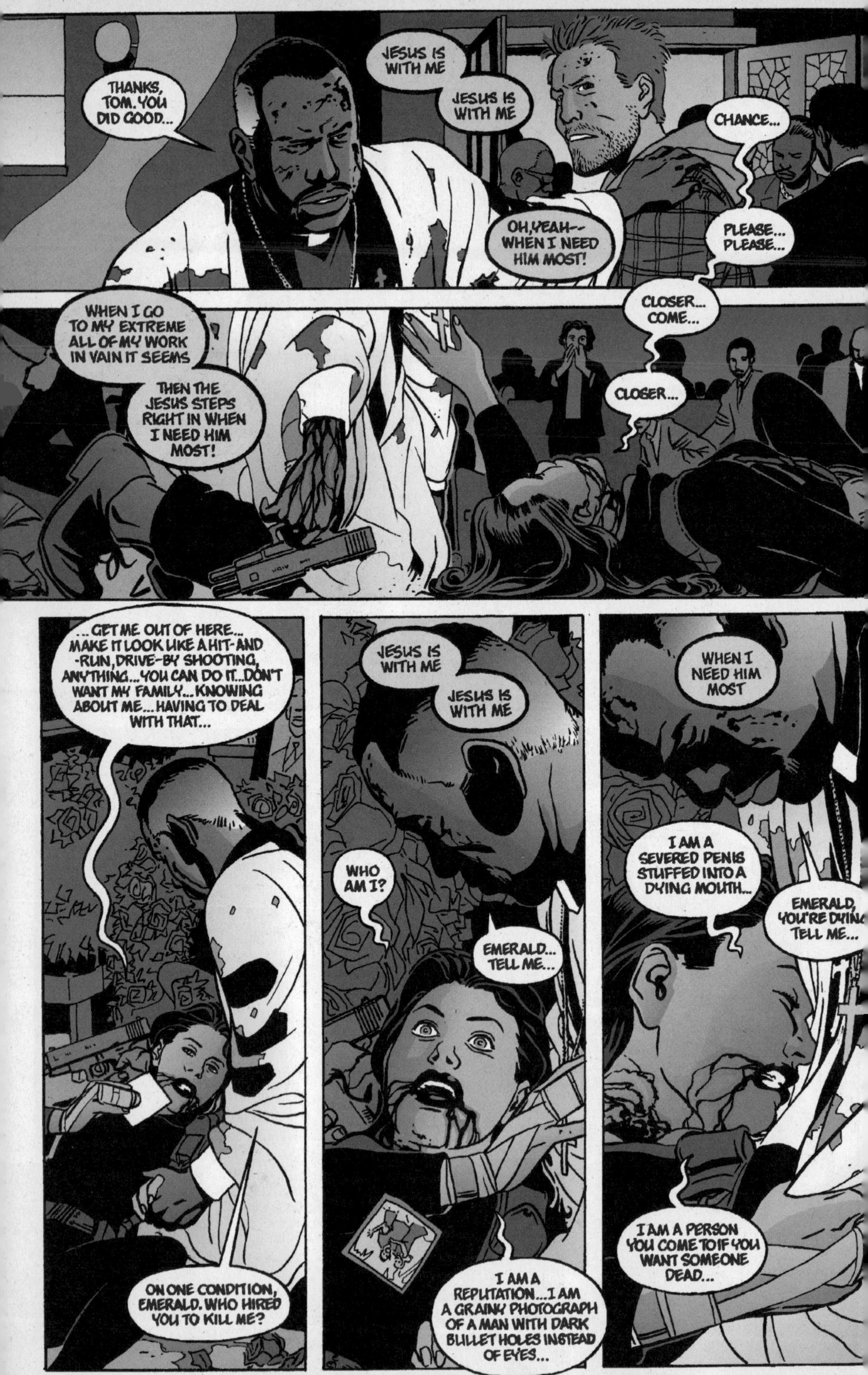
THANKS, TOM. YOU DID GOOD...
JESUS IS WITH ME
JESUS IS WITH ME
CHANCE...
OH, YEAH-- WHEN I NEED HIM MOST!
PLEASE... PLEASE...
WHEN I GO TO MY EXTREME ALL OF MY WORK IN VAIN IT SEEMS
THEN THE JESUS STEPS RIGHT IN WHEN I NEED HIM MOST!
CLOSER... COME...
CLOSER...
...GET ME OUT OF HERE... MAKE IT LOOK LIKE A HIT-AND-RUN, DRIVE-BY SHOOTING, ANYTHING... YOU CAN DO IT... DON'T WANT MY FAMILY... KNOWING ABOUT ME... HAVING TO DEAL WITH THAT...
ON ONE CONDITION, EMERALD. WHO HIRED YOU TO KILL ME?
JESUS IS WITH ME
JESUS IS WITH ME
WHO AM I?
EMERALD... TELL ME...
I AM A REPUTATION... I AM A GRAINY PHOTOGRAPH OF A MAN WITH DARK BULLET HOLES INSTEAD OF EYES...
WHEN I NEED HIM MOST
I AM A SEVERED PENIS STUFFED INTO A DYING MOUTH...
EMERALD, YOU'RE DYING TELL ME...
I AM A PERSON YOU COME TO IF YOU WANT SOMEONE DEAD...

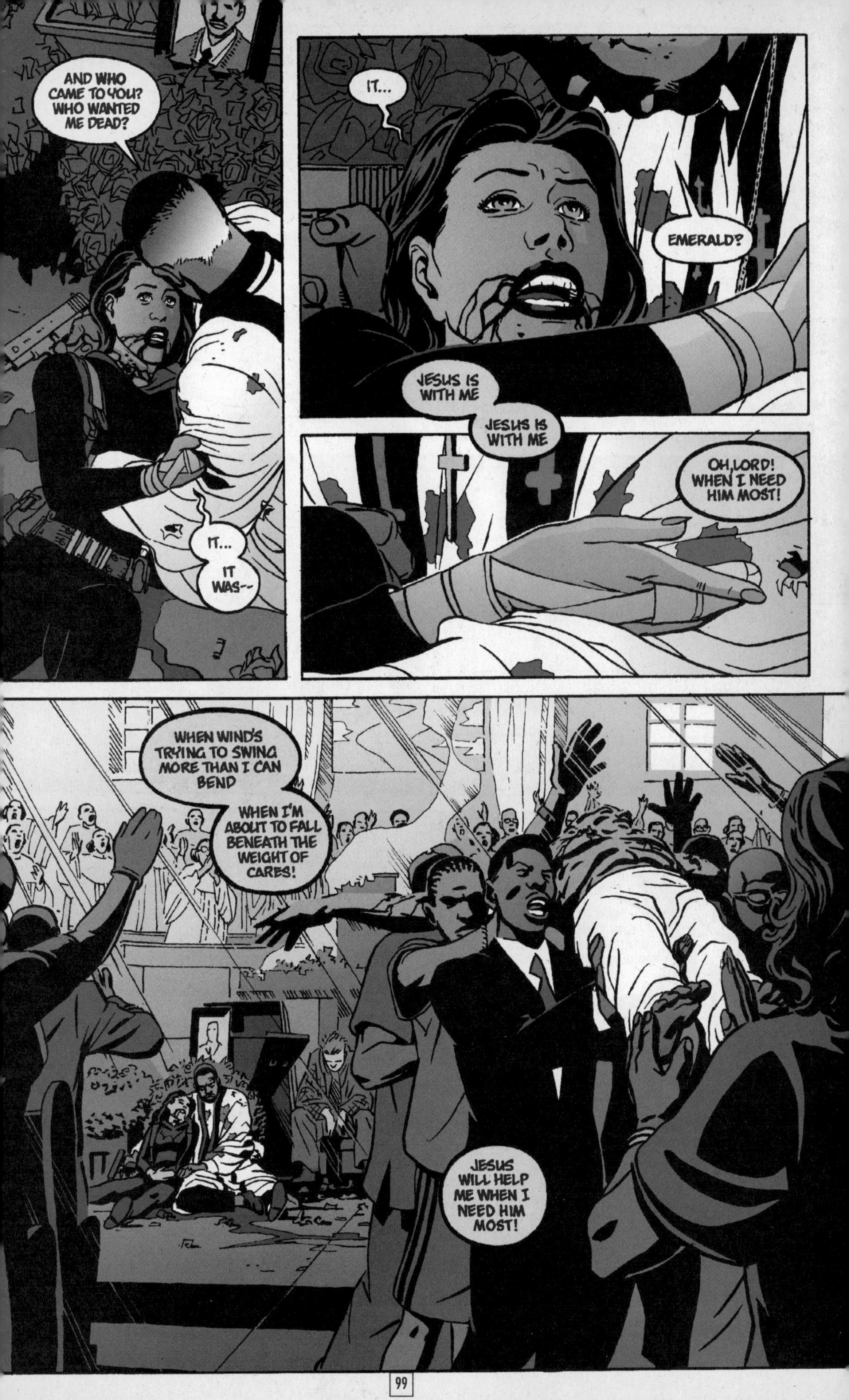
AND WHO CAME TO YOU? WHO WANTED ME DEAD?
IT...
IT WAS--
IT...
EMERALD?
JESUS IS WITH ME
JESUS IS WITH ME
OH, LORD! WHEN I NEED HIM MOST!
WHEN WIND'S TRYING TO SWING MORE THAN I CAN BEND
WHEN I'M ABOUT TO FALL BENEATH THE WEIGHT OF CARES!
JESUS WILL HELP ME WHEN I NEED HIM MOST!

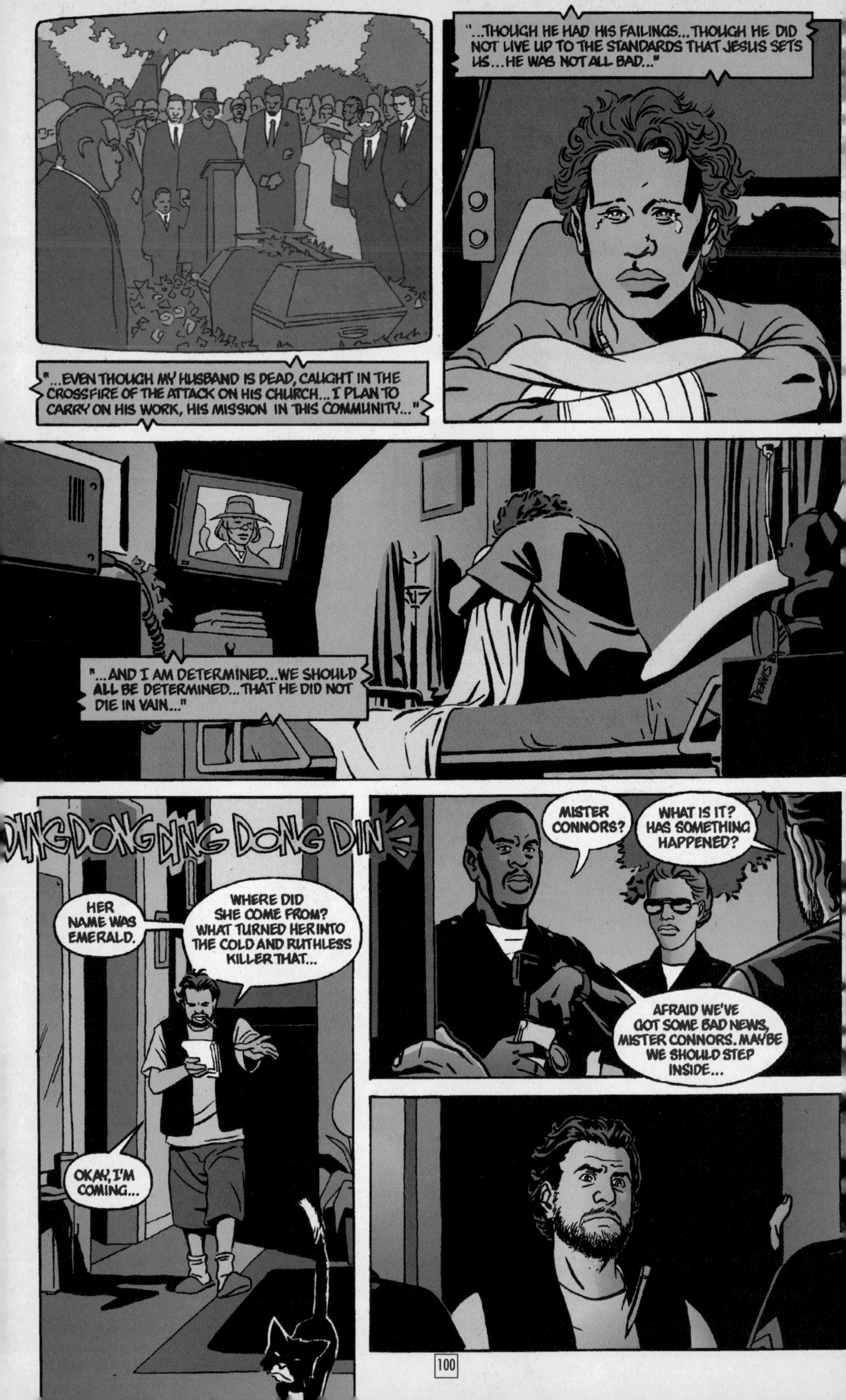
"...THOUGH HE HAD HIS FAILINGS... THOUGH HE DID NOT LIVE UP TO THE STANDARDS THAT JESUS SETS US... HE WAS NOT ALL BAD..."
"...EVEN THOUGH MY HUSBAND IS DEAD, CAUGHT IN THE CROSSFIRE OF THE ATTACK ON HIS CHURCH... I PLAN TO CARRY ON HIS WORK, HIS MISSION IN THIS COMMUNITY..."
"...AND I AM DETERMINED...WE SHOULD ALL BE DETERMINED... THAT HE DID NOT DIE IN VAIN..."
DENNIS
DING DONG DING DONG DIN
HER NAME WAS EMERALD.
WHERE DID SHE COME FROM? WHAT TURNED HER INTO THE COLD AND RUTHLESS KILLER THAT...
OKAY, I'M COMING...
MISTER CONNORS?
WHAT IS IT? HAS SOMETHING HAPPENED?
AFRAID WE'VE GOT SOME BAD NEWS, MISTER CONNORS. MAYBE WE SHOULD STEP INSIDE...

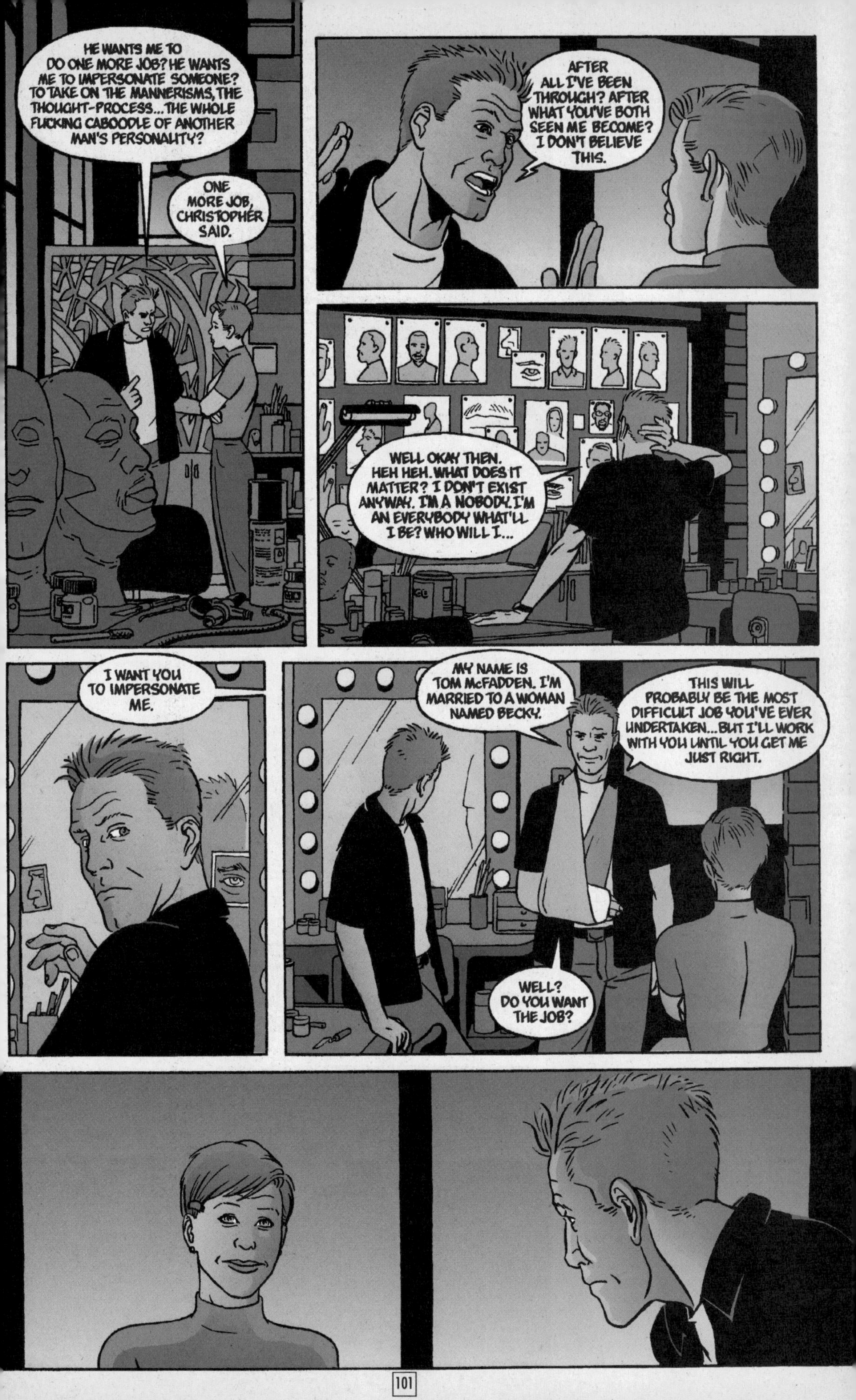

HE WANTS ME TO DO ONE MORE JOB? HE WANTS ME TO IMPERSONATE SOMEONE? TO TAKE ON THE MANNERISMS, THE THOUGHT-PROCESS... THE WHOLE FUCKING CABOODLE OF ANOTHER MAN'S PERSONALITY?
ONE MORE JOB, CHRISTOPHER SAID.
AFTER ALL I'VE BEEN THROUGH? AFTER WHAT YOU'VE BOTH SEEN ME BECOME? I DON'T BELIEVE THIS.
WELL OKAY THEN. HEH HEH. WHAT DOES IT MATTER? I DON'T EXIST ANYWAY. I'M A NOBODY. I'M AN EVERYBODY WHAT'LL I BE? WHO WILL I...
I WANT YOU TO IMPERSONATE ME.
MY NAME IS TOM McFADDEN. I'M MARRIED TO A WOMAN NAMED BECKY.
THIS WILL PROBABLY BE THE MOST DIFFICULT JOB YOU'VE EVER UNDERTAKEN... BUT I'LL WORK WITH YOU UNTIL YOU GET ME JUST RIGHT.
WELL? DO YOU WANT THE JOB?

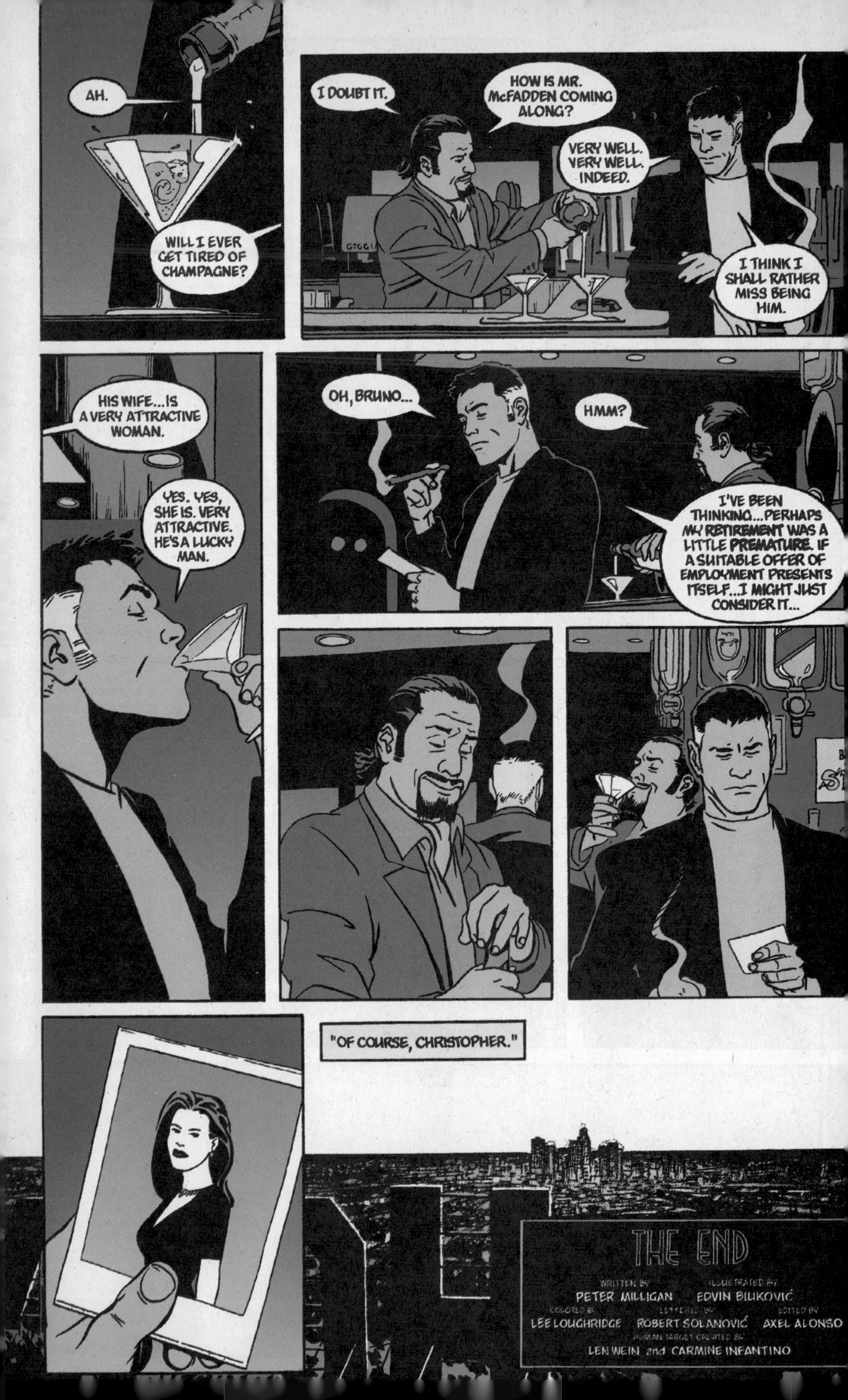
AH.
WILL I EVER GET TIRED OF CHAMPAGNE?
I DOUBT IT.
HOW IS MR. McFADDEN COMING ALONG?
VERY WELL. VERY WELL. INDEED.
I THINK I SHALL RATHER MISS BEING HIM.
HIS WIFE...IS A VERY ATTRACTIVE WOMAN.
YES. YES, SHE IS. VERY ATTRACTIVE. HE'S A LUCKY MAN.
OH, BRUNO...
HMM?
I'VE BEEN THINKING...PERHAPS MY RETIREMENT WAS A LITTLE PREMATURE. IF A SUITABLE OFFER OF EMPLOYMENT PRESENTS ITSELF...I MIGHT JUST CONSIDER IT...
"OF COURSE, CHRISTOPHER."
THE END
WRITTEN BY
PETER MILLIGAN
ILLUSTRATED BY
EDVIN BIUKOVIĆ
COLORED BY
LEE LOUGHRIDGE
LETTERED BY
ROBERT SOLANOVIĆ
EDITED BY
AXEL ALONSO
HUMAN TARGET CREATED BY
LEN WEIN and CARMINE INFANTINO